# Devon and the Slave Trade

# DEVON AND THE SLAVE TRADE

*Documents on African enslavement, abolition and emancipation from 1562 to 1867*

## Todd Gray

*for Paul, Jenny, Sarah and Lauren*

First published in Great Britain by The Mint Press, 2007

New edition, first published 2020

© Todd Gray 2020

The right of Todd Gray to be identified as author of this work has been asserted by him in accordance with the Copyright, Designs & Patents Act 1988.

All rights reserved. No part of this publication may be reproduced in any form or by any means without the prior permission of the copyright holders.

ISBN 978-1-903356-75-3

Cataloguing in Publication Data
A CIP record for this title is available from the British Library

The Mint Press
Taddyforde House South
Taddyforde Estate, New North Road
Exeter, England EX4 4AT

Typeset by Kestrel Data
Cover design by Delphine Jones

Printed and bound in Great Britain
by Short Run Press Ltd, Exeter

# CONTENTS

| | | |
|---|---|---|
| *Preface* | | vii |
| *Foreword* | | ix |
| *Introduction* | | 1 |

**PART ONE**
ACQUISITION: SLAVE VOYAGES — 15

1. Sir John Hawkins' three voyages to Africa and the West Indies, 1562 to 1568 — 17
2. African Devonians, the Guinea Company, 1588 to 1598, and merchants of Barnstaple, Colyton and Exeter — 26
3. Devon slaves in Morocco, 1637 — 31
4. Seven 'ten per centers' from Plymouth, Dartmouth and Exeter, 1698 to 1712, and the account of the *Daniel & Henry*, 1700 — 40
5. Devon's slaving voyages from 1747 to 1786 — 53
6. Regulating slave transportation: Lieut. John Incledon-Webber of Barnstaple and the voyage of HMS *Pomona* to Africa and the West Indies, 1788 to 1789 — 57
7. Arthur Frankland's anti-slaving voyage on HM Sloop *Jaseur* to East Africa, 1830 — 74
8. Brazilian Slavers at Plymouth and Exeter, 1845 — 77

**PART TWO**
INVESTMENT: PLANTATIONS AND TRADE — 83

1. Devon cloth and petitions from Ashburton, Dartmouth, Exeter and Plymouth regarding the Royal Africa Company, 1708 to 1711 — 87

2. Sale of a sugar plantation in Grenada 93
3. An Antigua plantation and the Swete family of Modbury, 1740s 95
4. The Rolle plantation in East Florida, 1780 to 1785 106
5. Captain John Stedman of Surinam, 1772 to 1777, and Tiverton, 1784 to 1797 112
6. Slaves on a Nevis Island plantation belonging to Mary Scarborough of Colyton, 1821 135
7. The account book of John Harrison, agent and attorney of Oldbury Plantation, Jamaica, 1831 139
8. The Topsham sugar factory and Samuel Buttell of Plymouth, 1684 to 1742 145

## PART THREE
## ABOLITION AND EMANCIPATION 149

1. The petition of William Castillo, formerly of Plymouth, 1758 151
2. William 'Bull' Davy of Exeter and the trial of James Somerset, 1772 154
3. An American Black Loyalist at Marystow, 1786 157
4. Expatriation and Equiano at Plymouth, 1787 159
5. The correspondence of Henry Addington, First Viscount Sidmouth, 1788 to 1824 161
6. Abolition, 1787 to 1792: Exeter, Plymouth, Tiverton, Kingsbridge, Topsham, Bradninch, Cullompton, Totnes, Dartmouth, Bere Alston, Crediton, Ashburton, Moretonhampstead and Honiton 165
7. Abolition to Emancipation, 1807 to 1833: Ottery St Mary, Plymouth, Exeter, Topsham, Stonehouse, Moretonhampstead, Tavistock, Ashubrton and Chagford 177
8. The freedom of four Africans at Plymouth in the early 1800s 190
9. A Plymouth missionary's view of South African slavery in 1815 195
10. 'The Ballad of the Negro' in a Marystow cottage in 1828 197
11. Compensation to Devon's owners of slaves, 1833 199
12. John Scott of Lympstone and Emancipation at Trinidad, 1837 201
13. Dahlia Graham of Senegal, the West Indies and Exeter Workhouse, 1854 207
14. Lord St Maur's diary of the American Civil War, 1861 210
15. Slave entertainment in Devon, 1867 212

*Conclusion* 215
*Notes* 218
*Index* 230

# Preface

I first became interested in Devon's involvement in African slavery when I began work in 1982 towards my doctoral thesis on the Atlantic in the 1500s and 1600s. It quickly became apparent that Devon's Elizabethan and Jacobean voyages of exploration, discovery and exploitation were too extensive to cover in one thesis with the result that I confined it to a study of exploration and fishing in the North Atlantic. Ten years later a chance meeting at the University of Exeter with the distinguished writer Maya Angelou inadvertently brought the subject back to the fore: her questioning the role Devon played in Africa reinvigorated what had become a dormant interest, and since then I have gathered information, albeit at a slow pace as more pressing projects took priority. The anniversary of the abolition of slavery gave the final push to completing this stage of research.

After twenty-five years this work finally came to fruition but despite this long gestation period, the results were intended merely as an introduction to the subject. The extensive period over which these events took place and the complexities of the topic made me all too aware that what I have produced was too limited in its scope and breadth to be anything but a starting point for discussion. The introduction of these documents was offered with the hope other historians will find them of use in furthering their own research and in pushing the subject further. Thirteen years later little further research has been undertaken or published. This book sold out some time ago but has been revised and reprinted because of a sudden demand occasioned by the Black Lives Matters movement. Now, as in 2007, there is a pressing need for impartial history.

I deliberately kept the use of the word slave instead of 'enslaved Africans' which became a preferred term in North America but was not yet as widely used here in Britain. This was because some of the documents included in the collection list individuals as having been born into slavery in the Caribbean and it would be misleading to term all of them 'enslaved Africans' and other terms, such as 'enslaved Americans of African descent' or 'enslaved African Americans', are too cumbersome. Other historical terms which appear in the documents have been reproduced, such as mulatto, negro, quadroon and sambo, which I hope readers will be sufficiently aware are considered inappropriate to contemporary society on either side of the Atlantic but are needed as tools to examine the past.

I would like once again to thank the His Grace the Duke of Somerset, the Right Hon. the Countess of Arran, the Right Hon. the Viscount Sidmouth, Mrs Diana Bury, Reverend Stuart Franklin, the Bristol Record Office, Devon & Exeter Institution, Devon Record Office, Everys Solicitors of Honiton incorporating Dunnings, National Archives, North Devon Record Office, Plymouth & West Devon Record Office and Westcountry Studies Library for permission to publish the accounts and illustrations. This book would not have been possible without the help and encouragement of a great number of individuals including Jamie Byrom, David Clements, Janet Henwood, Professor Richard Hitchcock, the late Professor Christopher Holdsworth, Professor Maryanne Kowaleski, Ian Maxted, the late Professor Robert Parker, Graham Parnell, Dr Tim Rees, the late Margery Rowe, Gill Selley, Professor Chantal Stebbings and Joyce Totterdell. I have also received help from the staffs of Bonhams, the Bristol Record Office, British Library, Devon & Exeter Institution, Devon Record Office, Exeter Cathedral Library & Archives, Exeter Central Library, Ilfracombe Museum, National Archives, North Devon Athenaeum, North Devon Record Office, Parliament Archives, Plymouth & West Devon Record Office, Somerset Record Office, Topsham Museum, University of Exeter Main Library and Westcountry Studies Library. Finally, this publication has been supported by a grant from Devon County Council which is gratefully acknowledged.

Dr Todd Gray
Exeter, July 2020

# Foreword

At its meeting on 19 July 2007, Devon County Council formally acknowledged Devon's involvement in the slave trade and agreed to support a number of activities, including the first publication of this book, to mark the bicentenary of the 1807 Slavery Trade Act which prohibited slavery in the British Empire.

Now, in 2020 we are reminded of the horrific legacy of slavery which, on an shockingly huge scale, exploited the peoples of Africa. "Black Lives Matter", people cried in response to the death of a Black man, George Floyd in America at the hands of a police officer. Because, despite over a hundred years of emancipation, Black people are still suffering at the hands of those who do not see them as an equal.

People have taken to the streets and questioned why we continue to celebrate those who played a significant role in the slave trade. In June, Plymouth City Council decided to rename Sir John Hawkins Square. Hawkins was born in Plymouth and led the first three voyages to Africa and the West Indies in the 1560s. His early involvement was soon to fall into insignificance when compared with the scale of slavery that followed and is more associated with the cities of Bristol, Liverpool and London. The trade still casts a long shadow given the legacy of profits in fuelling the development of much of Britain's commerce and architecture which we can still see today.

Whilst it is insensitive to celebrate people who had a substantial involvement in slavery, we must not eradicate them from our history altogether. The story needs to be told and understood, so that we can acknowledge our painful history and understand people's feelings and struggles. As William Wilberforce said in 1791, "you can choose to look the other way but you can never again say that you did not know".

Sadly, despite the abolition movement and Slave Trade Act, slavery still exists in society but in a different form. A victim of modern slavery will have their movements controlled or restricted by another and can be found working in industries, right under our noses, like nail bars, car washes, hospitality and care. The chains are no longer metal, they are emotional and financial. This year the Council has published our Modern Slavery Statement setting out how we will take steps to eradicate it from society and supply chains.

This year also marks fifteen years since the opening of the Devon Record Office at Great Moor House in Exeter. The records office was a great source of information for Dr Gray and we are pleased that historians are using the county's outstanding archives and hope it will encourage others to do so too. There is so much history to write about and perhaps now that Exeter, Devon's county town, was awarded UNESCO City of Literature status in 2019 we may see more written, including the positive histories of Black, Asian and minority ethnic people's contributions to Devon life alongside the more uncomfortable stories.

Events this year have again demonstrated the overwhelming kindness, compassion and understanding of Devon's people and communities in supporting and caring for each other. Learning and understanding our past is a further example of our support and care for each other here in Devon.

I welcome Todd's ongoing explorations of Devon's history, particularly his work to understand the role of those often marginalised in the past, and I thank him for bringing this into view. This is a timely republication and I am pleased that the Council is playing a small part in telling this important part in our history.

Councillor John Hart
Leader of Devon County Council
July 2020

# Introduction

Devon's role in African slavery is an uncomfortable topic. The brutality, with its graphic details of barbaric and inhumane behaviour, makes for uneasy and distressing reading. On a personal level, the subject is potentially difficult for anyone with ancestors who were slavers or for those whose family had invested in slave plantations and might still have residual wealth. It is also particularly problematic for those who can trace their family history to individuals once defined as the legal property of other men and women. It is difficult to imagine the conditions these slaves endured and upsetting to contemplate one's own family's experiences. There is also another emotional hurdle: in reconciling themselves to the past, descendants of those enslaved are faced with trying to understand Africa at the time and the possible collusion of other Africans in bringing their own ancestors into slavery. Moreover, some individuals will be the descendants of both the enslaved and slavers. Few people can find it an easy topic.

This book centres on one county's involvement in African slavery in its various forms. It includes material on its people in Africa and in other parts of the Atlantic world. In consequence the geographical range is extensive: it refers not only to Britain and Africa but also to North and South America as well as the Caribbean Islands. Nevertheless, the focus is squarely on Devon; the emphasis is on how this one county was involved in slavery including the effect on Devon itself. As a local study the material has implications not merely for these foreign places but it may prove informative to historians of other parts of Britain trying to understand how their area differed from the well-documented places such as London, Liverpool and Bristol. The county's links to slavery were not merely through its mariners' endeavours in Africa, as plantation investors and merchants trading in slave produce but it was also connected via its people being involved in navy patrols in regulating or abolishing the transportation of slaves, in one man acting as a Caribbean magistrate overseeing emancipation, as abolitionists and as consumers taking part in sugar embargoes. Similar overlooked histories could be replicated across Britain. Some individuals were not born in Devon but arrived at a later point. Perhaps the most striking example is Captain John Stedman who moved to Tiverton in 1784. He had Scottish and Dutch parents, had been a slave owner in South America and while there had undergone an informal marriage act with a slave. Their five-year relationship produced a son born into slavery. Stedman later bought his son's freedom and subsequently publicly acknowledged and raised him in Devon although he remained against abolition. His printed biography and private journal provide insights into how one individual accommodated himself, privately and publicly, with the institution of slavery. Doubtless there are other similar examples waiting to be revealed throughout Britain.

All historians interested in slavery should be drawn to a Devon study because of one man: Sir John Hawkins. As the first Englishman to participate in African slavery, he has given the county the dubious distinction of developing slaving in spite of that trade's subsequence dominance by other English cities. There are several striking elements of Hawkins' voyages. His personal role in the three voyages was of the utmost importance: Hawkins' tenacity and force of will were crucial in carrying through each expedition. There is another element which needs to be understood even at the risk of diminishing his significance. Hawkins was greatly dependent upon financial and political support from London, logistical help and general cooperation from Spanish merchants on both sides of the Atlantic and the assistance of Africans in providing slaves. He needed strong entrepreneurial skills in attracting this help and although these were matched by his successor in English maritime endeavour, Sir Francis Drake, a changing political climate provided new opportunities, in privateering, which made slaving less attractive in the latter sixteenth century. Hawkins showed the way but

*Introduction*

it would be several generations before the conditions were right for his successors to engage in slaving.

The importance of Hawkins' voyages should not be underplayed but where this study has perhaps unexpected appeal is that a number of other aspects are unknown. These overlooked topics not only provide important comparative details but widen our understanding of the impact slavery had on one particular area. Even so, it cannot be claimed that enough material has been found to claim that Devon's past was dominated by slavery: the documents which have been examined suggests the county was involved in the transportation of less than a tenth of a percent of all Africans transported across the Atlantic. Instead, Devon appears to have a history of engagement with it in a number of different ways. As a maritime county, and one which was particularly active and important during the sixteenth to eighteenth centuries, it would be surprising had it not had some level of interest but what may be more surprising is that Devon did not participate more fully. Only a handful of slaving voyages have been identified and one of the common themes among them is they were organised only in part from the county: in many expeditions either the ships, financial backers or crew were not Devonian. There is only one detailed account, that of a ship from Dartmouth, and that appears to show a marked naivety if not ineptness or incompetence on the part of those slaving. It is telling that after a single attempt at slaving not one of these Devon ships re-engaged in the trade.

The book's means for examining this past is through the introduction of what are largely unknown documents. This is a necessity because, as will be explained below, there is little printed research on it. What has instead taken its place in Devon has been an occasional debate in the public arena, over the course of the past ten years, over the taking of personal or collective responsibility for the past; the anniversary of abolition has this year brought this to the fore and overwhelmed any sober examination of Devon's role in African slavery. There have been excited discussions on the degree to which it is vital, necessary or appropriate to acknowledge the past and the need for, or validity in, contemporary Devonians making such a gesture. One historian recently categorised this as 'the cult of apology'[1] and there has been widespread local antagonism to apologies. The county's leading newspaper deplored the 'emotionalism' of apologies and the missed opportunity of using the event for education.[2] One local ceremony to mark the 200th anniversary of abolition involved two clerics from Exeter Cathedral but the Dean noted he was not apologising because he believed apologies were shallow given they involved 'something somebody else did years ago'.[3]

Over the past decade discussion of this topic has not been concerned with debating its history because that history has not been defined. Instead it has been dominated by the rights and wrongs of apologies. The response partly results from the nature of contemporary Devon and has implications for this study of African slavery in the county: it is likely that similar studies of more multi-cultural parts of Britain would have different reactions but there is little detailed research on the role of African slavery in the country outside the known slaving centres. The issue as to how appropriate apologies are in a Devon context was concluded by Devon County Council's decision, on July 19 2007, to mark the anniversary of abolition by passing a resolution. It noted:

> Devon County Council welcomes the theme of reflecting on the past as well as looking to the future. We believe that recognising the history of the Slave Trade and those who opposed it deepens our understanding of our heritage, celebrates our diverse cultures and increases our commitment to address inequalities and oppose all forms of contemporary slavery and exploitation. Devon County Council acknowledges the historical involvement of Devon - its ports, its people, its landowners, and the industries in the Atlantic Slave Trade and the arrival of slaves and former slaves who settled and became part of our communities. We will support activities which mark the Bicentenary and encourage our staff, elected members and residents of Devon to engage in them.

This has coincided with what could be a gradual consensus that public apologies are outdated and that a more sophisticated approach is needed to address the past.

There are other challenges in studying slavery in regards to Devon. As one of the largest counties in England it has considerable differences in topography. This has influenced the development of its communities in creating very distinct places. It has two cities, Exeter and Plymouth, which are little alike: one the long-standing regional capital in terms of religion, justice and the economy while the other became dominated by the navy from the late 1600s. The rural areas have two different moorlands in Dartmoor and Exmoor while the two coastlines along the Bristol and English Channels are also little alike. Farming, tin-extraction, cloth production, fishing and trade dominated the late medieval economy but new opportunities presented themselves with the opening up of the greater world in the sixteenth century. Compared to London and the South East, Devon was disadvantaged by its geography in taking part in medieval trade to the Baltic and the Netherlands but it suddenly was well-placed with trade to Africa and the Americas. Closer proximity gave a financial advantage which Devonians took up particularly in regard to Newfoundland fishing. In the sixteenth and seventeenth centuries fish, tin and cloth were sold to European markets but only fishing continued to be prosperous through to the end of the eighteenth century. It was just at this time, in the early eighteenth century when tin and woollen cloth were losing their prosperity, that slavery took off in other parts of the country, notably in Devon's near rival, the port of Bristol. Devon's economy needed redevelopment but it appears to have fallen back onto privateering in the continual wars against France and Spain (1702 to 1713, 1716 to 1720, 1739 to 1748, 1756 to 1763, 1778 to 1783, 1793 to 1797, 1798 to 1802) than turn to slavery. The reasons for this are unclear.

The greatest obstacle in addressing Devon's involvement with Africa is that the central question remains unanswered - that is, to what extent did it participate in slavery? It remains problematic to acknowledge or apologise for a past without first determining what it comprised. There are two contrasting views. Many assume that except for the Elizabethan voyages of Sir John Hawkins there was no involvement, others categorically assert that the local economy was built on it.

Neither position is true. These views have been expressed in spite of the lack of any published work based on primary evidence. The only exception has been a project of the Friends of Devon's Archives that requested its members to provide references from their own research. This has yielded some very valuable information but it is still incidental instead of methodical.[4] In spite of Devon having one of the richest and most extensive collections of documents in Britain we simply have not known the extent or character of local involvement in slavery because no researcher has undertaken the work. It is directly because of this gap in knowledge that there was no mention made of slavery in the standard history of the county, Professor W. G. Hoskins' *Devon*.[5] This was not apparent when the book was written but his omission has become more noticeable as time has gone by: as society itself changes so too does the study of history. New subjects open up. In the early 1950s, when Professor Hoskins was writing, there was also less written about the lives of ordinary people, of the history of gardens, food or of minorities. We now have work on the history of some ethnic or cultural communities in Devon most notably of the Jewish community.[6] Professor Hoskins wrote his seminal work when history was more the preserve of academics and at a time when record offices were dominated by University specialists and certainly not of genealogists who undertake nearly all local research today.

Hoskins wrote when the Commonwealth was replacing the Empire and although Britain was then becoming more multi-cultural, it is important to note Devon was less affected by immigration from the Indian sub-continent and the West Indies. Half a century later it remains one of the least changed populations in England.[7] This is not to say people of African descent have not lived in Devon during the last four centuries but their number has been low. Historical references can been found only to isolated individuals. The list of baptisms for Winkleigh for 1818 is telling: it noted 'Samuel Thomas, illegitimate son of Elizabeth Parker and John Thomas the Negro undoubted father'. The presumption must have been he was the father because the baby was of mixed race and John Thomas was the only black in the village.[8] Interestingly, an individual of that name was baptised in Plymouth in 1783 and noted as 'a black man'.[9]

Nevertheless, Devon has been influenced by the political response from Westminster in trying to address the challenges posed by the changing ethnic mix across the country. Since the late 1990s an emphasis from London on increasing social sensitivity has prevailed, often derided as 'political correctness', and in Devon there has been more attention paid to minority history. The lack of research has led to astonishing assumptions being made regarding Devon's history. One noticeable example of this took place in 1997 when human bones were found on a beach near Ilfracombe. It was pronounced, before evidence was fully examined, that these were the remains of black slaves from St Lucia who drowned in the wreck of the *London* in 1796. Public calls were made, led by Member of Parliament Bernie Grant and the African Reparation Movement, to return the bones to the West Indies. Tests later suggested they were not from the West Indies and questioned

*Introduction*

whether they were local fishermen.[10] Nevertheless the Dagara Peace Commission for the Peoples of the Afrikan Diaspora, a delegation from Ghana, performed a ceremony on 22nd April 2001 at Ilfracombe. The event's advertisement enticed the public to 'witness the true magic of the Dagara Peace Commission'. Participants were encouraged, in a departure from English custom, to 'bring £5 or £7 worth of silver coins in 10, 20 or 50 pieces to the memorial. As part of the Dagara tradition during the ceremony people are expected to give the chief mourners coins or cowry shells throughout its duration'.[11] That year the group performed a similar ceremony at Exeter Quay. The public message was that there were strong local links with slavery but it would have been misleading to have claimed slaves were sold on the quay given there is no evidence it happened. Devon was part of a national tour and the assumption was Exeter had a history similar to the major slaving ports. A more valid ceremony would have noted local imports of sugar and tobacco some of which, but not all, was produced with slave labour,[12] or to mark the sugar factory on the Exe river.[13] Finally, one recent booklet erroneously claims that in Devon 'people at all levels of society were involved' and that 'probably most families benefited from what became known as 'The Trade'.'[14]

This conclusion was reached without examining local archival or printed sources. A cursory glance at the written work would have led any reader to question how extensively Devon was involved. No existing study of a city, town or village concludes that slavery was important nor does any work on local industries indicate Africa was an export market. For example, the definitive study of the local cloth trade makes no mention of exports to Africa.[15] More recently, the editors of Devon's extensive two-volume maritime history have assumed there was no slave history and concluded it was due to 'perhaps because Devonians preferred to leave the slave trade to their less sensitive neighbours at Bristol'.[16] If there were a substantial history which has been deliberately ignored then this would have necessitated collusion of all of the many hundreds of historians who have worked on Devon over the last five hundred years. It would also raise questions as to why they would have acted *en masse* in this way in contrast to their counterparts in London, Bristol and Liverpool who have acknowledged and documented their slaving history.

It is in this vacuum of knowledge, in the wide gap between what some want to believe and what can be understood from published research, that this book has been written. The aim is to address the lack of reliable information on Devon's history by providing points for discussion in introducing relevant documents from local and national archives and also printed accounts. They have been reproduced in part or fully in the following pages and provide a tentative framework on particular areas. The initial conclusions contrast sharply with the claims stated above: they indicate Devon was involved in less than 0.03 per cent of African slaving.

It has been too easy to make assumptions given so little is known of Devon's role in African slavery in particular and of black history in general. As with any minority history, the search for information is complicated by the very scarcity of evidence for the individuals concerned: it is difficult to find details about the majority of the population but it becomes much more so when limiting it to one group which, it is safe to assume, has never comprised as much as one per cent of the population.

Three examples drawn from different types of documents illustrate the potential for hasty or incautious use of material. First, the burial of Joan Gale in Sidmouth on the 17th of February 1604 is of interest because she was described as a 'poor dark woman'.[17] The natural conclusion would be she was of African descent but the survival of a small number of other documents helps us to better understand her. Included amongst the millions of local records are petitions from the seventeenth century that mention three other dark people. One is from George Shaffe who described himself as a poor dark person who needed financial assistance. It is only through reading two other documents does it become clear skin colour did not determine being dark: petitioner Elizabeth Evans noted 'her darkness being God's visitation' had existed for 13 years while Thomas Greene claimed he had been dark for a 'long season'. In all three instances it was the world which had gone dark: the implication is that each had developed cataracts which had impeded their sight.[18] Secondly, the word black can also be misleading. In the sixteenth century it could refer to men and women with dark hair; a 'black' man or woman may not necessarily be what we assume today. In 1586 a Devonian named Thomas Rowclifffe testified he 'knew Leonard French very well and was well acquainted with him being a tall man of black complexion and serving as a soldier in Knockfergus in Ireland'. It would be easy to make assumptions regarding the ethnicity of French had not another witness, Richard

*Introduction*

Vowells, also testified. He said 'that one Leonard French late of Totnes and sometimes dwelling in this city being of stature tall and grosse and of a blackish complexion ... that he was about the age of 44 years as he thinketh, had a black beard and the hair of his head black and the grain marvellous black'.[19] Even the appearance of the 'Black Dwarf' in Exeter in 1819 was not what it may appear to be: *The Black Dwarf* was a radical pamphlet regarding the reform of national politics and sold in a shop in South Street. It caused a stir but not because of racial issues.[20] Finally, the identities of Africans can be easily hidden in documents. James Blackamore worked as a household servant in one of Devon's great houses in the 1640s. He frequently appears in the household's accounts, mostly straightforwardly with both his first and second names, but in a few instances there is added information: he is referred to as 'James the Blackamoor'. This was similar to names given other servants such as Welsh Dick and Irish Tom.[21]

It will take many years of further research before a reasonably accurate assessment can be made of Devon's involvement in African slavery. Other documents will be discovered and these will provide new details that will alter our perception of the subject. Those that form this collection, which cover four centuries, have been arranged in three parts with thirty-one sections. The common thread is each is concerned with Devon.

Part One concerns the acquisition of slaves. Eight separate themes are discussed comprising John Hawkins' three voyages of 1562 to 1568, the Devon merchants who were part of the Guinea Company from 1588 to 1598, a list of British slaves at Morocco in 1637, details of twelve slaving voyages of 'ten per centers' and others from Plymouth, Dartmouth and Exeter from 1682 to 1715, a list of slaving trips made from 1747 to 1786, and an account of the trial of foreign slavers at Exeter in 1845. There is also the account of a North Devon naval officer of his experiences patrolling the African coast in the late 1780s. His journal is revealing of African culture and the relationships between Africans and the Europeans in the midst of slaving. There are also two extracts from naval vessels on later anti-slavery voyages.

Part Two relates to investment through plantations and trade. Five accounts survive for estates in which Devonians had financial investments. These comprise plantations in Antigua in the 1740s, the Rolle plantation in East Florida in 1780, Nevis Island from 1812 to 1823, Grenada from probably about 1800, and Jamaica in the 1830s. There are also extracts from Captain John Stedman's account of Surinam in the mid 1770s and of his subsequent life in Tiverton with his son Johnny, a former slave. The Devon cloth trade is also examined through a series of petitions from Ashburton, Dartmouth, Plymouth and Exeter from 1708 to 1711 regarding the Royal Africa Company. Finally, there is a short section on a sugar refinery at Topsham at the end of the seventeenth century.

Part Three is concerned with abolition and emancipation. It includes a petition from a slave who was baptised in Plymouth in 1755, comments made during court proceedings which involved 'Bull' Davy of Exeter defending James Somerset in 1772, extracts from the correspondence of Henry Addington, first Viscount Sidmouth, from 1788 to 1824 and a short note on the experiences of Equiano, the well-known former slave who came to Plymouth to repatriate former slaves to Africa in 1787. Abolition is looked at through a petition from Ottery St Mary of 1814, a collection of papers for Plymouth from 1814 to 1826 and meetings and campaigns in other parts of Devon, notably Exeter. There are also records relating to the emancipation of slaves in the 1830s: it includes letters regarding the freedom of four Africans in Plymouth between 1811 and 1823, details of compensation paid to owners of slaves in the mid 1830s, an account by John Scott of Lympstone who assisted with emancipation at Trinidad in 1838, a description of a former slave who lived in Exeter in the early 1850s and the diary of Lord St Maur during the American Civil War. The last item concerns minstrel performances in Exeter by a group of former American slaves in 1867, two years after they were granted their freedom.

Even with this collection of documents, it cannot be said that the extent and character of Devon's involvement in African slavery has been conclusively determined. Yet, it can reasonably be stated that while it was not as important as it was to London, Bristol or Liverpool, there was still activity which needs to be acknowledged, addressed and understood. In the documents are individual examples of how Devonians related to Africans. In some cases Africans are seen cooperating in enslaving other Africans, in positions of power dictating terms, as the victims of warfare and kidnapping, and in resisting slavery by committing collective suicide. The relationships of Devonians to the enslaved are also varied including the comments by abolitionists to the concept of slavery, in the words of gratitude spoken to one Devonian who was in Trinidad on the morning of emancipation

*Introduction*

and in the enthusiastic words of a theatre critic who relished 'slave entertainment'.

Perhaps one of the most obvious outcomes of studying the following documents is to question the nature of freedom during these 300 years. It is difficult for modern society to understand how England not only lived with but welcomed the enslavement of millions of Africans. Part of the answer lies in the distinctions in freedom at the time: there were varying degrees of liberty and slavery was one of several forms of 'unfree' or coerced labour. There was a spectrum in which slaves were at one end and paid labour at the other. In between were many with varying differences in their legal status.

There were several kinds of forced labour. Most Africans were taken into 'chattel slavery' which was defined by the League of Nations in 1928 as 'the status or condition of a person over whom any or all of the powers attaching to the rights of ownership are reserved'. Other degrees of forced labour include debt bondage in which a free citizen remains so in theory but his or her status was in abeyance until a debt was worked off. Indentured labour was common in Britain and in many colonies white indentured servants preceded or co-existed with slavery. Serfdom had disappeared from Britain but in the early 1800s serfs could be found in other parts of Europe: tenants were unable to change their obligations by law, custom or agreement to live and labour on land held by another individual to whom they gave service.[22]

In the early 1800s different degrees of freedom in Britain were not determined merely by race but also by wealth, religion and gender: it was not the case that whites were free and blacks were enslaved. The final end to black slavery under British law came at a time in which the political rights of the general population were being addressed. Until then only the wealthiest men had the right to vote. In the 1830s, the decade in which freedom was finally granted to slaves in the British Empire, rights were also being granted to a greater number of individuals in Britain. Even so, it took until nearly a century later, until 1928, for every adult to have the right to vote: reforms in 1832, 1867, 1884 and 1918 gradually extended voting but only to portions of the population. Eventually the poor and women were included. For example, in 1867 the right to vote was given to all men who had property in urban areas rated annually at five pounds or twelve pounds in rural areas. All others were excluded including the poor. In 1928 the franchise was finally extended to women over the age of 21 and to all men who had been resident for at least six months. Even so, the 1832 Reforms forced through greater political rights for non-Anglicans: until then, for example, only men who attended the Established Church were allowed to become mayors of Exeter.

One of the following documents is from the account of a Plymouth man, Frederick Hooper, who was an aspiring missionary and visited South Africa in 1815. He failed to understand how the ruling white elite could deny black Africans access to Christian worship, but it is clear from his writing that distinguishing blacks and whites in terms of Christians and Pagans made it easier for some to justify slavery. In this respect race and religion were two factors which helped determine slave status.

Being born white in England did not necessarily guarantee freedom. The case of one particular Braunton man was unusual but is nevertheless insightful. In the late 1600s he petitioned the county justices for financial assistance because of his circumstances.

> The humble petition of Peter Caverly of Braunton in the county aforesaid, humbly showeth to your good worships that he, the said Peter Caverly, at the first beginning of the wars here in England was enlisted a soldier in the service of King Charles the first of every blessed memory and was in most of the greatest fights that were in England also in Ireland was a commission officer and so continued his faithfulness and loyalty to the great hazards of his live, as by many wounds and shots which he received in his body the scars and markets whereof on his body do still visibly appear, and yet not withstanding all this his undaunted courage and zeal for his majesty's service, carried him still along so far until at last by that tyrant Cromwell's army was taken prisoner in Ireland and carried into St Sebastian in Spain and sold for a slave and after a considerable time of enduring much misery there, by the good hand of providence came back again to his native country . . .[23]

In effect, Caverly was sold into slavery for political and religious reasons. His ethnicity was not the determining factor.

The ending of slavery in Britain and the Empire was a gradual process that took several generations. It came at a time, in the late 1700s and early 1800s, which saw tremendous developments in personal freedoms

*Introduction*

for millions of people on both sides of the Atlantic. In addition to the emancipation of black slaves there were great changes in Eastern Europe and Russia as well as in North America and throughout Europe. The American and French Revolutions of the late 1700s preceded these reforms and their rhetoric, at least, emphasised the importance of freedom and equality.

There was a long process of obtaining full rights for Africans in Britain and her colonies. A milestone in the end to slavery in England came in 1772 when James Somerset, a slave born in Virginia but who lived in Britain, was granted his freedom through a legal ruling. It raised expectations of the other 10,000 or so slaves in the country.[24] Abolition was formally proposed in 1788 but it took fifty years for full emancipation to occur. Three hundred years earlier William Hawkins had watched Africans being taken across the Atlantic by the Portuguese. During those centuries millions of men, women and children were enslaved before some of them, and their descendants, were finally freed in 1838. Devon, as will be seen in the following pages, played a part, less important than some parts of the country it must be admitted, in the acquisition of slaves, in investing in plantations and in trade. It also was involved in the movement for abolition and emancipation. Part of this history is revealed through the following documents.

'This air is too pure for a slave to breathe in'
William 'Bull' Davy of Exeter, 1772, speaking of England

# PART ONE

# ACQUISITION: SLAVE VOYAGES

This section comprises documents relating to the taking of slaves in Africa. A comparatively small number of Devon slaving voyages can be found in documentary sources. These are discussed in three of the following sections and relate to the Hawkins' voyages of the 1560s, a group of 'ten per centers' in the late 1600s and early 1700s, and voyages in the late 1700s. There are also sections devoted to the arrival of Africans to Devon which possibly relate to local merchants who were part of the Guinea Company in the late 1500s, rescued slaves of the Barbary Corsairs, the journal of a naval officer off the African coast in 1788, an account of a naval voyage to East Africa in 1830 and the trial at Plymouth of a group of Brazilians accused of slavery in 1845.

In this section, the number of known African slaving voyages and slaves taken is discussed in greater detail in three sections relating to the 1560s, the turn of the eighteenth century and from 1747 to 1786. They will show that forty voyages have been identified (3 in the 1560s, 12 from 1682 to 1715, and 25 from 1747 to 1786) and that these comprise less than 0.3 per cent of the estimated 12,000 slaving voyages which sailed from Britain. This drops to 0.25 per cent if a group of French vessels, which have been included in the 25 ships as they left from Plymouth for Africa, are excluded.[25] It has been estimated that between 13,887,500 and 14,650,000 slaves were transported from Africa to the Americas[26] but it is impossible to provide an accurate number of those connected with Devonians. The slaves were partially recorded: only on five Devon vessels were they numbered and this amounted to only 1,076 men, women and children. A more accurate estimate would be 3,836. This would comprise less than 0.03 per cent of all Africans transported across the Atlantic.[27] Assessing Devon's part in slaving in terms of numbers alone diminishes what cannot be calculated, and it needs to be considered, and that is the unrecorded human suffering caused to those involved.

# 1

# Sir John Hawkins' three voyages to Africa and the West Indies, 1562 to 1568

Through Sir John Hawkins Devon can lay claim to the first known voyage by an English ship to transport Africans as slaves to the Americas. No evidence has yet been found that any other Devonian repeated this movement, despite the high profits made, until generations later. It is easy to understand why neither he, nor another Englishman, wanted to repeat the astonishing efforts undertaken to complete the voyages. The organisation and potential hazards were too problematic for others to follow.

In 1493 an agreement between Portugal and Spain divided the newly-discovered parts of the world between them and excluded all other countries from exploration, colonisation or trade in the New World. From the 1490s Spain extracted a staggering amount of silver, gold, pearls and jewels from the Americas and by the middle of the 1500s Hawkins, like many other Europeans, wanted to share in this bonanza. There was little that could be done without flouting Spanish or Portuguese law until England officially waged war with Spain in the 1580s. Until then there was a risk that any activity in waters or land claimed by Spain or Portugal could be declared illegal by the Iberian or English governments: voyages by English sailors could potentially be acts of piracy with the consequence of a death penalty.

It was within these restrictions that Hawkins acted. He had a personal advantage over other men in that his own father had sailed to Africa

The Hawkins' coat of arms featuring an African girl with chains, 1566
(North Devon Record Office)

and Brazil on three occasions in the 1520s and 1530s. In 1527 William Hawkins sailed the *Pole* of Plymouth to Guinea in Africa where he probably first saw the transportation of slaves to the New World: Portuguese traders were engaged in taking them to Brazil. By that date the Portuguese had taken Africans to the New World for at least 22 years. They had already transported them to Madeira or Portugal itself since at least the 1440s; more than 140,000 Africans had worked in sugar plantations or as domestic servants. The plantation system of forced labour had, in effect, been transferred from the Portuguese islands in the Atlantic to the New World.[28] Hawkins returned to Brazil in 1530 and 1532 and although not welcomed by the authorities he managed to trade in the West Indies. The voyages were profitable and he died a wealthy man in 1554.

Eight years later his son, Sir John, sailed from Plymouth for Africa in the *Solomon* of Plymouth along with the *Jonas* and the *Swallow*. Hawkins was financially and politically supported by a syndicate of London investors which included Benjamin Gonson, treasurer of the Royal Navy. Hawkins knew the voyage violated Spanish and Portuguese law but he had another advantage: he was actively supported by the Ponce family, Spanish merchants who were resident in the Canary Islands. They were longstanding business associates but in this particular voyage the Ponces were partners and their help, including providing shipping and topographical intelligence, was most likely instrumental in the success of the enterprise. Through them Hawkins employed a Spanish pilot who was familiar not only with Africa but the West Indies. In effect, although headed by a Devonian, the voyage was a complex partnership of influential people in London commerce and government, Spanish merchants and Devon mariners. It was Hawkins however who received the glory at the time and the opprobrium since.

On all three occasions Hawkins used similar methods. He purchased or seized slaves in Africa and after transporting them to Spanish colonies in the Caribbean offered them for sale to plantation owners. What is astonishing is the degree to which he had to engage in guile, pretence and force to achieve these purchases. Moreover, following the success of his first voyage the colonists knew the Spanish government would severely punish any cooperation and Hawkins had to perform a public show of force in order for the colonists to later claim they had been unwilling partners in trade.

Accounts were written of all three of Hawkins' voyages.[29] The briefest report is of his first voyage of 1562 but it is still revealing. For example, Hawkins gave clear reasons for slaving: he had been 'amongst other particulars assured that Negroes were very good merchandise in Hispaniola [Cuba], and that store of Negroes might easily be had upon the coast of Guinea, resolved with himself to make trial thereof.' The ships left Plymouth for Tenerife and then:

> 'Passed to Sierra Leone upon the coast of Guinea which place by the people of that country is called Tagarin, where he stayed some good time, and got into his possession, partly by the sword, and party by other means, to the number of 300 Negroes at the least, besides other merchandise which that country yieldeth.
>
> With this pray, he sailed over the ocean sea unto the island of Hispaniola and arrived first at the port of Isabella. And there he had reasonable utterance of his English commodities as also of some part of his Negroes (trusting the Spaniards no further no further then that by his own strength he was able still to master them). From the port of Isabella he went to Puerto de Plata where he made like sales, standing always upon his guard. From thence also he sailed to Monte Christi (another port on the north side of Hispaniola and the last place of his touching where he had peaceable traffic) and made vent of the whole number of his Negroes for which he received in those 3 places by way of exchange such quantity of merchandise that he did not only lade his own 3 ships with hides, ginger, sugars and some quantity of pearls but he freighted also two other hulks with hides and other like commodities which he sent to Spain. . . . And so with prosperous success and much gain to himself and the aforesaid adventurers, he came home . . .'

The account of Hawkins' second voyage, of 1564 to 1565, was written by John Sparke and shows more clearly how difficult these expeditions were and why other men were subsequently disinclined to continue. The ships sailed from Plymouth on October 18 1564 and returned in late September 1565. The account comprises more than 10,000 words and gives considerable details on Africa and the West Indies. At the end of November Hawkins' ships arrived at Cape Verde and Sparke noted:

'these people are all black and are called Negroes, without any apparel saving before their privates. Of stature goodly men and well liking by reason of their food which passeth all Guineans for kine [cattle], goats, pullen [poultry], rice, fruits and fish . . . To speak somewhat of the sundry sorts of these Guineans: the people of Cape Verde are called Leophares and counted the goodliest men of all other saving the Congos which do inhabit this side of Cape De Buena Esperanca. These Leophares have wars against the Ieloffes which are borderers by them . . . Here we stayed but one night and part of the day for [on] the 7th of December we came away in that pretending [intending] to have taken Negroes there perforce [by force]; the *Minion's* men gave them there to understand of our coming and our pretence [intention], wherefore they did avoid the snares we had laid for them.'

Afterwards the ships sailed to the island of Sambula. The description of it includes details of the struggles between the Africans as well as reveals the state of slavery there. Sparke explained that some of the Africans he took were already slaves:

'In this island we stayed certain days, going every day onshore to take the inhabitants with burning and spoiling their towns. Who [the island's inhabitants] before were Sapies and were conquered by the Samboses (inhabitants beyond Sierra Leone). These Samboses had inhabited there three years before our coming thither and in so short space have so planted the ground that they had great plenty of meal, rice, roots, pompions, pullen, goats . . . and sundry other in no place in all that country so abundantly thereby they lived more deliciously than [any] other. These inhabitants have divers [many] of the Sapies which they took in the wars as their slaves; whom only they kept to till the ground in that they neither have the knowledge thereof nor yet will themselves. Of whom we took many in that place but of the Samboses none at all, for they fled into the main[land].'

Sparke also recorded that the Samboses also made slaves of their own people as a form of punishment for crime.

'when they sit in council the king or captain sitteth in the midst and the elders upon the floor by him (for they give reverence to their elders) and the common sort sit round about them. There they sit to examine matters of theft. Which, if a man be taken with to steal but a Portuguese cloth from another, he is sold to the Portuguese for a slave.'

Hawkins' men continued along the coast for several months to gather a sufficient number of Africans. Sparke noted a particularly fierce battle to gain slaves on the 27th of December:

'the Captain was advertised by the Portuguese of a town of the Negroes called Bymba (being in the way as they returned) where was not only great quantity of gold but also that there were not above forty men and a hundred women and children in the town. So that if he would give the adventure upon the same he might get a hundred slaves. With the which tidings he being glad because [in order that] the Portuguese should not think him to be of so base a courage but that he durst give them that and greater attempts. And being thereunto also the more provoked [enticed] with the prosperous success he had in other islands adjacent, where he had put them all to flight, and taken in one boat twenty [slaves] [al]together, determined to stay before the town three or four hours to see what he could do. And thereupon prepared his men in armour and weapons together to the number of forty men well appointed ... [They had as] guides certain Portuguese in a boat who brought some of them to their death. We landing boat after boat and divers [many] of our men scattering themselves, contrary to the Captain's will, by one or two in a company. For [they had] the hope that they had to find gold in their houses, ransacking the same. In the meantime the Negroes came upon them and hurt many being thus scattered. Whereas if five or six had been together they had been able (as their companions did) to give the overthrow to 40 of them. And being driven down to take their boats [they] were followed so hardly by a rout of Negroes (who by that took courage to pursue them to their boats) that not only some of them but others standing onshore (not looking for any such matter by means that the Negroes did flee at the first and our companions remained in the town) were suddenly so set upon that some with great hurt recovered [fled to] their boats. Other some not able to recover the same, took [to] the water and perished by means of the ooze. While this was doing, the captain (who with a dozen men) went through the town, returned, finding 200 Negroes at the water's side, shooting at them in the boats and cutting them in pieces which were drowned in the water. At whose coming they [the Africans] ran all away. So he entered his boats and before he could put off from the shore they returned again and shot very fiercely and hurt divers of them. Thus we returned back somewhat discomforted although the Captain in a singularly wise manner carried himself with countenance very cheerfully outwardly as though he did little weigh the death of his men nor yet the great hurt of the rest although his heart inwardly was broken in pieces for it.'

Hawkins lost seven men and had gained only ten slaves. Two days later the ships set sail for the Caribbean. The vessels were beset by a lack of wind which caused a shortage of water. But Sparke noted 'Almighty God never suffereth his elect to perish' and strong winds brought them to the Americas. The water shortages were particularly difficult given the considerable number of Africans onboard and the writer noted that many feared too many slaves would die of thirst.

After Hawkins' difficulties in obtaining slaves and crossing the Atlantic he had further problems in selling the slaves to the Spanish. The colonists had instructions from Madrid not to trade with foreigners and the governor of the first island enforced this law. Hawkins was forced to spend two months through the West Indies until he came to an island where he was able to negotiate the sale of what he called 'certain lean and sick Negroes' who would have otherwise, he argued, died onboard. He went on to sell more of this slaves and the voyage was also highly profitable.

On this third, and final voyage from 1567 to 1568, there were even greater difficulties in selling slaves in the West Indies and obtaining them in Africa. Hawkins wrote this account himself, possibly because of the disastrous events in the West Indies of which he felt betrayed by the Spanish. He noted the subterfuge needed in the Caribbean:

'partly by the Spaniards' desire of Negroes and partly by friendship of the treasurer we obtained a secret trade whereupon the Spaniards resorted to us by night and bought of us to the number of 200 Negroes.'

His account of first obtaining slaves is of great interest. Hawkins noted he had problems in acquiring 150 Africans. This forced him to accept the offer of a local king:

'there came to us a Negro, sent from a king oppressed by other kings his neighbours, desiring our aid, with promise that as many Negroes as by these wars might be obtained, as well of his part as of ours, should be at our pleasure. Whereupon we concluded to give aid and sent 120 of our men. Which [on] the 15 of January [we] assaulted a town of the Negroes of our ally's adversaries which had in it 8,000 inhabitants. It being very strongly impaled and fenced after their manner but I was so well defended that our men prevailed not but lost six men and forty [more were] hurt. So that our men sent forthwith to me for more help. Whereupon considering that the good success of this enterprise might highly further the commodity of our voyage, I went myself and with the help of the king of our side assaulted the town both by land and sea and very hardly with fire (their houses being covered with dry palm leaves. [We] obtained the town, put the inhabitants to flight, where we took 250 persons (men, women and children) and by our friend the king by our side there were taken 600 prisoners whereof we hoped to have had our choice. But the Negro (in which nation is seldom or never found truth) meant nothing less. For that night he removed his camp and prisoners so that we were fain to content us with those few which we had gotten ourselves.

Now we had obtained between four and five hundred Negroes wherewith we thought it somewhat reasonable to seek the coast of the West Indies and there for our Negroes and other merchandise, we hoped to obtain whereof to countervail our charges with some gains . . .'

This may have been the last slaving voyage from Devon, or England, for some time. The accounts of Hawkins' use of trade and force to obtain slaves and his relationships with local rulers illustrates some of the complexities of slaving but the lack of any original reports from Africans hinders our understanding of how Europeans were able to successfully engage in slaving.

There are other considerations to keep in mind. Clearly the European technological superiority was for Hawkins an advantage, particularly in trading goods with Africans such as guns. Of greater importance was the African practice of engaging in warfare which resulted in enslaving defeated people. The cooperation of some Africans in willingly selling slaves was essential to Hawkins' success. This was partly the result of an existing demand for slaves from Muslims in northern Africa: Arab slave traders were active in Africa before, during and after the Europeans. In addition to their keeping slaves, Africans sold them to Christians or Muslims. The removal of rival populations not only weakened Africans' neighbouring enemies but strengthened their positions by increasing their numbers in proportion, provided a secondary income and rid a community of unwanted people. Some of these Africans had been convicted of committing crimes and subsequently sold by the state as slaves. There was an English correlation: since the early 1600s the English had similarly expelled their own convicts to the New World and, from the late 1700s, to Australia.

Sir Francis Drake participated in the three voyages but contradictory accounts make it impossible to determine his precise activities. He was probably in his mid twenties at this time and was only a crewman on the first two voyages while on the third it appears he captained a vessel and engaged in slaving in Africa. However, Drake was a junior figure in all three fleets and it is likely that his participation would have gone unnoticed had he not become prominent in the following three decades. There is uncertainty as to whether the final voyage was profitable and it may have been the financial uncertainties in forcibly selling slaves that subsequently pushed Drake towards privateering.[29]

## 2

# African Devonians, the Guinea Company, 1588 to 1598, and merchants of Barnstaple, Colyton and Exeter

In 1588 Queen Elizabeth I granted six Devon merchants and two London merchants trading rights to the river of 'Senega and Gambra in Guinea'. These men comprised William Brayley, Gilbert Smith, Nicholas Spicer and John Doricot of Exeter, Richard Dodderidge of Barnstaple and John Yonge of Colyton. For ten years they held this license. During that time Africans were brought to Devon possibly through this association. If so, then this is the next indication of participation in the slave trade. However, there may be another reason for their arrival in Devon.

It was about this time that evidence appears in parish registers. The name of Dodderidge appears in the first African reference in Barnstaple's parish register, the baptism of 'Grace, a neiger servant of Mr Richard Doddridge' on 6 April 1596. He may have been responsible for distributing several additional Africans amongst three of his neighbours. The register noted baptisms for:

'Elizabeth an nigor with Mrs Ayer' on 10 April 1598
'Mary, daughter of Elizabeth, a nyger, with Mrs Ayer' on 22 May 1605
'Chaterin, a nygor with Mr Lanyon' on 26 February 1605/6
'Elizabeth, daughter of Susannah, a nygor' 10 November 1606

There is also a burial noted on 22nd May 1596 for 'Peter Mingus servant to Mr Norrishe'. In the margin is noted the single word 'negor. The entries were recorded twice and there are slight differences between them such as the baptism of 'Chaterin, a nygor with Mr Lanyon' otherwise 'Katherine a Negro, servant to Mr Lanyon'. There was also a burial in July 1605 of 'Marie, daughter to Elizabeth, a negro, servant to Mrs Ayre, 8th day base'. Interestingly, a copy noted she was illegitimate but failed to record her race nor does that for Peter Mingus' burial.

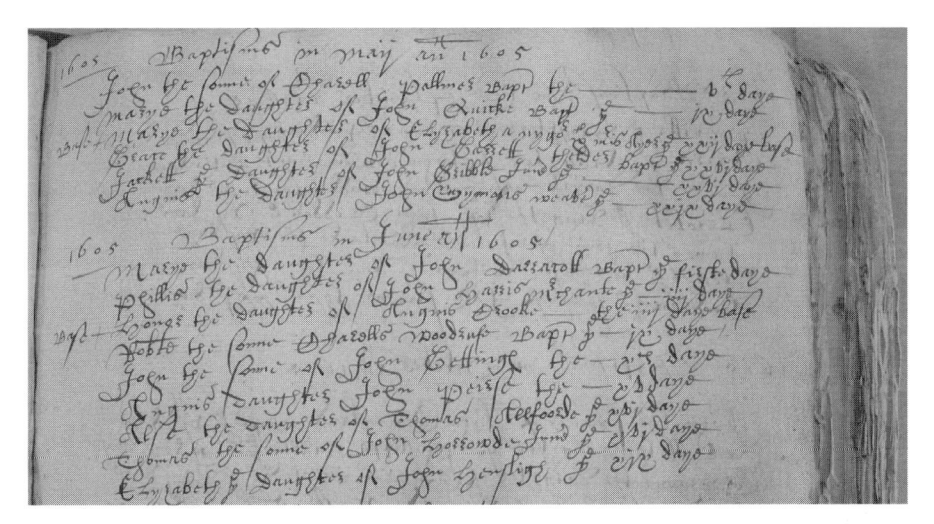

Entry in Barnstaple parish register for Mary, daughter of Elizabeth 'a nygor', 1605 (North Devon Record Office)

The appearance of these seven Africans was, no doubt, of considerable interest to this port of some two thousand residents but they were not commented upon by Adam Wyatt, the town clerk then compiling a chronicle of the main events in Barnstaple's history. A second piece of evidence makes this African presence in North Devon all the more remarkable. Nicholas Wichalse of Barnstaple wrote his will on 28 August 1570 and in it made a bequest to 'Anthonye my negarre'. This shows that eighteen years before Dodderidge was granted trading rights in Africa there was already a connection between Barnstaple and that continent. Moreover, Anthony was not enslaved but free: Wichalse gave him five pounds on condition he remained in the service of his wife Mary 'otherwise yf she mynde not to kepe hym to give hym five marks [£3 7s 6d] and lette hym dep[ar]te'.

However, it is possible that the other Africans came to Barnstaple through prize ships and not through the Guinea Company. On 26 December 1590 Wyatt noted:

> 'There came in over the bar of Barnstaple and arrived at Appledore a ship of this town called the Prudence of 100 tons and belonging to Mr Dodderidge of this town and others. She sailed over the bar of Barnstaple in a reprisal voyage on St Mathew's Day this year having in her 80 men or above and brought in a prize with her being a Portugal ship of about 80 tons which had been at Castellmayne upon the coast of Guinea, having in her 4 chests of gold to the value of 16,000 pounds and divers chains of gold with civet, ambergris and other things of great price with much grains [of gold], elephant tooth etc. Such a value as the like prize hath not before this time been brought into this port. This ship was brought up unto the quay of Barnstaple aforesaid the third day next following; the said chests of gold did weigh about 320 pound weight of gold, besides many chains of gold whereof the company made pillage.'

The timing of the licence, at the time when England and Spain formally were at war, limited trade opportunities in Africa. It is possible the Africans noted in the parish registers were onboard this particular prize ship, seized as Portuguese property and brought to Barnstaple with the rest of the cargo. Under these circumstances Dodderidge would have had few financial opportunities for selling them given England had no need for plantation slaves as it had no colonies and nor could they be sold to Spanish or Portuguese merchants given the state of war between the three countries. A group of Africans in Barnstaple might well have been a dilemma for Dodderidge and parcelling them out as servants would have relieved him of a financial burden let alone have given a monetary return. Another of the Africans, Peter Mingus, belonged to John Norris, another privateer.[34]

It is interesting in this context that in none of these registers does the word 'slave' appear. Unfortunately no information has survived to indicate whether these individuals were being paid for their labour or what restrictions they lived under. For example, it is not known how freely they could move from one employer to another, if at all. A belief developed in England that baptism was the key to freedom. If this was a mechanism for manumission then these individuals should be seen in a different light.[35] It may be useful to compare them with another African who worked in a household in close proximity to Barnstaple. In the 1640s the Earl and Countess of Bath employed James Blackamore, otherwise known as James the Blackamoor, as a cook at Tawstock. He received a salary comparable to those given to other household servants. It is interesting that his position was a high status one but one which involved work behind the scenes and not in the public eye.[36]

There are also references in Plymouth's church register to Africans and the first ones appear before the eight Devon merchants had their Guinea licence. The earliest is for a burial of 'Bastien, a blackamoor of Mr William Hawkins' which was recorded on the 10th day of December in 1583. Five years later another burial followed, that of 'John Anthony, a neyger' on the 18th of March in 1587/8. Ten further references could be related to the granting of the license, to slaving or the seizure of foreign prize ships; the merchants were legally entitled to include other men in their license and possibly it was through this connection that these additional Africans appeared in Plymouth but equally these servants may have come to Plymouth through prize ships or slaving. The parish register noted baptisms for:

'Helene, daughter of Cristian the negro servant of Richard Sheere, the supposed father being Cutbert Holman, base [illegitimate], 2 May 1593
Cristien, daughter of Mary, a Negro of John White's and the supposed daughter of John Kinge, a Dutchman, base, 17 November 1594
Fortunatus, son of a Negro of Thomas Kegwins, the supposed father being a Portugall, 24 December 1594
Susan, daughter of a Blackmoor, 1 July 1596
Katheren, daughter of Don Pedro, a bastard Neger, 4 October 1596
Richard, son of Mary a neger, base, the reputed father Roger Hoggett, 23 June 1603'

There are also burials noted in the register:

Lazia Carbew, a Negro, 11 March 1591/2
Cristian, daughter of Cristian, Richard Sheer's blackamoor, 14 April 1594

a blackamore at Captain Sparks, 30 November 1601
Mary, a blackamore at Mr Stallenge, 6 December 1601

Plymouth's references continue through the century with the next such entry being a burial on the 19th of August 1640 for 'a neager who was employed by Mr Abraham Jennings'.

Less conclusive evidence has been found for Colyton or Exeter having had resident Africans resulting from this trading venture. The first reference for Colyton is the burial on 1 June 1619 for 'Katheren, the blackamoor servant of Sir William Pole, knight, Antiquary of Colcombe' and for Exeter it was even later: in the parish register for St Mary Major appears the burial in 1632 for 'Thomas, the son of a Blackamoor'. There may have been Africans in these and other parts of Devon not noted as such in parish registers or were denied Christian sacraments and thus were not recorded in parochial documents.

There were also Africans living in the unlikely location of Hatherleigh. This remote town had three early references in its parish register: on May 13th 1604 'Grace, a blackamoore' was baptised followed by 'Rebecca, base daughter of Grace a negro' on 10 August 1606 and 'Honor, base daughter of Grace a negro' on 8 May 1611. Rebecca died not long after she was born; she was buried on 23 December 1607 as was her sister Honor on 6 February 1613. The family with whom they lived has not yet been identified.

The Africans' presence in Devon coincided with the arrival of other foreign nationals. Parish registers also show baptisms of 'Raleigh' a native American at Bideford in 1588,[37] of 'Adrian the Indian' at Stoke Gabriel in 1597, of 'Gifferdandgorge an Indian' at Plymouth on 22 October 1602 and the burial of 'John an Indian of the Fort' in Plymouth on 23 February 1613/14. These men were named after Devon men Sir Walter Raleigh, Adrian Gilbert, Sir Ferdinando Gorges and possibly Sir John Popham of Somerset. The native Americans were in Devon as publicity tools to engage possible investors in overseas ventures. There is no evidence that there was a similar service provided by the Africans. Instead it is likely they performed servants' duties similar to those which already employed many Devonians.

# 3

# Devon slaves in Morocco, 1637

At about the same time as Africans were being forcibly transported to the New World, other Africans were similarly taking Devonians to North Africa. From the early 1600s until the second decade of the nineteenth century North Africans captured English men and women and enslaved them. The captors are now popularly known as 'Barbary Corsairs' but at the time as 'Turks' because of a loose political association between the North African states and Istanbul; the implication was that they were Muslims. The English captives were brought to Morocco, Algeria, Libya and Tunisia where they were either imprisoned or sold on.

From 1625 the Devon coast was a prime location for these thousands of seizures. Kidnapping took place at sea but not on land in England, unlike in Ireland or on the Continent. Some of this took place within sight of the English coast. Religious and racial differences heightened the hysteria which built up over the fleets of marauders and the conditions in which these English slaves lived were comparable to those of the Equatorial Africans in the New World. Documentary evidence suggests that the number of Devonians enslaved in North Africa exceeded the number of Equatorial Africans taken by Devonians in the New World. In the seventeenth century several thousand men, and some women, from Devon were enslaved and this number continued to grow over the next two centuries.[38]

One account, published in 1721 as *A Description of the Nature of Slavery Amongst The Moors & The Cruel Sufferings Of Those That*

Engraving of the tortures given to European slaves in Morocco, 1637

*Fall Into It*, noted a number of captured Devonians including those onboard the *Norton* of Topsham. It had sailed on July 2nd 1720 from the Isle of Rhé with salt for Newfoundland. The crew included Thomas Ayres, Nicholas Selby, Thomas Brown, Henry Hardin, Ellis Keen, Southy Lightfoot, Ellis Flee, William Lyle, George Tilly, Henry Hollwill, Richard Page and Thomas Short. Several of the men had already died by publication of the account. Many dozens of other Devon ships had a similar fate during the eighteenth century.[39]

The seizure of Europeans by Africans remained an emotive issue for several hundred years. In the years following the final defeat of Napoleon in 1815 diplomatic negotiations between the Great Powers of Europe included the issue of African slavery but the delegates were more concerned with Africans enslaving Europeans.[40] Devonians had more than two hundred years to ponder the justification of Africans and Europeans engaging in the slavery of each other. The forced movement of Devonians to North Africa neatly coincided with that of Africans to the New World and raises questions on how some Devonians could complain of the violation of their freedoms while at the same time others were involved in similar operations in Africa.

Ransoms were paid for some Europeans and occasionally Devonians returned home but it is thought the majority died overseas. On two occasions the English government intervened through the use of naval force to obtain the release of slaves and one list[41] has survived of the names of 89 Devonians who were rescued out of more than 300 captives from throughout the country. Place names were also recorded on this list and Topsham was written in its older form of 'Apshom'. 'Sally' refers to Sallee, the port for Rabat in Morocco.

*Devon and the Slave Trade*

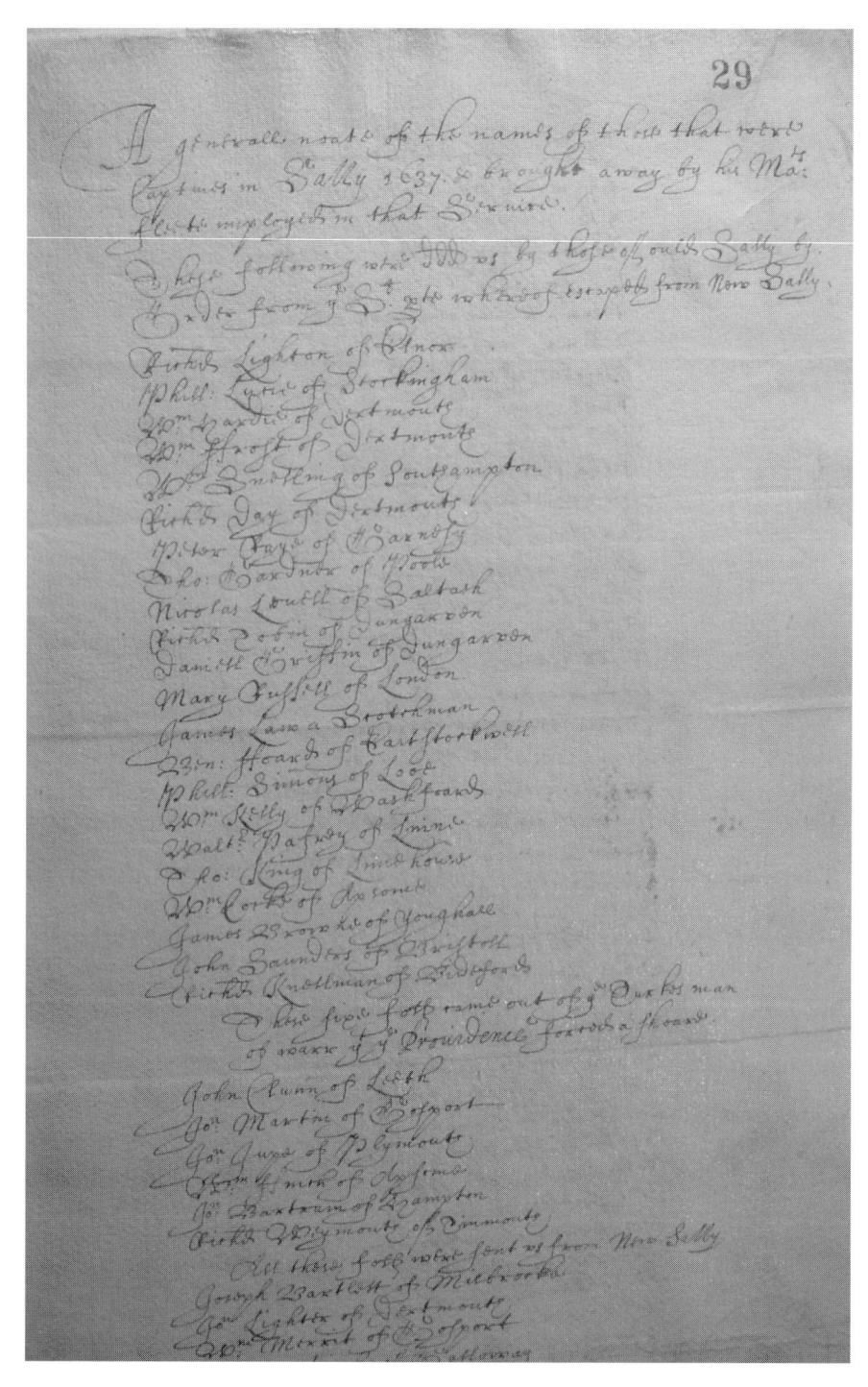

List of captives from Morocco, 1637 (National Archives, SP71/13/29)

*Acquisition: Slave Voyages*

'A general note of the names of those that were captives in Sally 1637 and brought away by his Majesty's fleet employed in that service. These following were delivered us by those of old Sally by order from the s. part whereof escaped from New Sally.

Richard Lighter of Elnor
Philip Lutie of Stokenham
Wiliam Hardie of Dartmouth
William Frust of Dartmouth
William Snelling of Southampton
Richard Day of Dartmouth
Mary Russell of London
Thomas Gardner of Poole
James Law, a Scotchman
Nicholas Lovell of Saltash
Ben Feard of East Stockwell
Richard Tobin of Dungarven
Philip Simms of Looe
Daniel Griffin of Dungarven
William Kelly of Washford
Walter Pafrey of Lime
William Cocke of Apsom

Thomas King of Limehouse
James Brown of Youghall
John Saunders of Bristol
Richard Knollman of Bideford

These folks came out of the Turks man of war that the *Providence* forced ashore:
   John Clunn of Leeth
   John Martin of Gosport
   John Jope of Plymouth
   William Firth of Apsom
   John Bartram of Hampton
   Richard Weymouth of Teignmouth

All these folk were sent us from New Sally
   Joseph Bartlett of Millbrook
   John Lighter of Dartmouth
   William Merrit of Gosport
   James Linch of Galloway
   William Bradshaw of Carnnathon
   Ann Bedford of London
   Katherine Richards of Youghall
   Thomas Man of Exeter
   Rebecca Man of Exeter
   John Hugh of Dungarven
   John Christopher of Helford
   Charles Hollyday of London
   Richard Barret of Exeter
   John Kerry of Minniard
   Thomas Trefife of Looe
   Peter Pill of Millbrook
   George Rickett of Kinsale
   Isaac Fickett of Jersey
   William Harris of Dartmouth
   Hanibal Thomas of Scilly
   Thomas Poodam of Apsom
   Robert Stephens, a Scotchman
   John Richars of Apsom
   Ralph Woster of London
   Thomas Isaacke of Wells
   Pascoe Celly of Plymouth
   Richard Beson of Jersey
   William Rabbe of Guernsey
   Richard Chappin of Apsom

Cornelius [Fitz] Morris of Youghall
Tristram Sharpe of Dartmouth
Edward Seaman of Looe
Christopher Wills of Dartmouth
George Cone of Apsom
Richard Wills of Helford
John Houdver of Fowey
Adam Hoode of Youghall
Humphrey Bate of Plymouth
Philip Strange of Barstalbe [Barnstaple]
Robert Mowbray of Leeth
Robert Bucland of Dartmouth
John Walker of Youghall
William King of Ipswich
Henry Pearcey of Dartmouth
Thomas Poulter of Worcester
William Benion of Carmarthen
John Harry of Dungarven
Edward Stone of Apsome
William Floss of Millbrook
Edward Toby of Dungarven
Teeke Drestell of Dungarven
Robert Miller of Chester
Jo: Butler of Looe
Ed: Drury of Dungarven
William Morris of Leeth
Jo: Cowen, a Scotchman
Edward Dungwell of Dungarven
Thomas D[?]gen of Dungarven
Jo: Browne of Bristol
Jo: Flattery of Torbay
Nicholas Rider of Plymouth
Adrian Stannill of Plymouth
Andrew Flattery of Torbay
Jonas Thomas of Lyme
Jo: Norris of Larpoole
James Snell, a Scotchman
George Hall of Dartmouth

Michael Downes of London
William Webber of Apsome
Robert Peece of Waterford
Nicholas Gray of Apsome
[torn]
Andrew Briant of Lyme
John Conworth of Dungarven
Nicholas Trathorne of Helford
Sampson Derry of Plymouth
Thomas Devorax of Washford
Jo: Boone of Plymouth
Jo: Wright of Plymouth
Jo: Winfield of Lerpen
Cormocke Fitz Thomas
Edward Barnes of London
Edward Quaite of Dartmouth
Richard Maddocke of Millbrook
Walter Waight of Millbrook
Mathew Adams of Plymouth
John Grister of London
William Crape of Dartmouth
Thomas Webber of Dartmouth
William Morsey of Youghall
Richard Scutt of Apsom
Jo: Baker of Plymouth
William Helvert of Apsom
Philip Doone of Plymouth
Peter Feres of Youghall
Joshua Thomas of Bristol
Dot. Miskoll of Dungarven
Thomas Butcher of Dartmouth
73 persons

William Trevor of Plymouth
Borne Ranke of Plymouth
John Primsom of Dartmouth
David Gardner, a Scotchman
Teeke Candre of Youghall
Christopher Galloway of Larpoole

*Acquisition: Slave Voyages*

Elias Fop of London
Jo: Challenge of Plymouth
Nicholas Quane of Dungarven
Abraham Cocke of Plymouth
Robert Burford of Bristol
Morris Toby of Dungarven
Thomas Eagles of Worcester
William Langford of Waterford
Jo: Pollard of Salcombe
Jo: Harris of St Germans
Philip Pearce of Denbury
Edward Toby of Dungarven
Samuel Grimeth of Ipswich
Thomas Grimelstone of London
Wal: Merchant of Milbrook
Jon: Waight of Dungarven
Thomas Vaughan of Miniard
78 persons

Jo: Byford of Bristol
Jo: Bagshot of Bristol
Grace Martin of the Bantry
Edward Whitterne of London
Robert Hogg of Leeth
William Nicholas of Weymouth
Thomas Eagles of Stroudwater
Jo: Morgan of Guernsey
James Kember of Plymouth
James Morris of Youghall
Hugh Morgan of Stonehouse
John Jones of Bristol
Michael Maglin of Youghall
Jon: Mearce of Kinsale
Richard Wood of Millbrook
Nicholas Griffin of Youghall
Da: Mursen of Dungarven
William Meskell of Dungarven
Josias Spicer of Plymouth
Thomas Loane of Taunton

Henry Goard of Plymouth
Thomas Walte of Aberday
Hugh Henson of Plymouth
William West of Abington
Christopher Page of Colchester
Henry Jenkins of Plymouth
Patrick Garland of Tredath
Jo: Thomas of Helford
John Laine of London
Richard Coop of Plymouth
Edward Adams of Apsom
Jon: Lerry of Guernsey
Jon: Clarke of Dartmouth
Jo: Harris of Looe
Jo: Langdon of Merriot
Robert Biger of London
Thomas Flowhaven of Dungarven
Thomas Cursie of Dungarven
Jo: Pitcher of London
Charles Edwards of Looe
Thomas Elliot of Plymouth
Abraham Harris of London
Ocdo: Stoud of Minehead
Edward Bampfeild of Weymouth
Jo: Carley of London
William Spicer of Apsom
George Phillips of Silly
William Waldkeeper of Edinburgh
Nicholas Muggin of Guernsey
[torn]
William Cratbert of Dartmouth
Thomas Smith of Hull
Peter Randell of Plymouth
Hugh Sander of Plymouth
Garrett Fittham of Dungarven
Robert Davie of Lyme
Edward Cranst of Plymouth
Edward Pope of Weymouth
John Howe of Millbrook

Stephen Cutten of Kinsale
Jo: Nouger of Jersey
Jo: Hunt of Dartmouth
William Lange of Plymouth
Richard Delling of Otterton
Thomas Coventy of Westchester
Thomas Lockie of Plymouth
Tippet Colsocke of Plymouth
Adrian Redes of Plymouth
Gregory Warde of Otterton
70 persons

Augustine Tricke of Barnstaple
Abraham Kembe of Guernsey
Stephen Elliot of Apsom
Jo: Stephens of Plymouth
Richard Stouth of Lyme
Robert Black of Guernsey
William Garrett of Poole
Jo: Browne of Bristol
Peter Rowland of London
Walter Noble of Youghall
William Grifin of Youghall
Thomas Browne of Weymouth
John Holman of Apsom
Valentine Goodwin of London
Edward Cartwright of Jersey
Derby Lane of Dungarven
Aubry Mudge of Newton Bushel
Richard Greene of Washford
Richard Ellford of Plymouth
Jo: Cary of St Ives
Henry Augery of Plymouth
Jo: Browne of Leeth
Henry Matten of Ashborne
Richard Boone of Plymouth
Richard Match of Dungarven
Walter Land of Plymouth
Richard Shilbe of Plymouth

Walter Michell of Plymouth
Richard Katherine of London
Grace Grimfield of Bristol
Jane Mellowes of London
George Hagon of Dealin
John Leekes of London
William Freeman of Poole
William [blank] of Tisbury
John Bowden of Dartmouth
Tristram Rose of Falmouth
Edward Tindall of London
Richard Moune of Dungarven
John Mersie of Dungarven
James Duncane of Apsom
William Lambe of Southampton
Robert Mervey of Plymouth
Walter Proude of Kinsale
Peter Clarke of London
Richard Coope of Linnington
Jane Dawe of Dorchester
Richard Fisher of Bathampton
Thomas Derdoe of Shaftesbury
Nicholas Randton of Bristol
50 persons

A separate list was made which gave the total number of people from each place.[42]

| London | 22 |
| Gravesend | 2 |
| Chatham | 1 |
| Gosper | 3 |
| Limington | 1 |
| Southampton | 4 |
| Lerpin | 1 |
| Jersey | 6 |
| Guernsey | 5 |
| Poole | 3 |
| Weymouth | 3 |

*Acquisition: Slave Voyages*

| | | | |
|---|---|---|---|
| Lyme | 5 | Westchester | 2 |
| Apsom | 18 | Colchester | 1 |
| Exeter | 3 | Ipswich | 2 |
| Teignmouth | 1 | Lynn | 1 |
| Newton Bushel | 1 | Hull | 1 |
| Tor[quay] | 2 | Aberday | 1 |
| Ashburton | 1 | | |
| Dartmouth | 22 | Scotland | |
| Denbury | 1 | Edinburgh | 6 |
| Salcombe | 2 | Leith | 5 |
| Plymouth | 38 | St Two | 1 |
| Millbrook | 9 | Ayre | 1 |
| Saltash | 1 | | |
| Looe | 8 | Wales | |
| Fowey | 1 | Carnarthen | 2 |
| Falmouth | 1 | Glamoris | |
| Helford | 5 | | |
| St Germans | 1 | Ireland | |
| Scilly | 2 | Dungarven | 27 |
| Barnstaple | 4 | Washford | 2 |
| Otterton | 2 | Galloway | 2 |
| Minyard | 4 | Youghall | 13 |
| Shaftesbury | 1 | Larpoole | 2 |
| Stroudwater | 1 | Develin | 1 |
| Taunton | 2 | Waterford | 3 |
| Bristol | 8 | Tredath | 2 |
| Wells | 1 | Kinsale | 5 |
| Tisbury | 1 | | |
| Worcester | 2 | 11 women | |
| Clifton | 2 | Majesty's subjects 302, Frenchmen | |
| Gloucester | 3 | 24, Dutch 8, Spanish 9 | |
| Abington | 1 | | |

# 4

# Seven 'ten per centers' from Plymouth, Dartmouth and Exeter, 1698 to 1712, and the account of the *Daniel & Henry*, 1700

In 1698 trade to Africa was extended from the Royal African Company to all merchants on condition a customs' duty of ten percent was paid on their Guinea-bound cargo. Those who sailed under this arrangement became known as 'ten per centers'. The arrangements continued until 1712 when the tax was abolished.[43] For these 14 years 7 ten per centers connected with Devon have been identified. The *Betty* of Exeter was first[44] followed by the *Dragon* of Topsham. The latter paid a duty of £67 14s 8d.[45] There is no comprehensive list of all these ships or of the people they enslaved and there may have been additional voyages, clandestine in nature, which have not yet been identified or which might not have been recorded. Even so, eighteenth-century sources provide better but still only partial information than those for the earlier periods.

In addition to the seven ten per centers there was an earlier voyage from Devon. In 1682 the *Speedwell* of Dartmouth sailed from Exeter for Cape de Verde (the Atlantic islands off Senegal) and was freighted by an Exeter merchant. The expedition went further: the ship sailed around the Cape of Good Hope to Madagascar where Africans and other cargo were taken onboard. It probably sailed to that island as it was out of the jurisdiction of the Royal African Company. In April the *Speedwell* arrived at Barbados with ivory and 170 slaves.[46] The

*Acquisition: Slave Voyages*

Plymouth in 1676 (Westcountry Studies Library, SC2300)

voyage was more successful than of many of the Devon ships which subsequently followed.

Arrangements for the voyages were complicated and reflected the complex manner in which trade was conducted at this time. It is striking that with the exception of George Barons, the Exeter merchant resident

Dartmouth in the early 1700s (Westcountry Studies Library, SC0499)

in the Netherlands, the remaining ten per centers did not repeat their involvement in Africa. The only exception was Roger Prowse who acted for John Burridge of Lyme Regis.[47] Few voyages were completely Devonian in composition; two left from Bristol but involved Devonians, one was a London vessel which sailed from Plymouth, another was a ship which went to Rotterdam from whence it left for Africa and four voyages were for a merchant originally from Exeter but who lived in Holland. Devon's involvement can best be described as partial. In comparison, the Burridge family of Dorset, which was involved in one Devon ten per center voyage, as well as another later slaving expedition, set out twelve additional voyages from London, Bristol and Lyme Regis[48] and Bristol had some 594 ships sail out in the same period.[49]

The voyages are summarised in the following table.

Ten per centers with a Devon connection, 1698 to 1712

| Date | Ship | Origin | Destination | Merchant |
|---|---|---|---|---|
| 1698 | *Betty* of Exeter | Bristol | Cape de Verde | John Ellard |
| 1699 | *Dragon* of Topsham | Exeter | Africa | Arthur Jeffery & others |
| 1700 | *Daniel & Henry* of Exeter (and Dartmouth) | Dartmouth | Guinea | Daniel Ivy, Henry Arthur, James Gould & others |
| 1700 | *Elizabeth Galley* of Bristol | Bristol | Guinea & Calabar | John Parminter & others |
| 1709 | *Dartmouth Galley* of Dartmouth | Dartmouth | Africa | John Harris & others |
| 1710 | *Sylvia* | Plymouth | Guinea | George Barons |
| 1711 | *John & Robert* of London | Plymouth | Gambia | Robert Burridge & others |

Sources: Elizabeth Donnan (ed.), *Documents Illustrative of the Slave Trade to America* (New York, 1965), II, 29, 31, 94; Nigel Tattersfield, *The Forgotten Trade* (1990), 369-74

The main commodities sent to Africa included Swedish iron, pewter and brass, bugles, cotton and linen cloth, alcohol, beads and coral. Cloth was carried on some of the ships and much of it was brought to Devon from other parts of the country, such as the worsteds, bays and fustians, or imported from abroad notably the cotton and linen. Only a small

Customs entry for the *John and Robert* of London, 1711, destined for Gambia from Plymouth (National Archives, E190/1070/12)

portion of the cargo can be identified as having been Devonian in origin: Exeter, the centre of the county's cloth industry, specialised in serge, particularly in a type of cloth known as a perpetuana. Serge was exported on one voyage. It left from Exeter; the *Betty* of Exeter brought serge to the Cape Verde islands. It appears Exeter's woollen cloth was not as marketable in Equatorial Africa as cotton cloth but even so, it still found a use: one commentator in the late 1600s noted Africans used perpetuanas to make girdles 'four fingers broad to wear about their waist'.[50] As discussed earlier, the cloth industry in Devon was then at its most prosperous and Exeter's cloth exports were concentrated on markets in the Netherlands, the Baltic and France but, tellingly, the most eminent historian to work on the local cloth industry makes no mention of Africa.[51]

The *Daniel & Henry*, sometimes described as being of Dartmouth and at other times as of Exeter, appears to be the only ship for which a detailed account has survived. It was part of 'Burwells book', an account by John Burwell who has been described as the 'ship's husband'.[52] The *Daniel & Henry* left Dartmouth on 24 February 1700 and returned 17 months later on 23 July 1701. Most of its cargo was supplied by London merchants and not by Devon men. This is similar to that onboard other voyages with the result that national importers/exporters were the financial beneficiaries rather than Devon merchants. The voyage of the *Daniel & Henry* was also not profitable for its investors: it made a loss of nearly £1,500 and those concerned did not repeat the exercise.[53]

Dartmouth's venture into African slavery was at odds with its principal trade at this time: the port, like Teignmouth, was overwhelmingly concerned in overseas fishing. It had progressed from medieval fishing in Ireland, the North Sea and Iceland to the development of New England and particularly Newfoundland. By 1700, when the *Daniel & Henry* left Dartmouth, many tens of thousands of Devonians had earned their livelihoods from fishing. It was, as Sir Walter Raleigh once notably stated, the main stay of the county. Although the voyage of the *Daniel & Henry* is not representative of the main thrust of Dartmouth, or Devon commercial enterprises, the documents of this voyage provide good insights into the nature of slaving at the time. It may be Devonians' unfamiliarity with the trade was responsible for the financial failure and the prices they paid for purchasing Africans were not representative of their more accomplished competitors. Nevertheless the details are revealing of how they conducted trade.

For its cargo the ship carried alcohol, knives, bars of iron, basins and tankards (water vessels), looking glasses, gunpowder, firearms (carbines), flanes (arrows), sheets, English woollen cloth (perpetuanas, says), Indian cottons (tapseil, salempore, nehallaware, niconees) and Flemish dornicks. In one instance tapestries were traded. Over the course of the two and half months the ship was off West Africa some of the cargo was exchanged for gold in the form of ackeys (a gold-based currency in Guinea) and in one instance 6 tackeys (half of an ackey).[54] At other times the cargo directly purchased slaves. The ship anchored at eight places. At each point the amount of goods or gold paid or exchanged was noted. In many instances the ackeys raised by selling items were recorded as in '3 lead bars 3A' which was shorthand for 3 ackeys. Some containers were noted such as firkins of tallow, cases for spirits, and barrels of powder. The basins came in various sizes, noted by poundage.

Included amongst the merchant's accounts is the following record.

John Burwell's account of the voyage of the *Daniel & Henry* off Africa, 1700
(Devon Record Office, 3327Aadd/PZ3)

'An account of the disposal of Captain Roger Mathew's cargo in the *Daniel & Henry* on the Gold Coast for slaves, 1700

| Date | Goods | Received |
|---|---|---|
| April 11th at Axim | 3 pieces perpetuanas, 4 sheets, 2 small knives | 1 man |
| April 18th at Dixcove | 2 half barrels powder, 1 small looking glass | 1 woman |
| April 10th at Axim | 4 looking glasses 3A, 3 bars lead 3A | 4 ackeys |
| April 11th at Dixcove | 6 small knives | 6 tackeys |
| | 1 dozen knives | 1 ackey |
| April 12th ditto | 17 looking glasses, 2 knives, 5A, 2 lead bars 2A | 7 ackeys |
| April 13th ditto | 1 nest trunks 8A, 1 firkin tallow 4A | 12 ackeys |
| April 14th ditto | 80 bars of iron, 1 sheet A128, 10 dozen knives 10A | 138 ackeys |
| April 15th ditto | 43 dozen knives A43, 3 sheets A3, 19 dozen knives A19, 5 firkins tallow A20, 1 half case spirits A2, 1 lead bar A1 | 88 ackeys |
| April 17th ditto | 2 half cases spirits A4, 6 dozen knives great A6, 2 firkins tallow A8, 1 firkin tallow & 1 small glass A4, 4 sheets A4 | 26 ackeys |
| May 1st at Commenda | 2 whole cases spirits & paid 24 ackeys gold | 1 man |
| 6th at Commenda | 48 dozen knives large, 39 sheets, 8 whole cases spirits | 3 women, 1 girl |
| 9th ditto | 64 sheets, 1 firkin tallow, 2 pieces perpetuanas, 1 ackey gold | 3 women, 1 boy, 1 girl |
| May 9th ditto | 33 sheets, 3 piece perpetuanas, ½ dozen large knives, & 43 ackeys gold | 2 men |
| | 1 say, 1 perpetuana & firkin tallow, 4 3lb basins, 2 tankards | 1 man |
| | 1 looking glass, 4T, 2 whole & 1 half case spirits 10A | 10 ackey 4 tackeys |
| | 1 dozen great knives & 1 looking glass 1A, 1 half case spirits 2A | 3 ackeys |

*Acquisition: Slave Voyages*

| | | |
|---|---|---|
| May 10th ditto | 2 whole cases spirits 8A, 10 looking glass 2A, 2 firkins powder 4A | 14 ackeys |
| Dixcove | Gave 32 A gold & 28A & 32A | 3 men |
| | For 2 chests corn gave 4 An. Gold | |
| May 10th | | |
| Anamabo | 2 pieces says & 4 3lb basins | 1 man |
| 11th | 1 say & a perpetuana | 1 man |
| 12th | 1 piece say & a firkin tallow | 1 woman |
| 14th | 2 firkins tallow & 16 ackeys gold | 1 woman |
| 15th | 6 half cases spirits, 6 pieces perpetuanas, 6 looking glass | 1 man |
| 13th | gave 22 ackeys gold for | 1 boy |
| May | | |
| Alsenferra | 7 dornicks | 1 girl |
| 16th | 3 firkins tallow & 36 sheets | 1 man, 1 boy |
| 17th | | |
| Tantumquerry | 16 sheets, 4 pieces says, 1 whole case spirits, 2 tankards, 1 firkin powder for 1 man & 2 women, & 4 chests corn | 1 man, 2 women |
| ditto | 1 half barrel powder, 1 firkin tallow & 8 ackeys gold | 1 woman |
| | 5 whole cases spirits, 3 whole dozen [blank], & 48 ackeys gold | 1 man, 1 woman, 1 boy |
| | 24 sheets | 1 woman |
| May 18th ditto | 2 whole & 3 half cases spirits & 1 ackey gold | 1 girl |
| May 20th ditto | 1 firkin tallow, 2 barrels & 4 firkins powder | |
| | 6 sheets | 2 men |
| | 2 sheets & 24 ackeys | 1 man |
| May 21st ditto | 1 flane, 6 great knives, 1 firkin tallow, 1 whole case spirits & 12 ackeys | 1 man |
| | 1 barrel powder 6 dozen great knives | 1 man |
| May 22nd ditto | 7 firkins tallow, 1 dornicks | 1 man |
| ditto Winnebah | 1 piece nehallaware, 1 ackey | 1 woman |
| | 1 barrel powder, & 4 ackeys gold | 1 man |
| 23rd ditto | 32 sheets, 7 firkins tallow & 28 dozen great knives | 2 men |
| 25th ditto | 1 piece dornicks & 32 ackeys gold | 1 man, 1 woman |
| 27th ditto | 1 firkin tallow, 1 barrel powder, 1 3lb basin | 1 man |
| 26th ditto | 2 dozen great knives, & 17 ackeys | 1 boy |
| | 26 ackeys for a young man | 1 boy |
| | 2 dozen great knives, & 24 ackeys gold | 1 woman |

|  |  |  |
|---|---|---|
|  | 5 pieces nehallaware, 3 dozen small knives | 2 women |
|  | 12 dozen small knives, 2 tankards, 2 dozen great knives, 2 firkins tallow, 25 ackeys gold | 1 man |
|  | 3 barrels powder, 1 dozen great knives | 3 men |
| 27th ditto | 2 dornicks, 2 firkins tallow, 32 dozen great knives | 2 boys |
|  | 5 firkins tallow, 2 3lb basin, & 2 tankards | 1 boy |
| 28th | 1 barrel powder & 2 tankards 1 man; 2 firkins tallow, 100 [?], 8 dozen great knives, 1 tankard, 1 woman | 1 man, 1 woman |
|  | 13 dozen great knives, 4 firkins tallow 1 woman; 1 barrel powder 1 man; 1 barrel powder, 2 dozen great knives 1 woman; 2 barrels powder 2 boys | 1 man, 2 woman, 2 boys |
| Winnebah June |  | [totals] |
|  | 1 barrel powder, 1 firkin tallow 1 man; 18 iron bars, 1 dozen great knives 1 man; 1 barrel powder 1 man; 26 dozen great knives | 3 men, 1 woman |
| 4th | 2 pieces nehallaware, 4 dozen great knives 1 woman; 21 iron bars, 2 firkins tallow 1 man, 1 girl | 1 man, 1 woman, 1 girl |
| 6th | 3 flanes 1 man; 1 firkin tallow, 15 sheets, 6 dozen small knives, 1 tankard 1 woman; 4 sheets, 1 perpetuana, 6 iron bars 1 woman; 1 barrel powder 1 woman | 1 man, 3 women |
|  | 2 pieces nehallaware, 8 looking glasses 1 woman; 8 pieces perpetuanas, 10 looking glasses, 3 1lb basins 1 man; 2 fanes, 1 3lb basin, 1 tankard, 8 looking glasses 1 woman | 1 man, 2 women |
| 13th | 4 pieces tapestry | 1 man |
| Allampo | 1 say, 9 2lb basins, 1 hanger 1 woman; 1 say, 8 3lb basins 1 woman; 1 tapseil, 6 dornicks 1 girl; 2 perpetuanas, 16 sheets 2 girls | 2 women, 3 girls |
|  | 1 perpetuana, 8 sheet, 1 tapseil 1 woman; 9 dornicks 1 woman 2 tapseils, 12 sheets 1 man; 24 1lb & 7 3lb basins, 1 piece niconees 1 woman | 1 man, 3 women |

*Acquisition: Slave Voyages*

| | | |
|---|---|---|
| June 15th | 1 say, 1 piece nehallaware 1 woman; 14 carpets 1 man; 8 tankards, 16 sheets 1 woman; 22 sheets 1 girl; 11 dornicks 1 woman | 1 man, 3 women, 1 girl |
| June 16th | 9 1lb & 1 3lb basins, 2 perpetuanas, 1 tankard 1 woman; 1 tapseil, 20 tankards 1 man; 1 nehallaware, 2 3lb & 12 2lb basins 1 woman | 1 man, 2 women |
| June 17th | 3 perpetuanas 1 woman; 8 tankards, 3 irons bars 1 girl; 2 perpetuanas, 8 sheets, 1 carpet 1 man; 11 dornicks 1 woman | 1 man, 2 women, 1 girl |
| June 18th | 2 topseils, 2 tankards, 1 niconee 1 woman; 2 pieces niconees, 1 3lb basins 1 woman; 2 pieces nehallaware, 1 3lb basin 1 woman; 1 sheet, 4 dornicks, 3 looking glasses 1 girl; 1 say, 2 tapseils 1 man; 1 say, 7 sheets 1 woman; 1 half barrel powder, 2 3lb basins, 3 looking glasses 1 girl | 1 man, 1 woman, 2 girls |
| June 19th | 1 case spirits, 11 tankards 1 girl; 1 say, 8 tankards 1 woman; 1 say, 6 tankards 1 woman; 12 looking glasses, 6 tankards 1 girl | 2 women, 2 girls |
| June 20th | 4 dornicks, 8 3lb & 3 2lb tankards, 1 case spirits 1 woman; 6 carbines, 1 hanger 1 man; 28 sheets, 2 brass pans 1 man | 2 men 1 woman |
| | 1 say, 8 tankards 1 woman; 16 3lb basins, 8 tankards 1 woman; 3 salempores, 3 3lb basins 1 woman; 4 firkins powder, 1 tankard 1 girl | 3 women, 1 girl |
| | 2 topsails, 2 dornicks, 8 3lb basins, 1 tankard 1 man; 1 say, 9 2lb basins 1 woman; 9 2lb basins, 2 tankards, 1 brass pan, 1 case spirits 1 woman | 1 man, 2 women' |

A total of 46 men, 50 women, 11 boys and 15 girls were collected during this time. More is known of the voyage of the *Daniel & Henry* because of the survival of the ship's logbook. Parts of it were edited in 1920 and it reveals that 452 slaves were taken on the Gold Coast before crossing the Atlantic. One month into that voyage, the logbook recorded, 'we have now thrown overboard 153 slaves' and four weeks later 'we have now at this day noon 183 slaves dead and many more very bad'. On arrival at Jamaica another 6 died and a total of 246 slaves were sold.[55]

The financial failure of the *Daniel & Henry* was not dissimilar to the experiences of the other seven Devon ten per centers. It is perhaps significant that the first of the 'Devon' ten per centers left from Bristol. In January 1698 the *Betty Galley* of Exeter left that port with a Bristol vessel, the *Beginning*, and sailed for Cape de Verde. The *Betty*, an 80 ton ships, was freighted by Charles and John Ellard, probably Exeter merchants. Nine months later it arrived in Barbados with 97 slaves and 400 tusks of ivory. Two months later it was in Plymouth with a cargo of ivory, pepper, sugar, ginger and molasses and then sailed to Exeter with ginger, sugar and tobacco. Neither Ellard appears to have engaged in slaving again and shortly afterwards the *Betty* became a privateer in the War of the Spanish Succession.[56]

This voyage was followed by that of the *Dragon* of Topsham which sailed the following year, in March 1699, from Exeter. The vessel was owned by a consortium of four Exeter men, one Exeter woman and a man from Falmouth. It was probably significant that the latter's brother, Thomas Corker, was the Royal African Company's agent on the Gambia but another factor in the fate of the voyage was the death of the captain, Christopher Butcher, also one of the ship's owners, four months into the voyage. Difficult relations between the two men also hindered the collection of slaves. The first mate, Henry Taylor, took over as Captain but disaster struck shortly afterwards when the slaves revolted during the Atlantic crossing; this caused the deaths of seven slaves and two crewmen. Five of them, still shackled, drowned when they leapt into the sea and their chains dragged them to the seabed. By the time the *Dragon* arrived in Barbados it had no more than 42 slaves, the majority of whom were the property of Thomas Corker and the investors owned only fourteen one of whom died before he could be sold. The voyage was further compromised by the health of the crew who had all died by October and the disappearance of their legal papers. The vessel was impounded in Barbados and was forced to sail to other Caribbean islands in order to reimburse costs. Taylor, described by one historian as 'a Jonah of the first water', had further bad luck when the vessel, more than three years after leaving Exeter and still unable to legally return to England, was captured by a French pirate. He was then imprisoned in a Spanish prison in the West Indies and released on Christmas Day 1702. Eight months later and four years after the ship left Devon he finally returned to England and was promptly arrested for financial impropriety. None of the Devon investors again invested in African slaving and one merchant, Arthur Jeffery, who had frequently traded in the Caribbean, went bankrupt and fled abroad to avoid his creditors.[57]

After the voyage of the *Daniel & Henry* the fourth of the ships to engage in slavery was the *Elizabeth Galley* of Bristol whose connection to Devon was it was freighted by John Parminter of Bideford, a tobacco merchant. There were two close connections between this voyage and two earlier ones from Devon. The vessel was named after Parminter's wife Elizabeth, the daughter of Daniel Ivy who was one of the investors in the voyage of the *Daniel & Henry*. The *Elizabeth* left Bristol in January 1700. Its captain was William Levercombe who two years earlier had been on the Bristol ship which accompanied the *Betty* of Exeter to Africa. The *Elizabeth's* voyage was also not successful: it sailed to Calabar, in what is now Nigeria, and was wrecked offshore.[58]

The fifth ship, the *Dartmouth Galley*, was also a financial failure: it was captured by French privateers off Guinea in January 1710. The vessel had left Dartmouth only four months earlier and the main investor, John Harris of Exeter, refrained from further activities in Africa.[59] The next Devon-associated voyage, the sixth, set sail from Plymouth. Some vessels had left that port as a matter of convenience but were ships registered elsewhere and freighted, invested and captained by men from other parts of the country. The *Sylvia Galley* was Plymouth's first ten per center and she sailed in 1710 for Guinea. The voyage was organised by George Barons, an Exeter merchant resident in Amsterdam. Although he was English the bulk of his trade passed through Rotterdam. The voyage must have been a financial success because it was repeated four years later. In the meanwhile the seventh, and last of Devon's ten per centers, set sail in April 1711 from Plymouth, the *John & Robert* of London, for Guinea. Incomplete records hinder understanding the financial viability of the voyage but it set sail again for Africa a few years later. Nevertheless it was Plymouth's last slaving venture for the period from 1698 to 1725.[60]

The freeing of trade in 1712 was followed by four slave voyages from Devon. In 1713 the *Anna* of Topsham sailed for Portugal and arrived in the Gambia in January 1714 after the captain was persuaded by a Portuguese merchant that he would obtain a better price for his cargo.

Royal African Company agents refused to assist him in slaving and the viability of the voyage is unknown as is the next voyage, that of the *Surprise Galley* of Exeter. The last two voyages were made by the *Sylvia Galley*, a small vessel of only 40 tons. It ran two trips in 1714 and 1715. George Barons, who had earlier used the same ship, was responsible for both trips and once again it was Rotterdam where the trade was centred. Barons and his family then appear to have withdrawn from the slave trade and concentrated on other cargoes in the West Indies.[61]

The identified voyages of Devon's ten per centers were nearly 4 per cent of all ten per centers for the years from 1698 to 1708.[62] Although marginal in national terms it remains the greatest number of voyages that Devon appears to have engaged in. They had a high proportion of failure due to financial incompetence, shipwreck and captures by pirates and privateers which was probably due to unfamiliarity with trade. The apparent hesitation of Devonians to participate in slaving may be due to these factors but intermittent war with France and disruption to trade as well as continual opportunities to engage in privateering during the war against the French from 1702 to 1713 were also important. Devon lost its main markets for cloth, Spain and Italy, during these war years. Exeter was able to compensate by redirecting cloth exports to Rotterdam while other ports, such as Barnstaple and Dartmouth, were more dependent upon fishing in Newfoundland. French privateers targeted Devon vessels in the Atlantic fishing grounds and off Barnstaple where so many ships were lost to the French that it became known to French privateers as 'the Golden Bay'. These ports, deprived of their staple trade turned to privateering. Of the 1,343 vessels which engaged in privateering 59 came from the South West. One of them, the *Dartmouth Galley* which had slaved, later found privateering so lucrative that one historian noted it had 'extravagant successes'.[63]

# 5

# Devon's slaving voyages from 1747 to 1786

In 1779 the *King George* set sail from the river Exe. It was advertised as 'a cruise of six months, now fitting out in the harbour of Topsham, and to be got ready with all possible dispatch, the private ship of war, *King George*'.[64] The ship was one of the many privateers which left from Devon in the eighteenth century and the owner was Benjamin Buttell who had inherited his father's sugar factory at Topsham. In the midst of yet another war, with the resulting disruption to trade, merchants turned to other means to make money. It was also an alternative to slaving. No information has been found to show Devon ships engaged in slaving voyages at this time but reports to the House of Commons and Board of Trade provide details of expeditions in the years before and afterwards. It remains an incomplete picture because of the loss of customs accounts for Devon for some years of the eighteenth century which hinders ascertaining a fuller number. Even so, they supply more information than we have had to date.

One historian has estimated that in the eighteenth century lesser ports in the country contributed as much as ten per cent of all slaving expeditions from Britain but the number from Devon appears to have been much lower in any one year. There were no Devon voyages noted for 1747 to 1749 but in 1750 it was reported to the Board of Trade that six ships, out of a total of 134 from Britain sailed for Africa from Chester, Lancaster, Glasgow and Plymouth.[65] Three years later another ship left Plymouth for slaving[66] and it was probably these vessels that a few years later the Commissioners at the Board heard 'that no trade has been carried on at Senegal since we took the place, no vessels for trade being around except two or three small vessels from Plymouth, Exeter and Liverpool, which only brought out some bad spirits which had helped to destroy the soldiery'.[67] Plymouth's participation was described by one historian as having been 'minute and sporadic'[68] at this time and yet it was Devon's main port in the trade.

There is more precise information available for the years from 1757 to 1776. In 1757 a total of 106 ships sailed from Britain for Africa and this included from Exeter the *Prince of Brunswick* of 90 tons which set sail for Senegal. There were also two ships from Plymouth, the *St John* of 40 tons and the *Amity* of 40 tons. The *Prince of Brunswick* was also recorded as having left from Plymouth. The following two years there were no Devon ships noted of the 231 voyages for Africa but in 1760 one of the 143 vessels was the *African* of 100 tons from Exeter. Two years later, in 1762, the *Senegal Packet* of 50 tons sailed from Exeter as did the *Ann & Elizabeth* of 40 tons from Dartmouth while from Plymouth the *Swallow* of 50 tons set out. The *Ann & Elizabeth* was also noted as sailing from Plymouth that year. In 1763 there were five Plymouth ships recorded: the *Messney* of 250 tons, the *Prince George* of 160 tons, *Le Rosalie* of 300 tons, *L'Amitie* of 180 tons and the *Duchesse de Gramond* of 350 tons. In 1764 the ships from Devon comprised two from Plymouth (the *Betsey* of 30 tons and the *Mary & Joseph* of 180 tons), in 1765 there were four from Plymouth (the *St Ann* of 200 tons, the *Brocenteur* of 100 tons, the *Besney* of 280 tons and the *Supplement* of 100 tons) while in 1766 the Plymouth ships were the *Heureaux* of 150 tons and the *Angelique* of 250 tons. *L'Heureaux Union*, recorded as being of 200 tons, also sailed from Plymouth in 1767.[69] The arrival of these eleven French ships, much larger than any of the Devon vessels, must have been connected with the Seven Years' War which had just ended. They were much greater in tonnage than any of the other Plymouth ships and their appearance at Plymouth raises many questions.

The voyage of the *African* from Exeter in 1760 may not have been its first voyage. In 1754, by the 28th of August, a ship of that name from Plymouth, sailed into Plymouth from Jamaica and brought a cargo of Muscavado sugar, rum and ivory. The only merchant named in the customs account was John Morehead.[70] It would be more surprising for a ship of that name to have had less than two voyages to Africa and it is likely there were other expeditions.

*Acquisition: Slave Voyages*

No other Devon voyages have been found until 1782 when one vessel of 90 tons sailed from Plymouth for Africa, in 1783 two ships of the same port with a combined tonnage of 360 tons left for the same destination and in 1785 another ship, also from Plymouth, of 300 tons sailed.[71]

These voyages are summarised in the following table.

Known slaving voyages from Devon to Africa, 1747 to 1785

|  | *Plymouth* | *Exeter* | *Dartmouth* | *National total* |
|---|---|---|---|---|
| 1747 | - | - | - | 72 |
| 1748 | - | - | - | 88/89 |
| 1749 | - | - | - | 80/83 |
| 1750 | 1 | - | - | 78/82 |
| 1751 | - | - | - | 85 |
| 1752 | - | - | - | 94 |
| 1753 | 1 | - | - | 117/118 |
| 1757 | 2 of 80 tons total | 1 of 90 tons | - | 106 |
| 1758 | - | - | - | 103 |
| 1759 | - | - | - | 128 |
| 1760 | - | 1 of 100 tons | - | 143 |
| 1761 | - | - | - | 122 |
| 1762 | 1 of 50 tons total | 1 of 50 tons | 1 of 40 tons | 119 |
| 1763 | 5 of 1,240 tons total | - | - | 163/169 |
| 1764 | 2 of 210 tons total | - | - | 163/171 |
| 1765 | 4 of 680 tons total | - | - | 135/159 |
| 1766 | 2 of 400 tons total | - | - | 141 |
| 1767 | 1 of 200 tons | - | - | 158 |
| 1768 | - | - | - | 146 |
| 1769 | - | - | - | 159 |
| 1770 | - | - | - | 162 |
| 1771 | - | - | - | 192/194 |
| 1772 | - | - | - | 175 |
| 1773 | - | - | - | 151/159 |
| 1774 | - | - | - | 158/167 |
| 1775 | - | - | - | 138/152 |
| 1776 | - | - | - | 115 |
| 1777-80 | data not found | | | |
| 1781 | data not found | | | 77 |
| 1782 | 1 of 90 tons | - | - | 69/74 |
| 1783 | 2 of 360 tons total | - | - | 130/135 |
| 1784 | - | - | - | 99/100 |
| 1785 | 1 of 300 tons | - | - | 116/117 |
| 1786 | undetermined | undetermined | undetermined | 146 |
| Total | 25 ships | | | 4,128 – 4,193 |

Sources: Elizabeth Donnan (ed.), *Documents Illustrative of the Slave Trade to America* (New York, 1965), II, 507; National Archives, BT 6/7 & 6/3/153; Sheila Lambert (ed.), *House of Commons Sessional Papers of the Eighteenth Century* (Wilmington, Delaware, 1975), vol. 67, 87.

Altogether this amounts to 25 voyages from Devon and comprises between 0.59 and 0.6 per cent of the total number of ships recorded as having left Britain for slaving in Africa during those years. The total number of ships drops drastically, to less than 0.4 per cent, if the eleven French vessels were excluded. There are good reasons to be suspicious of their identification as Devonian. They were significantly larger than the Devon ships; their combined tonnage was 2,440 whereas the Devon ships were only 700 tons. Their participation at this time, at the signing of the First Treaty of Paris, is curious and their subsequent absence as Plymouth slavers suggests a lack of identification with Devon. It is possible they were using the port as one of convenience. As with the War of the Spanish Succession, the Seven Years' War turned commercial vessels into privateers: 1,679 ships from throughout the country became privateers and 62 of them were from the South West.[72] The interplay of dislocated trade routes and renewed opportunities for privateering must have been a factor in the middle of the eighteenth century as it had been in its first decade.

# 6

## Regulating slave transportation: Lieut. John Incledon-Webber of Barnstaple and his voyage on HMS *Pomona* along the African coast and to the West Indies, 1788 to 1789

In 1788 Parliament passed legislation to limit the number of slaves to be carried on British ships. The intention was to reduce their suffering but not to end slavery. It was in pursuit of enforcing the law that HMS *Pomona* sailed from England in the summer of 1788 for the African coast. Lieutenant John Incledon-Webber, whose family lived at Braunton in North Devon, was one of those onboard and his journal survives of the six-month voyage to West Africa from what is now Senegal to Angola.[73] In only one instance did he record finding English ships, both from Liverpool, which had contravened the new regulations. He did not appear to have regarded the voyage as a success. There is a detailed account of relations between the colony of Freedom in Sierra Leone and local Africans. The details of negotiations with a neighbouring ruler differ from those given by another mariner.[74] Many naval journals and logbooks did not stray from recording weather and navigational concerns. For instance, that of the *Benjamin* which left Plymouth in June 1689 and sailed along the African coast recorded little additional material of interest.[75] Incledon-Webber, however, was more concerned with social aspects.

According to Incledon-Webber none of the crew had been to the

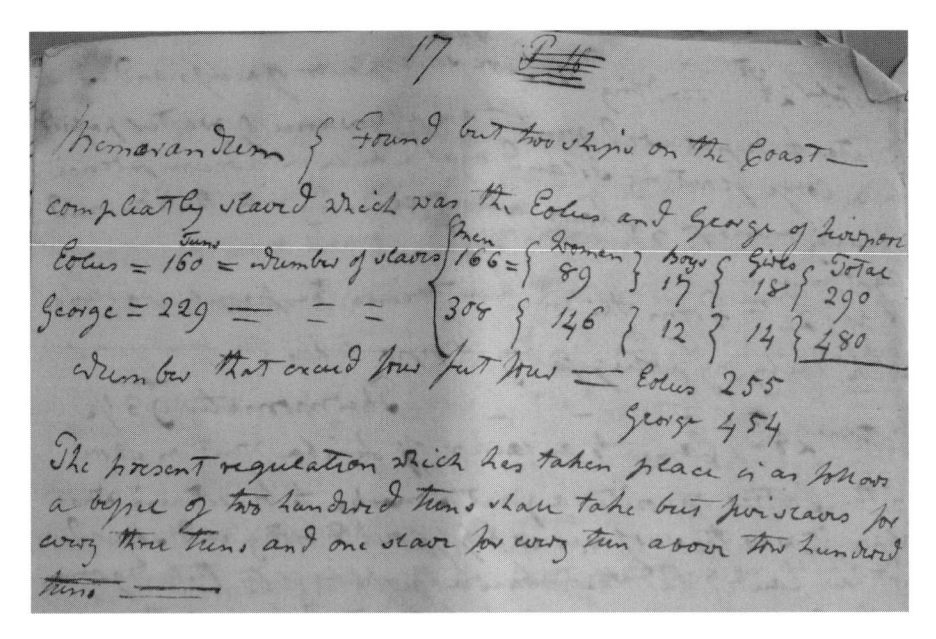

John Incledon-Webber's journal (North Devon Record Office, 3704M/O5)

Slave Coast. A considerable number died from disease and the voyage appears to have been an arduous task. Incledon-Webber admitted in one passage that there was resentment of the Quakers for their being there ('that the villains of Quakers, which were the occasion of our voyage, were doomed to spend their remaining days on the burning plains of Africa is the wish of every man in this ship'). He wrote that he purchased a young girl as a slave and had a Portuguese boy to attend him.

Perhaps the greatest contribution that the journal makes is in describing the African societies and the navy's relations with them. The captain seldom left the ship and it was left to Incledon-Webber to go onshore. Because of this descriptions are particularly detailed and informative. His use of language is interesting in that the account has archaic words, such as *dash* (a payment) and *slops* (cheap seamen's clothing), and ones which have changed their meaning including *palaver* (a public meeting held to decide a dispute). Among the places visited was the black colony of Freedom which Equiano had been organising in Plymouth earlier that year (see pages 159 to 160). In a few instances parts of the paper have not survived and there are missing words. Incledon-Webber died within six years of finishing this voyage.[76]

'Remarks on running down the coast of Africa in HM Ship *Pomona* employed to deliver the late Acts of Parliament relative to the slave.

On Wednesday the 27th August Arrived at the mouth of the Gambia, found it very difficult to make it [to] the land being so low and the water shoal stood in for Cape St Mary's which is known by some remarkable high cabbage trees on the pitch of the Cape. Attempted to go up the river to Barra Point but was prevented by the shoalness of the water, was nearly being on shore and losing the ship. Sent the second Lieutenant with the cutter manned and armed up the river to James Island and came to off Cape St Mary's where we observed a number of cattle and some of the natives.

Thursday the 28th Went on shore at the Cape to try if we could trade for some beef and refreshments, was received on landing by the priest and three men with a white flag as a signal for trade. Bartered with them some gunpowder and tobacco for four bullocks, some fowls and some yams, hauled the seine and caught a number of fine fish, shot some partridges and a couple of ducks, found the natives were subjects of the King of Banian and were Mohammedans. The soil appeared very fruitful, it being the rainy season we saw it in its highest perfection, but the natives appear to be very indolent and very superstitious. By way of cooperation after I had purchased the bullocks having the butcher on shore [I] ordered him to kill a bullock and cut it up for the ship's company's dinner; which we attempted by bringing the bullock to a large tree near the shore in order to cut his throat and dress him; the natives perceiving we were going to kill it sallied forth from their town – man, woman and children making the most dreadful howling it is possible to conceive and one of the head men of the village ran to the tree and cut the rope which the animal was fastened with, crying 'no good white man the devil' thereon which I ordered him to desist and take him to another tree where we killed our bullock in peace and happy to find they had got the devil so snug in Africa. The tree was so large that with difficulty 12 men could take the circumference of it, the tail of the bullock was requested by the priest and hung upon their tree, I suppose as an atonement for the insults we had offered to His Majesty.

Returned onboard, heavy rains with much thunder and lightning, thermometer 88°½ Shot a base of partridges. Found the cutter was returned from James Island which the officer found deserted, only one ship laying there in a most deplorable state, having buried all her crew. One onshore a wreck having been cut off by the slaves and the white people murdered to a man. Sent her three hands, two men taken sick. This is what they style the rains or the sickly season. Sailed for the river Sierra Leone.

Friday 5th September Arrived in the river Sierra Leone and anchored in Frenchman's Bay, found here four English ships and one French brig. Went on shore to cook at the watering place in the Black Colony of Freedom, founded by that worthy man Jonas Hanway[77] and patronised by a Mr [Granville] Sharp of London. Learnt from the settlers they had suffered amazingly from sickness, being reduced from upwards of four hundred and fifty to fifty families. The governor by [the] name [of] Lucas, a black man, informed me it was one of the most unhealthy situations imaginable. They had rains six months of the year without easing but for a few hours; and the remaining six months not a drop but on the contrary a burning season. From some observations I made on the King of Robanna's town I found their homes made more commodious than the new colony. They were all plastered below to keep out the damp, and every house a fire in it. Another thing, the ground their houses stood on was old ground, and not liable to the damps that most accrue from a new situation like the colony of Freedom and though the inhabitants were black yet they were perfectly strangers to that climate and constitution. In short I estimate their sickness in great part to proceed from sleeping in huts hastily run up in a fresh soil where vegetation was too active and so unwholesome that it consumed the men before it could nourish the plants take it all and all it is a very bad situation to form a colony. The governor made me a present of some cucumbers and I had an opportunity of returning him some English potatoes.

Monday 8th Went onshore by order of the Captain having informed him of a misunderstanding that prevailed between the colony and the King of Robanna relative to the watering place. In short it was a finesse of the black fellow the King of Robanna. King Cojou, another prince situated near the colony, had sold this land and watering place for so much rum and different sorts of goods. A few days before our arrival the old King of Cojou died and remained unburied at this time. The King of Robanna on his oath sent word to the governor that he expects to be paid for the ground the colony of Freedom stood on and the dash for the ship's watering as King Cojou had no right to dispose of the ground, it being part of his Kingdom. Therefore expects he would pay him similar to what he had King Cojou. I found that the young King Cojou, the present man, was concerned and no doubt was to have half of the goods as I alluded to before it was a finesse of the black fellow's. A king's ship coming in frightened them confoundedly as they had threatened to burn the colony unless immediately complied with. Here rested the grand palaver which was to take place; accordingly at sunrise we fired a gun as a signal that the two kings of Robanna and Cojou should meet at the courthouse in the colony for settling this affair. All the masters of merchantmen attended and a very grand palaver it was. We found there was nothing to be done for the tranquillity of the colony but complying with the King of Robanna's demand and accordingly sent him the cask of rum, tobacco and powder with some flints and slops. Ratified the treaty afresh which we assured should be as lasting as the sun which was over our heads. In fact, the matter was that they had not rum enough to bury the old King therefore if the colony had not made up the rum and the merchantmen, most or all trade would have been stopped.

Returned onboard very fatigued although in company with two crowned heads the whole day. Received an invitation from their Majesties to attend the funeral of King Cojou which the next morning I attended and to my great surprise found he had been dead ten days and on enquiry that it was always customary to keep their kings a certain time to collect their friends from the different nations and make a grand cry. He was preserved from purification by herbs and looked as fair as it is possible to conceive. His son and wives acted as principal mourners and I suppose at least there was twelve thousand people collected at his town. He was conveyed from his house on a bier of fine muslin and very finely dressed through a lane of all his subjects the strangers being without the lane excepting the two kings, an officer of the ship and myself who acted as mourners being at each end of the corpse but he stank so confoundedly that I was obliged to fall back amongst the women and take some brandy which station I preferred during the whole ceremony. The place of his interment was under a large tamarind tree, what they call a palaver tree, as they held their courts of justice under them, and palaver signifies country law. The grave was a square hole about three foot by fourteen, in the middle they laid him on a couch on each side all sort of provisions to support him to the other world. After all this had been arranged four slaves were introduced and put to death as attendants and four of his wives. They appeared to me to [be] very old and would have shortly followed him of their own accord. The ceremony being ended they covered him with a vast deal of . . . interment in the earth in short every luxury was given to him . . . journey. When a howl burst forth that no man could ever conceived. The multitude separated, the women into the bush where they began to howl, the men some dancing others firing guns, some going in fact in less than an hour men, women and children were all drunk and a person would suppose hell itself was on the banks of the Sierra Leone such a sight I never saw before and never wish to experience it again. Returned onboard having promised the King of Robanna to breakfast with him next day.

Wednesday 10th Went onshore to haul the seine and caught a very fine turtle and plenty of fish near the King of Robanna's town, breakfasted with him on coffee and Cassada [Cassava, the starch obtained from the manioc root or tapioca] with some dried venison. [He] made me a present of some very fine pine plants, returned him some tobacco and brandy, shot a King Bird and some quails, returned onboard and sailed for the Gold Coast.

Heavy rains, thunder & lightning. The thermometer up to 89.

Monday 11th Passed by Cape Appollonia, the first settlement on the Gold Coast, When saluted by the fort with 17 guns [we] returned 15 and stood on for Anamabo.

Wednesday 24th Arrived at Anamabo when saluted by the fort with 17 guns, returned 20. I was waited on by the lieutenant governor who invited the captain and officers onshore after dinner attended the captain as far as the surf in our own boat when we disembarked into the governor's canoe with twenty black fellows to paddle her, who carried us on short through the most tremendous surf I ever behold. Was received on our landing by the governor, lieutenant governor and a vast concourse of natives. On our entering the fort was received by a guard and saluted with 17 guns, returned 20. Drank tea and coffee when we walked in the black town, embarked at sunset, was saluted with the same number of guns as at our landing, returned 20 from the ship.

Thursday 25th By desire of the governor, a king's ship being in the road, attended a palaver of all the old men of the Fantu [Fanti] and Cormantine nations relative to the settling trade which had been at a stand some days owing to the depredations of some of the Cormantine nation. The French that have erected a fort in that country since the war were certainly at the bottom of the whole as they do their utmost to distress our trade. The palaver was settled on in the course of a few hours, when the governor knowing the country language prepared me for a sight of the justice which attended country palaver. Three slaves were brought under the palaver tree and stabbed with daggers through their spinal marrow, then disjointed, their heads, hands and feet, legs and thighs were then separated and each member sent to the different villages of the two nations. Where their robberies were committed [their remains were] to be hung up in terrorum by way of convincing them that should they be found out disturbing trade they would be served the same way. After this affair was over we returned to the black town where I was shown the place for executing criminals for murder. It was under a large palaver tree surrounded with a fence of bamboo, without it was a stone bench on which they cut off the criminal's head when it was imposed without the fence until it was dry, then hung on the tree. There were then hanging up within the fence. By this I find they take blood for blood. Took leave of the governor and returned onboard very much fatigued. Sailed for Accra. Thermometer at the fort 89°, in the ship 88°.

Friday 26th Arrived at Accra. Was saluted by the fort with 17 guns, returned 20. Went on shore to procure stock for the people. Found a very fine country and a small breed of horses peculiar only to this place and what is very extraordinary they will not live either twenty leagues to the northward or southward of this place. I unfortunately found the governor to be a very great rogue imposing on us in every sense of the word, found plenty of game, shot an antelope, and some quails, procured some stock and sailed for Grand Topo and Whydah.

The fever has broke out in the ship, buried four men, twenty in the list. Thermometer 89°, 2 degrees beyond what it generally is.

Monday 29th Came to an anchor off Grand Topo, was doubtful what place it was. Therefore went onshore with the cutter and this being a savage coast came to a grapnel close in with the surf when a large canoe came off and invited me to go onshore to the Danish factory which was a black man's house. [I] was received very civilly by the black Capuchin [caboceer] which is the head trader of the town. Found him at breakfast, partook of coffee, Cassada and Indian corn made into corn mixed with Cassada, some Irish butter and very good French brandy. Was agreeably deceived in the account I had received of these Negroes. Found the Capuchin a very intelligent fellow having in his youth been at Liverpool and spoke very good English therefore had an opportunity of interrogating him concerning the African trade and particularly if in case Great Britain had resolved on abolishing the slave trade other nations also had come into it, what would they then do with their slaves when there was no mart whatsoever for them. He very coolly replied we will cut the throats of the old and infirm, the young boys and girls we will reserve to bring in our yams and corn. He then enquired our business on the coast as he heard they were not to slave any more from England. I told him it was to prevent English ships from taking so many onboard at one time (as they get sick and died). He replied 'Oh, we have plenty in the bush.' I endeavoured to inform myself how they distinguished their property and what regulations had been handed down to them by their forefathers and how they lived before trade was known. He replied I don't know. It is enough for me if I can live myself. They are without doubt the most lazy set of beings in the world and at the same time very expert and keen in trade insomuch that they know the value of a Guinea as well as any white man. As for agriculture they cultivate no more than will just rub through the year and sleep the other half. I here saw a chain of slaves which had come down the country a six months' journey. There was the father, mother, husband, wife, child all blended together perhaps sold to different merchants or even in the same ship they are separated and when they arrive in the West Indies sold at different islands and never see one another more. This is the slave trade. But the people in this trade are callous to every idea that these people are used ill. They only reply with a dam that if they were not to buy them the natives would cut their throats.

This is the country for the famous Whydah cloths which I found from the Capuchin were made back some month's journey in the Eyo's country and brought down here for trade, some of them so fine that you may draw them through a ring and cost four man slaves which is upward of eighty-eight pounds sterling. The manufacture is the more extraordinary as it is all done without a loom. The Capuchin wives made me a present of a small one and another I traded for these people are very civil, their women handsome and obliging. Further down the Bight of Benin they are very different, not one Negro better than Cannibals.

Returned onboard and sailed for St Thomas [Sao Tomé]. The barometer 88°½.

I cannot help remarking the ignorance of the White People at the different factories on every thing relative to the produce and customs of this country. They appear not to have the least curiosity though some of them have spent the best part of their lives in it. Nine out of ten whom visit this extensive continent visit it for slaves. This is the grand object of their voyage. It engrosses all their attention and occasions them even to overlook the productions of the place. Indeed had they a turn that way there would be little opportunity to satisfy their curiosity as the trade is carried on at present. Admitting they had a turn for Botanical or Chemical pursuits which this country affords an amazing field for. The interior trade is carried on by what they call Capuchins and only a Negro path for perhaps a six men to journey back into the country from whence they convey down their slaves and elephants' teeth, the gold dust is taken up near the coast and I could learn they had but one mine which is not a great way from Anamabo. It is mostly found after the heavy rains particularly a mountain to windward of Accra called the Devil's Hill which projects into the sea. They likewise trade in gum, almond, palm oil and the black Capuchin informed me he procured in 86 some *gum guaiacum*. As for spices the only ones I could hear of was the cassia or wild cinnamon which is very common. Their cotton far surpasses whatever I saw in the French island and [I] was informed they had lately found out in the country of the Eyo's six month's journey a pod which bore a red cotton preferable to any dye which they intermixed in their Whydah cloths, and made them come very high. Indeed I endeavoured to get a sight of some but could not, they being very rare to be met with. The Negroes are very tenacious of their property which they ill tell you was left them by their fathers and jealous to the last degree of any White Man getting footing amongst them or of penetrating into their country. Some of them are very rich, what they call the takers, one in particular was pointed out to me at Anamabo as worth ten or twelve thousand pounds and yet is of no service to them being obliged to bury it and often take sulky prior to their death and is lost to their heir and family by not discovering where it lays.

Arrived at St Thomas to take in wood, water and refreshment, found to island to abound with everything but very unhealthy. Trucked [traded] all our old cloths for stock, fruit, monkeys, parrots and parakeets. Went round with the barge to wait on the governor about 3 leagues from the ship, was saluted on landing by the fort with 15 guns and received by the lieutenant governor, conducted up through pair of stairs to the governor's apartments, he having retired to the upper storey being the rainy season. Found him an intelligent man, a renegade Englishman, and a captain in the Portuguese navy. Dined with him, returned onboard. On my return was shown a house by the lieutenant governor where the captain of the *Phoenix*, 40 gun ship, and five of his officers and six attendants came to reside a few days to refresh themselves. By what I could learn it was about the year 63, it being the rainy season in the course of five or six days they were all taken in and died excepting one man, a mulatto. It strikes me this must have been Mr Clivedon's brother. Since I received this intelligence I happened to peruse a treatise wrote on tropical diseases by Doctor Lyme and find he takes notice of this extraordinary circumstance and that the mulatto was in the royal hospital at Portsmouth but not being cured he returned to Guinea with an idea he had been poisoned and that none but the Negroes could cure him. It is an idea which prevails with all common seamen when they have contracted the Guinea disorder which is generally an intermitting fever accompanied with violent shocks of an ague. I have remarked during this voyage which no ship whatever performed before or experienced so much the viapitudes of a tropical climate particularly so being the rainy seasons on the windward coast and likewise on the coast of Angola accompanied with most tremendous thunder and lightning, heavy dews at night and very cold which being exposed too without the greatest care and plenty of bark is the bane of all European constitutions. In short, everything in this country, even the water, to be at variance with all Europeans that have occasion to visit this climate and that most of our people which have fall sick are the most lazy and corpulent men that have been always used to the seas round our island and others that have never been at sea before. Among them much to lamented by us his country and his friends was a very promising young man, a Mr Whiteford, eldest son of Sir John Whiteford of Ayrshire in Scotland, he was [a] man to be regretted, being an intimate friend of Domet's. The duty being particularly worse on the Commissioned Officers in this voyage being not only exposed to the constant rains but in danger of catching the most malignant distemper which prevails in a young man by being obliged to visit every ship and mastering their slaves where often every disease is prevalent that mankind are afflicted with – a service which no king's officer ever had to perform before and I hope never will again. That the villains of Quakers which were the occasion of our voyage were doomed to spend their remaining days on the burning plains of Africa is the wish of every man in this ship.

October 10th Having completed our wood and water, sailed to the island of Prinass [Príncipe].

October 11th Arrived at Prinass and was saluted by the Portuguese fort with 17 guns, returned 20. We found one English ship there bound to St Christopher's completely slaved [full of slaves]. The captain went on shore for the second time only this voyage sailed for Loango on the coast of Angola. Thermometer at 10 clock 92°¾.

October 19th Arrived at Loango, found there six French ships, very difficult to water and the English [have] no trade here. Thermometer 92°.

October 20th Sailed for Mayumba.

October 21st Finding the shore so difficult of access and no water to be procured, went to an allowance of water, passed by a large floating island near a mile in circumference. Heavy rains for 48 hours without ceasing with thunder and lightning.

October 24th From the incipient rains, the people falling sick daily, my Portuguese boy Tippio taken ill of a fever. Thermometer 93°½.

October 28th Came to anchor off Timba, went onshore in the cutter, opposite a great smoke began to be certain what place it was the surf was so high could not land should not have landed had there been a possibility the Negroes being little known and not to be trusted. Four of them came down to the beach, and with difficulty I learnt of them that Cabinda, where we now were bound for, was to windward of us. Returned onboard. Very hot, the thermometer at 94°.

October 29th Saw eight sail of ships at anchor to windward of us which we took for Cabinda but found out on our arrival it was Melimba. A very fine day, dried all our clothes, quite a treat. This day caught a bonito and a dolphin, hooked two very large sharks, but the Captain unfortunately shot away both the lines, what is astonishing this is the first fish we have caught at sea during our voyage.

**Memorandum**
Found but two ships on the coast completely slaved which was the *Eolus* and *George* of Liverpool.

**Number of slaves**

|  | Men | women | boys | girls | total |
|---|---|---|---|---|---|
| *Eolus* 160 tons | 166 | 89 | 17 | 18 | 290 |
| *George* 229 tons | 308 | 146 | 12 | 14 | 480 |

Number that exceed four feet four    *Eolus* 255
                                      *George* 454

The present regulation which has taken place is as follows, a vessel of two hundred tons shall take but four slaves for every three tons and one slave for every ton above two hundred tons.

The distance run by H.M.S. *Pomona* from the third of August to the 11th of December being as great a run as ever ship made being 4 thousand 7 hundred leagues, 15 hundred of which was on the coast of Africa. Nearly a month is to be deducted from this (being at an anchor).

Came to an anchor at St Melino after being absent six months during which time we had been constantly at sea and ran until our arrival at Portsmouth seven thousand three hundred leagues January 29th.

Recapitulation accounts of the deaths. This is a greater loss of men than six ships have lost in six years owing to our being on the coast all the rainy seasons. Twelve going to the hospital tomorrow.

The master Mr Disdale, 3 petty officers & surgeon, 25 private men.
Total 5 officers, 25 private men 30

October 30th Came to an anchor at Melimba found there 9 French ships, went on board of the largest to enquire what place it was and the distance from Cabinda. Found all our charts very erroneous. The

French man exceeding polite, breakfasted with him, returned onboard and made sail for Cabinda.

October 31st Arrived at Cabinda, found there five French ships and a good roadstead, plenty of wood and water but little refreshment having sent out boats for water without waiting on the king as had been customary with the merchant ships. He came down with a large body of men to prevent us from watering not knowing that King's ships never pay for water and having never seen a ship of war on that coast before, he insisted at first that we should not water without paying the dash. Was obliged to go onshore and settle the matter by bringing the king onboard to dinner with all his attendants, made them very drunk and saluted him on his going on shore with eleven guns. The palaver being settled we had leave to wood and water and everything the country could afford.
   Thermometer 92°½ Lat. 5 45L

October 31st Went onshore in the morning to haul the seine, caught a vast deal of fish and a fine turtle. Breakfasted with the king, found their huts very clean and preferable to any I had seen on the continent of Africa, the women handsome and the men very polite which I attribute to their intercourse with the French, the English having given up the trade for slaves on the coast of Angola. On enquiry I found for this reason: the slave on this coast are used to live very well and with little work, the country back producing every luxury. Therefore when they arrive at the West India Islands and are put to labour, from not being used to it they pine away or take sulky and will not eat so there is little good to be had of them, the country on the seacoast affords very little.
   I shot a few partridges and saw some quails but being the rainy season was obliged to return onboard, heavy rains with tremendous thunder and lightning.
   My Portuguese boy Tippio recovered well enough to go onshore and play at a dance with the natives. Found the water to have a disagreeable taste from its being the rains and a great number of trees growing in the river.

November 1st We were informed by the officer on the watering party that there was an Englishman confined in arms onboard one of the French ships that he wished to be taken out, sent the second Lieutenant to demand him as being a British subject. The Frenchman refused to deliver him when he was told in case he did not by fair means we would come in with the ship and take him by force, he replied that he would defend him to the last man. And armed all our boats, went in and boarded him, found the man in irons a native of Lancaster, knocked him out and brought him onboard and brought him onboard, hoisted in the boats and sailed for the river Congo and Ambris.

NB made the king a present of a barrel of gunpowder with which he was very much pleased and desired to be remembered to his brother [King] George [III] in England, that he would be always a friend to the English and desired that when we came again his brother would send him some guns by us. His name Mackfourer, King of Cabinda. He had a Governor and a Commodore in his train and is one of the petty kings under the dominion of the great King of Congo, one of the most powerful chiefs in Africa. A peculiar custom prevails with them, when going to drink they form a circle, the governor in the middle pours whatever the liquor is into his hand and tastes it when he sprinkles the whole circle, then they push about the bottle and drink health and success to you.

November 3rd Came to an anchor in the mouth of the great river Congo off Cape Tadrone, heard of a English ship being up the Zaire sea, could not speak [to] her. [there] came alongside a war canoe with a man slave and a girl. Bought the girl for a keg of rum & of brandy, a pair of pistols and a dozen bottles of powder. Sailed the fourth for Ambriz.

November 5th Arrived at Ambriz, found there two French ships and no brigs, one English brig from Liverpool. Found she was the only English vessel that had been there for four years. The French as I remarked before have engrossed all the trade on the extensive coast of Angola to this place. And are in a fair way of having it likewise to windward, so much for the act relative to the slave trade. The country here has a pleasant appearance but when you get onshore [it is] very sandy, plenty of quails, and hares, the first I heard of in Africa excepting at Accra. Shot a brace which proved very acceptable although they were not hunted. I could find no difference in them from ours in England excepting being smaller. Found here great plenty of turtle. Thermometer 94°½

November 6th Sailed for Santa Paula or Luanda.

November 8th Arrived at La Vraiz Croizis, a large fort belonging to the Portuguese. Spoke [to] a French brig from Bordeaux [which had sailed] last from St Philip de Benguela. I found by her that they are obliged to smuggle all their slaves on this coast, the Portuguese having possession of all the coast of Angola.

November 9th Arrived at St Tulla de Luanda, the capital of Angola, belonging to the Portuguese. Waited on the governor to request he would furnish us with fresh provisions and some water. Found him a polite man, his lady a French woman with all the vivacity which is peculiar to that nation. Breakfasted with them, when he ordered his aide-de-camp and secretary to attend me and provide everything I should stand in need of. Procured six bullocks, two dozen fowls, some yams and onions with a launch load of water, returned to dinner which was mostly ragouts strongly impregnated with garlic. After a few glasses of wine took my leave as in this country they all retire to lay down, went and drank coffee with an English lady, a merchant's daughter at Lisbon and wife to the governor's secretary. They were all astonished at an English man-of-war being in this part of the world. Found this place very unhealthy, everybody afflicted with fevers and agues, not a grain of bark in the province nor a man of the faculty the physician and surgeon being lately dead. Exchanged a cask of porter for a cask of port. Returned onboard.

November 10th Made the governor a present of two dozen of porter and a cheese. Received some sweetmeats from his lady. Returned onboard and with great satisfaction took our farewell of the coast of Africa after having traversed this continent from Longitude 14° 42 north to the Latitude of 10° 00 south with bad charts and not a soul in the ship ever on the coast before and what is more with little advantage to government. Saluted the fort with 15 guns and made sail for Barbados. Thermometer 94° ½

The last places we have been at are looked on by the Portuguese to be the most unhealthy in the world, particularly Loango, Malimba, Cabinda and St Tailia de Luanda. The grass which grows on this coast is almost always three or four feet high and receives abundant dews during the night. And is almost certain death to a European that goes into it before the sun has exhaled the vapours. Even the natives do not care to go out until the sun has been up some time. The very sea is impregnated with the fishes that come out of the great rivers particularly Congo at the distance of ten or twelve leagues and has a yellowish cast which they tell you is very unwholesome to bathe in. The days are excessively hot, the nights damp and cold which is a dangerous alternative. I observed the natives always kept fires in their houses by night and were very desirous of trafficking for blankets. Ships on this coast often lose two ship's companies before they can proceed on their voyage which I partly attribute to their watering at an improper time being exposed to the dews and the rains. Likewise inaction and wearisome-ness which they ought of all things to discourage for exercise is as necessary here as in a northern climate.

November 28th Arrived at Assencion, a barren sandy island without wood or water, went on shore with the boats for the night and found 20 turtles. Made sail for Barbados.

December 11th Arrived at Barbados, found H. M. Sloop *Bonetto*, the commodore and squadron just sailed for Grenada. Died the surgeon's mate, the third officer we lost in this voyage. Exceeding happy in getting once more amongst our own colour.

December 25th Dined with General Naylor, found his lady very partial to birds, sent her two pair of parakeets.

26th Dined with Doctor Crawford, found a large company particularly a new married couple, the woman old enough to be his grandmother and very fat which occasioned a smart thing to be said that he had married a woman with a vast deal of substance.

27th Dined with Honest Jake Blacket, a merchant, made the country gentlemen intolerably drunk, went to the Mulatto dance and supped with them.

28th Dined with Mr Marks, the navy agent, found out [he was] a Westcountry[man].

29th Dined with Governor Parry, General Mathews, General Naylor, Captain Newcombe, Domet & Rickets of the navy with a number of

*Acquisition: Slave Voyages*

army officers and civilians. Domet for a wonder got drunk and [?] over a soldier.

Nb arrived here the 24th, HMS *Maidstone*, Captain Newcombe from Grenada with General Matthews, commander in chief of the troops and governor of Grenada.

30th Weighed and sailed for Old England.

January 6th Met with a gale of wind at S West Latitude 29° - 30°, in attempting to cross the deck against the pathway and cut my skin from the knee to the ankle. Obliged to keep my bed being bruised very much.

January 8th Wind shifted to the NW blowing very hard. Master and Captain sick, [?] laid up, Second Lieutenant only capable of keeping the deck. Ship very leaky owing to our being so much contained to the same ship's company. Quite [?] out not able to bear the cold and very short of compliment from sickness.

10th The gale blowing very hard carried away our quarter galley and the mouldings. Not a place in the ship to sleep dry in and the seas making a fair breach over her.

# 7

# Arthur Frankland's anti-slaving voyage on HM Sloop *Jaseur* along the East African coast, 1830

In the late eighteenth and throughout the nineteenth centuries naval ships were given tasks to first oversee and gradually stop the slave trade. Many voyages set out from Plymouth or have Plymouth connections. In 1824 Henry Woollcombe, a leading figure in Plymouth's anti-slavery movement, received a letter from his nephew, then aboard a naval ship patrolling in the West Indies. He wrote to his uncle of good news regarding anti-slavery success: he had taken some 737 slaves ('I have taken two more since the one in the Bann, one with 143, the other with 260 slaves onboard making altogether 737 human beings I have been the means of rescuing from slavery') being transported. He was particularly pleased with the bounty money he would receive from seizing the ships: he estimated he would have more than a thousand pounds as his share.[78]

Six years later, in 1830, Arthur Frankland sailed on HM Sloop *Jaseur* along the coast of East Africa and through the Mozambique Channel on a voyage 'for the purpose of suppressing any slave trade that might be going on'. The vessel was not engaged in stopping slavery but merely in ensuring there was no transportation of slaves. Frankland recorded his experiences in a journal which was later deposited at the Plymouth & West Devon Record Office.[79] Two particular extracts are revealing of his attitudes towards Africans and of the slavery then being practiced in Portuguese Mozambique.

Frankland was greatly interested in the natural history of African and also in the Portuguese colonists. At one point Frankland noted:

> 'At sunset we returned to the town much pleased with our trip. The natives are continually at war with one another and sell their conquered enemies to the white men for anything they can get, many of the tribes are in the possession of gunpowder received in exchange for slaves. The black Portuguese troops (I saw no European soldiers though I believe there were some in the town) seemed to be in a most wretched state of discipline, sentries were lying down in the sand and some were actually talking to their friends on one side of the street with their muskets on the other.'

Sometime afterwards he recorded another experience.

> 'The Europeans described their slaves as great rogues and always absconding. Senor Raphael said that it frequently happened that when you enquired why the dinner was not brought to table, you would find that two or three of your slaves had walked off with it into the interior. Whatever their faults may be poor devils, the Portuguese (the most cruel of slave masters) take good care to inflict dreadful punishments on them in return. Being anxious to ascertain their mode of discipline I enquired of Senior Raphael (who understands English well) what were the usual chastisements, he replied excessive Flogging with stripes of bullocks' hide tied in several knots. With this formidable instrument, slaves were frequently flogged to death and Senior Raphael actually told me in the coolest and most unfeeling way imaginable that he himself had on several occasions caused his own slaves to be flogged in the above manner until life was extinct.
> 
> I would have made further enquiry into this horrid fact, had it not been for the First Lieutenant, who seeing me getting into a rage, changed the conversation. There was a small cat of nine tails of the above description hanging over the Governor's dinner table *in terrorem* and I must say that having just heard of

the manner in which it had very likely been used it completely took away my appetite.

The present governor has been at Tupamborne about six years and formerly made a good thing of it, but he much complained of the suppression of the slave trade which had ruined everybody, he also stated that at present with the exception of ivory and a few gems, there is no trade worth taking up. Slave dealing must have been lucrative enough. I purchased from a dealer several articles with which he procured slaves. Ten glass bead necklaces worth two shillings each were considered equivalent to a full grown black. Pieces of brass and copper rings are also exchanged in the same manner. The neighbouring tribes keep up a constant warfare merely for the sake of selling their prisoners to the Portuguese and now even bring them in great numbers to the settlement, though they have been told the exportation of them is no longer allowed. Such is the anxiety of the natives to possess pieces of iron, copper or brass, that it had frequently happened that a slave from Trehamban had escaped to his relations in the interior, but had been brought back to his master by his own father who would receive some trifling present of the kind for his trouble.'

# 8

# Brazilian Slavers at Plymouth and Exeter, 1845

In the summer of 1845 slave trading, seven years after emancipation of the slaves, returned to England via Devon. Ten prisoners were accused of murder and taken from Plymouth to the Devon Assizes in Exeter. At 7am on the morning of July 24 1845 they left the county gaol and were brought to Rougemont Castle where they were tried before a jury of 'half Englishmen, half foreigners'. The prisoners, many of them Brazilians, were charged with murder. Five were convicted. British naval ships were legally entitled to treat ships suspected of slaving as pirates. Five years after the trial slavery was abolished in Brazil[80] but not before a wave of public indignation in Devon over the acts committed by the slavers.

The jury was told of a treaty between Britain, Portugal and Brazil of 1823 that outlawed slaving. Nevertheless, the *Felicidade* was found on 27 February to have been on a slaving expedition off the African coast. The vessel was boarded by men from HMS *Wasp* and taken. A few days afterwards the British captured another slaving ship, the *Echo*. That ship had 434 slaves onboard. There were not enough British sailors to crew the two vessels and it was because of this shortage that some of the crew of the *Felicidade* felt enabled to attack and overcome their British captors. It was these men who were later recaptured and charged with the murder of eight British naval men on 3 March 1844 while sailing the *Felicidade*.

PORTRAITS OF THE THIRTEEN PIRATES, WITH LIEUTENANTS STUPART AND WILSON.

Slavers on trial in Exeter, 1845 (*Exeter Flying Post*, 31 July 1845)

*Acquisition: Slave Voyages*

One of the crew was Sobrina de Costa, an African and former slave, who worked with the Brazilians in slaving. His evidence was reported.

> 'it appeared from questions by Mr Manning [he] was a slave but has become a Christian and been baptised. In his examination in chief by Mr Godson he said *I was born in the interior of Africa and was free there but when a little lad was sold as a slave and sent to Babia, where I was slave to Juan de Costa. In the beginning of this year I went in a French barque with a French captain to the African coast.*'

Portraits of the men by Mr G. Dorrington of 143 Blackfriars Road in London appeared in the local newspapers and in the *Pictorial Times*. The *Exeter Flying Post* noted:

> 'The above are portraits of the men who are convicted of a deed which will long be remembered in the annals of crime, including also those who became Queen's Evidence, and likewise Lieutenants Stupert and Wilson. The public attention has been strongly aroused respecting the details of this dark and fatal 'tragedy', which has thus suddenly launched into eternity eight of our Fellow Countrymen, and we are sure the Features of the Perpetuators of the Deed, and of the other parties already named, will be regarded with much curiosity.
>
> No. 1 is the Portrait of Lieut. Stupart, of the Wasp, who took the *Felicidade* and subsequently of the *Echo*, and by his orders Mr Palmer and some British Seamen went on board the former vessel where the direful slaughter afterwards occurred.
>
> No. 2 Lieutenant Wilson, of the *Star*, by which vessel the *Felicidade* was at length taken and thus a knowledge of the melancholy fate of the British became known. The *Felicidade* seemed as if it were destined to become the scene of further horrors. Lieut. W. was ordered to proceed in her to Sierra Leone, a gale arose and the ill-fated vessel sunk beneath its fury. The poet's thoughts seem here realised 'truth is strange, stranger than fiction' – amidst the miseries and calamities of this event the calmness and intrepidity of British Seamen overcame every

obstacle and rose superior to the danger which threatened every moment to overwhelm them. A raft was constructed and for twenty days did these brave men struggle with an accumulation of miseries and suffering. The fierce rays of an African Sun scorched them by day and the chilling damp of night formed an awful contrast during the hours of darkness. Their parching thirst was only assuaged in a little degree by a few drops of rain, and extraordinary to relate their food was some sharked which they contrived to catch. Five men sank beneath such a dreadful state and they were at length picked up by the *Cygnet*.

No. 3 Cerqueiro, the Captain of the *Felicidade*, who was present at the slaughter and became a Queen's Witness – he detailed the particulars of the scene to the Commander of the *Star*, and states he refused to participate in the plans of the Serva to accomplish the death of the British.

No. 4 Sobrina Da Costa, an African Negro, also a Queen's Evidence, and witness to the slaughter.

No. 5 Florenco Ribeiro,* was wounded by the handspike of the Quartermaster.

No. 6 Manuel Josi Alves, was knocked down and thrown overboard by the Quartermaster in the beginning of the fray, he swam round the stern, as it is stated, and got into the boat – afterwards came on deck and ferociously took up the blood in his hand and drank it, because he had not had his satisfaction.

No. 7 Sebastian de Santos was acquitted.

No. 8 Francisco Feriera de Santo Serva,* the captain of the *Echo*, and, together with the crew, was afterwards transferred to the *Felicidade*. He it was who proposed the murder, and was on deck the whole time, calling the men from below and inciting them to fully accomplish the awful scene in which they were engaged. Serva determined on seizing the *Felicidade* himself and assumed the command, until the vessel was finally taken by H. M. *Ship Star*.

No. 9 Emanuel Francois Rosaigre, a black and native of Pondicherry, a Queen's Witness, gave his evidence in French, his native language, very clearly evincing a great degree of intelligence.

No. 10 Antonio Joaquim,* actively engaged in the fray.

No. 11 Janus Majaval,* he was indicted as a principal, the best looking of all the prisoners, and is said to be a nephew of the celebrated General Espartero, his countenance displayed a more than ordinary acuteness, and he was evidently one accustomed to think and act with promptitude and decision. He struck Mr Palmer, the Midshipman, with a carving knife on the left side, and then threw him overboard.

No. 12 Jove Antonio, the youngest of the prisoners, being only 18, was acquitted.

No. 13 Juan Francisco,* took a principal part in the murder.

No. 14 Manuel Antonio acquitted.

No. 15 Jozi Maria Martinos,* a very determined participator and engaged throughout the deadly affray.

Those marked thus * were condemned to death.'
One local newspaper editor reflected:

'There is something in this fearful tragedy which is revolting to the better feelings of humanity – the traffic in slaves is brutal and repugnant to all the principles of morality and religion. That it should be sometimes stained by the harrowing details of crimes of the deepest dye cannot be very surprising if we briefly reflect on the way in which that trade is carried on, and also on the men who invariably compose the crews. Desperadoes in character and accustomed to deeds of reckless cruelty, the crew of a slaver presents perhaps a greater amount of crime and atrocity than can be met with elsewhere amongst a similar number of men.'

It is interesting to compare the trial of these men with the other prisoners who were being charged and sentenced at the same time in Rougemont Castle. One individual named Thomas Nicholls was imprisoned for two months at hard labour for stealing two geese, Henry Diment was transported out of the country for seven years for stealing two spades at Crediton, John James was transported ten years for stealing a jar and brandy at Ottery St Mary and William Braddon was transported for fifteen years for stealing a sheep.[81]

The Brazilians were never executed: the legality of the trial was subsequently questioned[82] and by the end of the year they received a royal pardon.[83]

# PART TWO

# INVESTMENT: PLANTATIONS AND TRADE

European imports of New World consumer goods in the seventeenth century accelerated a demand for labour in the Americas. Keen competition developed between Europeans trading in sugar, tobacco, coffee and chocolate production and this added pressure to make commodities more economically viable. This also resulted in the gradual replacement of white indentured servants with unpaid labour. Early in the seventeenth century at least one Devonian, John Delbridge of Barnstaple, sent local men and women to settle in the West Indies[84] but these white colonists could not provide sufficient labour at a cost or level which was needed. Coerced labour quickly became the major part of English colonial populations in the Caribbean in the seventeenth century.

As with the rest of England, Devon men invested in plantations that used this slave labour. The word 'plantation' applied to a variety of economic endeavours such as those in sixteenth-century Ireland which a considerable number of Devon families had such as the Courtenays of Powderham. The latter owned an extensive amount of land in County Limerick.[85] The great families of Devon, such as the Chichesters, Gilberts and Raleighs, led colonisation in the sixteenth century and by the seventeenth there were many gentry families with branches in Ireland.[86] Devon also specialised in 'Fishing Plantations' in New England and particularly Newfoundland. One such place was the Greens Cove Fishing Plantation in Newfoundland in the 1750s and Robert Trelawney had a similar operation at Richmond Island in Maine. Many dozens of other Devonians had comparable ventures.[87] The word plantation is now almost exclusively applied to slave operations in the American South or in the West Indies but to Devonians it would have first indicated their older ventures in the North Atlantic where the greater number lay.

These were different from the plantations of the American South, the West Indies and South America which used slave labour although the brutality used against the native populations of North America and Ireland was also neither just nor fair. The seizure of lands in the North Atlantic colonies has also left a long legacy for the descendants of the original occupiers. Given the longstanding importance of Ireland to Devon and that fishing was an established and core industry, it is likely that the county invested more in Irish land and in fishing plantations across the North Atlantic than it did in the southern slave plantations.

The city of Exeter was asked on two occasions to invest in endeavours which would have included slaves. In 1638 they were approached regarding a plantation in Tobago and one hundred years later Robert Parker, an official of the Royal African Company, wrote seeking financial help with operations in Guinea.[88] No evidence has yet been found to show the city took up the offers.

However, evidence survives showing a number of Devonians invested in plantations which used slave labour. No doubt there were others which have not yet been identified[89] but it cannot yet be stated how extensively Devon participated in plantations. One who did was John Ellis of Mamhead whose will of 1810 noted 'I give and devise my plantations or sugar work situate in the parish of St Mary in the island of Jamaica and commonly called or known by the name of Newry together with all and every the messuages lands, tenements, slaves, cattle stock, utensils, implements of planting and other appurtenances'.[90] Another is William Pollard, a younger son of the King's Nympton family, who emigrated across the Atlantic and his descendants continued to own slaves in Bermuda and Barbados.[91] Doubtless there were other Devonians who left the county and their subsequent families had similar histories. Other families began their Devon associations after becoming wealthy through investing in plantations. Perhaps the best known is the Lopes family of Maristow in West Devon. Some two

*Investment: Plantations and Trade*

hundred years ago Sir Mannaseh Masey Lopes moved to Devon and he purchased some 32,000 acres in South West Devon. He was descended from Jewish settlers in Jamaica where the family had sugar plantations.[92] There are also records in Devon's archives which show individuals from other counties, who may have had Devon connections, as being slave owners.[93]

Six accounts relating to slaves in the Americas have been identified which provide extraordinary details on the nature of the plantations. Two were owned by younger sons of wealthy Devon families, one by a man who moved to Devon from Holland, another by the widow of a Bristol merchant and two are of documents which are held locally but have not yet had a Devon connection identified. Trade petitions from Devon relating to Africa have also been included as these point to Devonian interest in the continent.

# 1

# Devon cloth and petitions from Ashburton, Dartmouth, Exeter and Plymouth regarding the Royal Africa Company, 1708 to 1711

Six petitions from Devon provide some indications of the county's involvement in Africa in the seventeenth and early eighteenth centuries. These documents relate to Devon's attempts to fit into national legislation which regulated African trade. Such trade was restricted by the government to particular organisations and it may be of interest that the first petition regarding Devon's trade with Africa appears to date from 1694.

The petitions were preceded by a series of these bodies which had exclusive rights but were distinguished by their failure to effectively capitalise on their monopolies. The influx of Africans into Devon in the late 1500s was not followed by a great increase in subsequent trade. Instead, early seventeenth-century trade between England and Africa was inconsequential.[94] There was an attempt to rectify this in 1619 when the 'Governor and Company of Adventurers of London trading into the parts of Africa' was formed. It had exclusive rights to trade and comprised 38 gentlemen and merchants including at least two Devonians. One of them was Sir Ferdinando Gorges, Governor of Plymouth Fort and later a resident of Bristol. Gorges was also the leader of the company which had exclusive rights to New England. His interest in Africa is curious as he was then being overwhelmed in organising the colonisation of New England. His biographer made no mention of an interest in Africa which might be explained by Gorges' taking administrative control of New England coinciding with being made a member of the African company.[95] Sir Warwick Heale of Wembury was another Devon member of both companies. The African initiative suffered from insufficient financing, was restructured in 1631 and again in 1651 but the lack of official records has contributed to an incomplete understanding of its activities. With the Restoration of Charles II in 1660 England's trade was once again reassessed and a new company, the Royal Adventurers into Africa, was formed. A new group of men were given the chance to make their fortunes through a trade monopoly but the Adventurers were also reorganised three years later with, for the first time, slave trading noted as an objective. One director was Sir John Colleton, a plantation owner whose family had property in Barbados and South Carolina and who retired to Exmouth. Included in the baptisms recorded for the parish of Withycombe Raleigh near Exmouth are those of 'Andrew Hector Harris, a black belonging to John Colleton, aged 37 years on 3 August 1748', of 'Elizabeth Marchant, a black belonging to John Colleton, esquire, aged 27 years' on the same date, of 'William, an Indian servant of Sir John Colleton' on 26 July 1731 and his burial on 28 May 1735.[96]

Nine years after reorganisation, in 1672, after yet another financial failure, the Royal African Company was formed. The granting of what were in effect official monopolies aroused the hostility of other merchants and financial interests including Exeter which in 1694 sent a petition against this monopoly. Petitions were later sent in the early eighteenth century from Dartmouth, Exeter and Plymouth regarding their African trade and asking that the trade remain open. One supported the Royal African Company; the petitioners expressed concern for the continuation of the Company which was then on the verge of insolvency. It had debts of more than £300,000 and the first petition, from Exeter fifteen years after its earlier effort, was sent a few months before a crucial meeting of the company's directors with the creditors.[97] The petitions, as noted in the House of Commons' journal, are reproduced below.

**'13 December 1708**
A petition of the Mayor, Bailiffs, Burgesses and other inhabitants of the town of Dartmouth was presented to the House, and read, setting forth, that the petitioners' trade and livelihoods chiefly depends

upon shipping and navigation; which has been greatly encouraged by merchants trading to Africa, fitting out their ships for the said trade; that if the Africa Company should obtain that trade to themselves, exclusive of other merchants, the port will be thereby deprived of any benefit there. And praying that the trade to Africa may continued open to all her Majesty's subjects, regulated in such manner as to the House shall seem meet.'[98]

**'10 January 1709**
A petition of the Mayor, Aldermen, and Common Council of the City of Exeter and also of the merchants and other traders in the woollen manufactures was presented to the House and read; setting forth, that by means of the Act, made in the reign of the late King William for opening a free trade to Africa, greater quantities of woollen manufactures have been vended to those countries than at any time before and praying, that a free trade to Africa may be continued, under such regulations as shall be thought meet'[99]

**'11 January 1709**
A petition of the Mayor, Magistrates, Common Council and other the principal merchants and trading inhabitants of the Borough of Plymouth, was presented to the House and read, setting forth that since the laying open the trade to Africa, divers ships have been fitted out from the port for that coast, to the great benefit of the said borough, and parts adjacent, employed in the woollen manufactures; that if the said trade to Africa should be granted to the Africa Company, exclusive of all others, the petitioners conceive it will much prejudice them and the woollen manufactures, to be a discouragement to navigation in general; and praying, that the said trade may continue free and open to all her Majesty's subjects, under such regulations as the House shall think fit.'[100]

**'2 February 1709**
A petition of the Weavers, Tuckers and other Artificers belonging to the manufacturing of Perpetuanos for Africa, living in and near *Exon*, was presented to House [of Commons] and read; setting forth, that the Petitioners have been greatly supported in their trade by the great quantity of woollen goods, usually exported by the Royal African Company, who (as the Petitioners are informed) have met with such

discouragements in their trade, that they will be forced to withdraw their effects, and decline the trade to Africa, to the utter ruin of the petitioners; and praying that the traffic of the said Company to Africa may be preserved and encouraged at the House shall think fit.'[101]

An agreement was reached to extend credit until 1 May 1711 for a final financial settlement. Two weeks before that deadline yet another petition was sent from Devon. It was in this year that the Company failed to buy any commodities, including Devon cloth, to export to Africa.[102]

**'14 April 1711**
A petition of the dealers in wool, serge-makers, wool-combers and weavers in behalf of themselves, and great numbers of poor people in and about the town of Ashburton in the county of Devon, was presented to the House and read; setting forth that of late years the trade on fine serges has been lessened, we have been employed in making coarse serges, commonly called perpetuanas, for the coast of Africa, which of late have been much increased, and the petitioners have not only by that manufacture of coarse wool, and many poor people are thereby employed in spinning for those coarse goods; and being informed, that endeavours are used to confine the trade to a company, whereby the quantities made will be lessened, and the petitioners exposed to the utmost straits: and praying to be favoured in the consideration of their case.
   Ordered that the said petition be referred to the consideration of the whole House, to whom the petition of the adventurers and creditors of the Royal African Company and others, subscribers for the support and carrying on that trade, is referred.'[103]

Devon's concern for the financial well-being of the Royal African Company related to its two trades. The Company bought African commodities, such as gold, ivory, dyewood and hides, for trading in England and this accounted for some two thirds of its income. Slaves for export to the West Indies were the greater single commodity. The Company purchased English and foreign goods in order to buy the slaves and goods.[104] It was these purchases in England that the Devonians complained about: local cloth was, according to the petitioners, of great financial interest. Devon's centre of the cloth industry was Exeter and it experienced an extraordinary expansion in trade in the late 1660s. Different types of woollen cloth were particular to distinct areas of Devon and Exeter became, by the late 1600s, a centre for perpetuanas. From Exeter more than a quarter of all English cloth was exported by 1700. Only London and Bristol had a greater amount of trade and Exeter was the third largest city in the country in terms of population, wealth and trade. The main cloth markets were the Netherlands and the Baltic. Cloth was sent to London, from which a great amount went to France, and other export markets were Portugal and Spain. The definitive work on the local cloth market by Professor Youings omits any mention of Africa as a trade destination[105] which is puzzling in regards to these petitions. The reasons could be explained by the continual economic ups and downs of the cloth trade. One of these concerned the export of English cloth to Germany which by 1707 was prohibited. A number of Devon places, including Ashburton and Exeter, petitioned Parliament against it as they and others did regarding the importing of Irish yarn in 1717. At this time Exeter also sent many other petitions regarding taxes on soap, candles, oil and dyestuffs. The Devon petitions on African cloth exports were written when the industry was being disrupted by other exports and on the point of terminal decline. The first years of the eighteenth century were the height of prosperity for Devon's cloth industry but by 1745 exports from Exeter were half of what they were in 1700. The rot had set in during the second decade of the eighteenth century, at the time of the complaints regarding African exports.[106]

Given no attention to Africa was given by Professor Youings in her study of Exeter's cloth, it could be argued that the Devon men were desperately seeking any means to rebuild their markets and were grasping at straws regarding African exports. However, records of the Royal African Company shed light on this discrepancy. They show that in the first two years of its operation, from 1672 to 1674, Devon cloth worth some £8,000 was purchased via agents and intermediaries. It has been estimated that at this time Exeter exported £2,000,000 of cloth annually which means that these cloth purchases destined for Africa comprised 0.4 per cent of the overall yearly value in Exeter. This later increased to at most 0.7 per cent in 1693, the year of the greatest purchases of perpetuanas. Overall, the sale of Exeter cloth for Africa were worth £161,000 from 1672 to 1704: this was equal to 0.4 per cent of overall production. The reason for Professor Youings not noting Africa as an export market was because it was included within London sales from whence it was exported. The principal historian of the Royal African Company considered it to be of 'marginal importance'.

Nevertheless, it was more important to the Royal African Company than to Devon: the cloth, most of it from Devon but not all, comprised some ten per cent of the Company's overall exports in value. Of greater interest was cotton, a more versatile fabric for Africa than woollen cloth. This originally was re-exported from Asia and some £10,000 worth was bought every year: this compares with just over £5,000 worth of Devon cloth. The subsequent production of English cotton in Manchester must have further rendered Devon woollen cloth less attractive. Other materials exported by the Company were not supplied by Devon. This included iron and copper from Sweden and Germany, firearms from the Dutch or London, and knives and sheaths from Birmingham. The remaining goods totalled only a few thousand pounds worth of incidental items.

In summary, these figures show the export of local goods was incidental to Devon's economy and only one type of Devon cloth was important to the Royal African Company. That interest lasted only a short while and made up only a small portion of the overall value.[107] What makes these exports of particular interest is that they coincided with the period of greatest interest by Devonians in African slaving. It is with these voyages that additional information can be derived. The information from the records of the Royal African Company relate to its own ships but Devon's voyages at this time were independent of it (see below, pages 40 to 56). While the number, only twelve, was marginal in terms of the Royal African Company's efforts, it still shows supplemental exports of local cloth. Nearly all of the vessels' cargoes were imported goods from London, Rotterdam, Ireland, Germany, Sweden or elsewhere but there were still some perpetuanas and possibly other local cloth which was not specified as such.[108]

## 2

# Sale of a sugar plantation in Grenada

Amongst the documents at the Devon Record Office is an undated lease for one year of a sugar plantation by the name of Revierre Antoine in Grenada between Edward Payne and Thomas Dawes.[109] It appears to have been written in about 1800. The island was described by one Devonian in 1825 as being 'distinguished amongst the British Antilles for its internal unamity and its liberal treatment of the coloured classes of the inhabitants. In this last point the planters of this island go beyond all their brethren; the free coloured man has every privilege of the white . . . indeed the prejudice of colour is fainter in this colony than in almost any other.'[110] The individuals which appear in the following document were not fortunate enough to be free but were the property of the plantation. They were listed alongside the livestock.

The Schedule or Inventory referred to by the above-written Indenture:

**Negro Men**
Bartholomew, London, Larrann, Fransoe, Jeak, Jean, Pierre, Noell, Augustus, Cola, Jean Frantoe, Claud, Ouagui, Domanique, Valentine, Silvert Antonie, Andre, Charles, Rancine Martin, Scipio, Bazil Marcisce, Peter Atkin, Daniel Robert, Johnny, Carpenter, Livelurdevois Pompee, Fanboy, Spadille, Philip, Livelur Grand Jane, Alexis, Simon, Laurrant, Hippolite, Nichola, Alexis, Coof, Cambridge, Sampson, James, (Cooper)

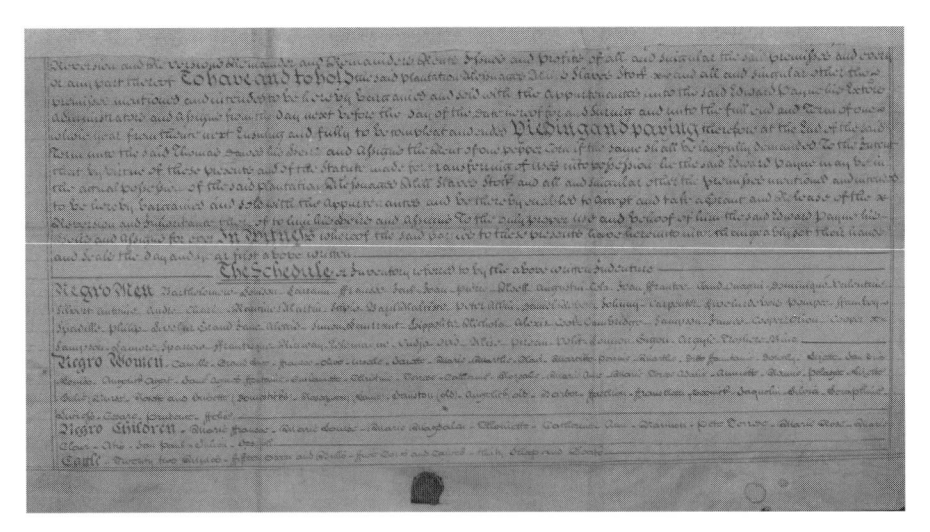

Schedule of the slaves in Grenada, *c*.1800
(Devon Record Office, 337b/1/435 (46/5)

Orion, (Cooper) Sampson, Lamore, Sparrow, Frantisque, Rigway, Telemaque, Cudgo, Ovio, Miso, Pirean, Polit, Lonnon, Gigou, Argyle, Troshere Bina.

**Negro Women**
Camille, Grand Luce, Fransoe, Olive, Urselle, Jenette, Marie, Marthe, Clair, Marcitte, Pernne, Marthe, Ditto Fountaine, Dorothy, Lizette, Jan Evive, Louisa, Angelick Agat, Jane Agnes Foutaine, Guilanette, Christine, Terese, Catherine, Rozealie, Marie Anne, Marie Teresa Adalie, Anniette, Rennie, Pelagee, Lizette, Gulie (Nurse), Rosette and Gabette (Domestics), Rosegway (Lame), Jauston (old), Angelick (old), Barbor, Fashion, Fransheen, Jaquelin, Silvia, Seraphine, Lucresso, Cesare, Prudence, Felix.

**Negro Children**
Marie Fransoe, Marie Louise, Marie Magdalan [Magdalene], Thomiette, Catharine, Ann, Rammon, Pete Terese, Marie Rose, Marie Clair, Jan Paul, Julion, Joseph.

**Cattle**
Twenty-two mules, fifteen oxen and bulls, five cows and calves, thirty sheep and goats.

# 3

# An Antigua plantation and the Swete family of Modbury, 1740s

One sugar cane plantation came to a Devonian with a curiously appropriate name through his marriage to a wealthy older Barbados widow: the Swete family of Modbury held Caribbean property through the marriage in London in 1699 of Maine Swete to Grace, the widow of Henry Le Conte of New York and William Wainwright of Antigua. She was then thirty-two years old and had been born in Barbados where her family had lived since the mid 1600s when Colonel Humphrey Walrond migrated from Sea near Ilminster in Somerset. Mrs Grace Swete's dowry included an estate in Antigua which had been the property of her second husband. The new couple moved to the West Indies and nearly thirty years later, by 1728 when Grace Swete died, her widower returned to England and married Esther Prickman. He was then a middle-aged man and his new wife was a much younger woman. They had a son, John, born in 1731 but four years later Maine Swete died followed by his son in 1755. Esther Swete was left as the only surviving family member and she passed the estate to Reverend John Tripe on condition he changed his surname to Swete. He is remembered chiefly as the leading advocate of the Picturesque Movement in Devon[111] and continued to own at least one Caribbean property: in his private letters he mentioned land in Jamaica in 1793.[112]

The Wainwright/Swete plantation on Antigua was described in a

Slaves in Antigua, 1737 (Devon Record Office, 388M/E1)

series of documents. One is an undated survey, but written not long after Maine Swete's death, which summarises its holdings.[113]

**Antigua**
We the underwritten (being well-acquainted with the estate of Main Sweet deceased & living in the neighbourhood thereof have at the request of Richard Oliver esquire met at the said estate & thoroughly viewed the same together with the canes, buildings, Negroes & cattle thereon do value and give our opinions on the same in manner & form following:

First, as to the canes upon the said estate
We find six pieces of plant canes containing as we imagine 50 acres but all of them except one piece seem to be planted at very improper times being either too early or too late for the ensuing crops, five of the said pieces of plant canes will be cut the ensuing crop & may possibly make sixty hogsheads of sugar most of them. However, save what we call standovers which is frequently owing to their being improperly planted and the best judges are often disappointed by an over calculate of such canes. The remaining one piece of plant canes being planted late cannot be supposed to come in till the year 1739 & will then be called standovers, they appear but ordinary considering the fine weather for many months past & the great dependence to be had on them.

There is only one piece of Rattoons or Second crop canes which are designed as plants for ground which is now preparing.

The mill very defective & all the other buildings appear in a most ruinous condition.

The Negroes consisting of 88 in number young & old we value at £1,743 Antigua Currency as may appear by the following schedule of particulars.

The cattle being 69 in number appear in good order & may be reasonably worth £10 Antigua money round.

The land at the body which we are told may be about 815 acres, we compute (including the mill and other buildings thereon & likewise

2 stills & old coppers in the whole) to be worth £12 per acre Antigua money. NB the situation of the body ponds is of no advantage nor adds anything to the value of the said estate.

There are some other Plantation Utensils which not being of any great value we omit appraising.

The land at Falmouth is reckoned 90 acres & values by us at £3 per acre.

All which being appraised to the best of our judgment & amounts to six thousand, four hundred eighty three pounds Antigua money. We certify under our hands this 29 day of November 1739.

Jon: S[?]ell
Rowell Hamilton
Henry Blizard
Robert Allen
Memorandum out of the above pieces of plants which is to be cut this year being full of the blast we imagine we will make very little.

The following list of 88 slaves was organised by sex and age with individual names and values given of the 26 men, 22 women, 18 boys and 22 girls. The physical state of two women, in regards to their ability to do work, was noted. A summary was made of the value of the entire plantation, at £6,483 of which the slaves made up some thirty per cent of the total. As in the previous document, slaves were sometimes listed by their colour distinctions including five Mulattas, two Creoles (who were either formerly, 1, the child of black South American parents born in the Americas, or 2, a person born and naturalised in the Americas of European or African race), and one Caramante (which has not been identified).

A List of Negroes & their value

MEN
Jackey, a driver £40
Jacob £45
Tombo £20
Johnno £40
George £30
Strephan £35
Aucomb £40
Pathro £40
Savy £40
Arrow £40
Quabena £30
Duranta £15
Sharper £25
Harry £30
Old Frank £15
Ammo £20
Appio £1
Caramante Cudgo £5
Billey £2
George £40
M. Johnny £40
Timan £40
Peroe £1
Bounty £40
Creole Cudjoe £25
Cuffy £1

WOMEN
Old Nanny the Doctress £10
Old Dawley £1
Old Nancey £1
Old Peggy £1
Mary £36
Mimboe £2
Sarah £36
Quasheba £36
Marose £36
Bobb £28
Guan £36
Betty £30
Rachell £35
Fattesman £25
Phillis £30
Jane £35
Buddeine £35
Little Jubba £36
Old Jubba past labour –
Young Nanny never works hath one leg & the other bad & said to be free
Pheba £35
Old Lead £20
Women £504

BOYS
Rowley £28
Sava £18
Duke £25
Antoney £14
Leon £2
Isaac £20
Cesar £11
Jacob £10
James £28
M. Frank £14
Little Sharper £12
Quacoe £7
Little Strephan £3
Little Johnny £1
Sampson £1
Colloe £10
Dickey £5
Steven £16
Boys £251

GIRLS
Andella £20
Silvia £28
Jenny £35
Matty £25
Mary Ann £14
Abby £18
Ritta £12
Cocoa £12
L. Jane £2
L. Betty £12
Bessee £10
Molly £14
Clorinda £25
Philleret £12
Patience £12
Sarah £5

Molly Terry £14
L. Dolly £1
Mulatta Hannah £1
L. Peggy £2
L. Lead £5
Little Hanna £1
Girls £288

Men £700
[Women] 504
[Boys] 251
[Girls] 288
Negroes £1,743
Cattle £690
Body land £3,780
Falmouth £270
Total £6,483

A second list also survives of the slaves and livestock which was dated 14 June 1744. The plantation machinery and tools were also recorded. The list is similar to the undated one but has slightly different numbers of slaves (80 instead of 88) with extended details on the ability of children to work. The livestock are recorded in the same manner as the slaves, by sex and age with their names given. In many instances their names are the same.

14 June 1744, a list of Negroes and Cattle and an Inventory of Plantation utensils by Mr Rowland Oliver

An Inventory of the slaves, cattle and plantation utensils on the estate of Maine Sweet Esquire, deceased.

*Investment: Plantations and Trade*

MEN
Jacob Driver, disabled in one hand
Stephen Old
Old George with a wooden leg
Young George
Mulatta Johnny
Old Seavez
Johnno Boson
Cubbinah
Bounty
Arnah ruptured
Timon
Harry
Rowley
James
Leon
Old Sharper
Colla
Petro
Cudgo
Cufee
Old Amimo
Duke
Tomboy with a rotten foot
Stephen

BOYS THAT WORK
Isaac
Seavez
Dickey
Quacow
Mulatta Frank
Jacob
Sharper
Caesar

WOMEN
Old Peggy very old and subject to fits
Old Lady Doctress
Old Dolly Good for Nothing
Old Jubba Do:
Old Nanny very old
Sarah
Marotte
Gayan
Quasheba
Jane
Silvia
Jubba
Clarinda
Marian
Abby
Rachel
Buddamay
Bab
Jenny
Bennabah Plantation cook
Tibbah
Betty
Old Mimba very old
Ritta

BOY INFANTS
Little Johnny
Sampson
Little Stephen
Green
Elsen
Little Bounty
Harry Gregory Mulatta
Tom Blackeyby Do:

GIRLS THAT WORK
Bessy
Coco
Black Moll
Patience
Moll Terry
Mulatta Hannah
England Jane of little or no service with sore legs
Little Layde
Betty Jack
Philoret

GIRL INFANTS
Little Sarah
Little Peggy
Little Hannah
Lucy
Johnto
Eve

CATTLE
Red Bulls
Rowlin
Tago

BLACK BULLS
Quick
Sandy

RED OXEN
Winter
Tombeck
Wilby
Ingin
Baker
Bold Face
Sowell

Old Captain
Readney
Gallant
Jewell
Punch
Lyon
Diamond
Bell
Fidler
Captain
Butler

BLACK OXEN
Dick
Brangill
Scipio
Back
Cole
Monday
Pybald

BLACK BULL CALVES
Sunday
Wier

RED BULL CALVES
Frye
Saturday
Jongs
Jenkins
Toby
Speedwell

RED COW CALVES
Combah
Bessy
Lady
Sarah

Mimbah
Tewget
Cotton
Hannah

BLACK COW CALVES
Ritta
Peggy
Speed
John Coomah
Moll
Grace
Canny
Silver
Katy
Ancilla
Cubbah

RED COWS
Madam
Blossom
Maria
Ingin
Doll
Daphne
Betty

Maggy
Surey
Flower
Mage
Pretty
Sibella
Mary
Phillis
Lucy
Cherry
Abbah
Rawbone
Hannah

BLACK COWS
Dullinda
Coobah
Nancy
Suse
Sheley
Pendah
Abbah
Venus
Bess
Sarah, Judy, Margo & Betty

PLANTATION UTENSILS

In the boiling house, three large coolers, two striking co: in good order, nine coppers in good order, four ladles one new the other very old, five scummers four old one new, two spouts in good order, two iron pots one with two holes in it, three block treble, double & single sheaved in good order, a parcel of old iron, a pair of large stilyards, a smith's anvil, a jack, two sledges & a hand hammer, two lamps & a shovel, a dozen & a half of cart nails, a smith's beak iron.

In the still house, two stills of & two tubs, six wooden cisterns, four ditto in the ground, six liquor casks, five large jars, a three cans, a lee cistern, twelve spouts fro the boiling house to the still house & three in the still house, two spare coppers & a large kettle, two small ladders, a parcel of nails for the use of the works.

In the mill, a ladder & two iron crows, seven spouts from the mill to the boiling house.

In the overseers room, a large old chest.

One new cart with yokes and chains.

A letter of 1745 written by the overseer to Mrs Esther Swete includes references to the usefulness of particular slaves and the need to increase their number.

Antigua, 24th July 1745
Madam,

I wrote you last by a sloop that I sailed with an express from English Harbour sometime in March last a copy of which and also a copy of the plantation accounts I sent you by Captain Hartley which I hope you have received. We have not yet finished the crop, I believe we shall make about 4 or 5 hogsheads of sugar more. The Negroes being so frequently ordered upon public work for the defence of our island has prevented the crop being taken sooner. I believe we shall make upwards of 70 hogsheads of sugar, 60 of them I have already shipped to Messrs Delamore. I am sorry I had not known sooner of your intentions of giving my brother the sales of part of your sugars. The next shall be consigned to your self that you may dispose of them as you think proper as prep[torn] we have no ship that takes in sugars for London. My brother writes me your desire I would purchase 3 or 4 young Negro wenches for your estate. I shall observe your order when any vessel arrives. We have had but few Negroes imported here since the French war and those has sold chiefly for bills of exchange. I should be glad to have your orders who I shall draw upon in case I should not be able to purchase upon any other terms then by Bills of Exchange. Your gang of Negroes greatly wants recruiting. If you were to order six young Negroes to be purchased every year it would be of great service to the estate. At present we can scarcely make 40 able Negroes. The rest are either children or so old they are incapable of working. Old George died a few days ago. He is no loss to the estate as he has been past labour for some time. The following sugars has been shipped this crop:

10 hh by Heartly, 10 per Bever, 10 per Almary, 10 per Coulter, 10 per Hubart, 10 per James Payne, I am madam, Your most humble servant, Rowland Oliver

# 4

# The Rolle plantation in East Florida, 1780 to 1785

From 1763 until 1783 Dennys Rolle was a principal colonist of East Florida. Rolle was a member of a wealthy and influential family in Devon but he himself was the eighth child. The family had two great houses in Devon at Stevenstone in the north of the county and Bicton in the south-east. At the age of 24 he inherited some 6,000 acres in Hampshire and Somerset, he married the following year and eight children were born over the following twelve years. A year after the birth of his last child, in 1763 when he was 38, Rolle acquired land in Florida from the government and in 1764 sailed across the Atlantic to develop what was becoming a new British colony. Three years before, in 1760, he had visited the American colonies and had been elected Member of Parliament for Barnstaple the following year. Whilst living in Florida he continued to cross the Atlantic and visit his home in Devon.

Rolle had originally attempted to acquire land in Georgia but settled for a grant of many thousands of acres in the new colony of Florida. He brought with him a small party of Devonians to settle the land, which was to be named Rollestown, situated between what is now Daytona Beach and St Augustine in north-east Florida. Rivalries with local officials and inept estate management doomed Rollestown to failure but it was the cessation of the colony to Spain in 1783 that ended Rolle's

Bicton in 1800, one of the homes of the Rolle family
(Westcountry Studies Library, SC0176)

adventures in Florida. He then applied for compensation and turned his attention to developing the Bahamas.[114]

Amongst the surviving papers for Rolle's Florida estate is a detailed account of Jericho, one plot of his property, and this listed not only cattle, horses, implements and machinery but also the human beings that he owned.[115] It was signed by William Wilson and William Bell who were apparently the overseers.

**'Jericho April 1st 1780**
Schedule of the property of James Penmen at his plantation sold this day to Denys Rolle Esq. and at present under our care and management.

| *Men* | *Women* | *Boys* | *Girls* |
| --- | --- | --- | --- |
| Damon | Cinna | Turpin | Bett |
| Caesar (Morris) | Phillis | Isaac | Dinah |
| September | Marria | Damon | Jeaney |
| Titus | Chloe | Hugh | Aga |
| Ishmael | Rose Morris's | Bob | Peggy |

| | | | |
|---|---|---|---|
| Sawney | Juddy | Joe | Lucy |
| Tom | Nancy | Ned | |
| Jacob | Kate | Pompey | |
| Sam | Clarenda | | |
| York | Sally | | |
| Briton | Dolly | | |
| Little Jacob | Rose | | |
| Jack | Molly | | |
| Little Caesar | | | |
| Philip | | | |
| Dick | | | |
| Barbara | | | |
| Will | | | |
| Charles | | | |
| Antigua | | | |
| Sam 2 years | | | |
| Little Jack | | | |
| Cromwell | | | |
| Luck | | | |

**Recapitulation**
24 men, 13 women, 8 boys, 6 girls 51 in all'

Another list, Nos. 201 to 202, recorded that Cimma, a 'house wench', and Phillis, a washerwoman, were valued at £80 each, that Maria, with her sons Ned and Bob and an unnamed six-year-old daughter, were valued at £100, that Molly with her sons Hugh and Joe were valued at £80, Chloe with her daughter Peggy were valued at £60, and Rose, Juddy and Nancy were valued at £50 while Kate and Clarinda were each worth £40. Bett and Jeanny were valued at £30.

There is also a list of 1 November 1785 which recorded 'dead and missing negroes' with a total number living at 98, dead and missing 69 as well as 'born 167' and 'an original number of 155'. Slaves were also recorded as being fit or unfit to perform 'tasks'. Some of the slaves were described as Mandingos, a term used to describe certain people of West Africa.

*Investment: Plantations and Trade*

'List of negroes the property of Dennys Rolle Esquire on this island.

| Men | Women | Boys | Girls |
|---|---|---|---|
| Damon driver 53 | Sally useless 49 | Little Damon 11 mo. | Dinah 13 |
| Little Jacob 22 | Dolly 19 | Ambrose (mullato) 6 | |
| Jemmy 34 | Marian 35 | Jemmy 4 | Betty 9 |
| Ben 36 | Pamela 35 | -Ben 7 | Nancy 4 |
| Billy 37 | | -Farewell 1 | Molly 1 |
| Mund. Caesar 31 | Pendar or Lucy 37 | | Celia 2 |
| Cyrus 33 | Lucy 31 | | |
| Romulus 31 | Madam 29 | | -Daphne 14 |
| Numa ruptured 31 | Phoebe 26 | | -Charlotte 4 |
| Jacob 37 | Cinna 33 | Isaac 16 | Betty 13 |
| Charles or Saul 33 | | | |
| Sampson 33 | | Misey 33 | Seapoy 12 |
| | | Polydore 10 | |
| | | Tom 7 | |
| | Lyddy 26 | | |
| Sawnny 39 | Rose (new wife) 14 | | |
| York 31 | Cyndar (new wife) 14 | | |
| | Sylvia 51 | Prince 10 | |
| Philip 34 | Nancy 31 | - Hugh 10 | |
| | | - Joe 1 | |
| Rose 35 | Simon 2 | Aga 8 | |
| Mingo 24 | Phillis 29 | | |
| Britain 33 | Thyme (new wife) 14 | | |
| Ishmael 35 | Myrtilla (new wife) 23 | Chance 2 | |
| Little Charles 23 | | | |
| Cato 24 | | | |
| | Judith (old) 61 | Abe 18 | |
| | | Jack 10 | Phobe 8 |
| Luck 35 | | | |
| Cromwell 53 | Rose 33 | - Abraham 10 | Jenny 11 |
| Tim 64 | | - Dick 6 | |
| Felix 39 | | | - Juddy 10 |
| | | | - Maria 7 |
| Turpin 19 | Daphne 15 | | |
| | Quashiba 34 | - King 10 | - Tyra 6 |
| | | | - Klara 4 |

September 35           Beck 32            Ben [blank]        Daphne 9
                                          Ned 7

                       Mundingas:         January 15         Phoebe 11
                                          Billy 15           Nanny 12
                                          Will 15            Jenny 13
                                          Monday 15
                                          Bucks 14
                                          Joe or Simon 15
                                          Harry 14
                                          James 14


Isaac run                                 Titus dead
Hercules dead                             King dead
Jackey dead                               [total] 29
Ansell dead                               Hannah sent to the Havana
Big Sam dead                              Phyllis (Toney's wife) dead
Little Jack returned to Penman            Maria (Jack's wife) dead
Jack run                                  Molly (Jack's 2nd wife) dead
Dick drowned                              3 Mandingo's not named dead
Barbara run                               Chloe (Scipio's wife) dead
Jacob dead                                Bess (Smart's wife) dead
Antigua dead                              Juddy (York's wife) dead
Owen dead                                 Lybrey (Trial's wife) dead
Will run                                  Dix (Felix's wife) dead
Tom run                                   Phoebe (John's wife) dead
Tryal dead                                Kindar dead
Prince dead                               Nanny (Billy's wife) dead
Old John dead                             Charlotte (Jack's wife) dead
Sam dead                                  Maria (Charles' wife) dead
Smart dead                                Chloe (Ishmael's wife) dead
Toney dead                                Moll (Tom's wife) dead
Bob dead                                  Kate dead
Scipio dead                               Clarinda dead
Pliny dead                                [total] 21
Jack dead
Big Caesar dead                           Hector, run and sold to the Indians
Little Caesar dead                        Quash (Sampson's wife) dead
Peter dead                                Mulatto John dead

*Investment: Plantations and Trade*

Andrew (Mun.) dead
Bob dead
March (Lyddy's child) dead
Pompey Caesar's child dead
Frank (Mandingo) dead
Peggy and Lucy, Jack's children dead
Kate – Madingo dead
Nancy – Mandingo dead

Sarah – Mandingo dead
Amy (Jack's child) dead
Nanny (Sampson's child) dead
Betty (Scipio's child) dead
Phillis (Tim's child) dead
Bella – Mandingo dead
Maria – Mandingo dead'

There is an oral tradition that after Rolle's subsequent failure in the Bahamas his son instructed the family land to be given to his slaves. The papers at the National Archive show that in 1836 John Rolle received £4,333 6s 9d in compensation for the loss of his 377 slaves in his Bahamas estate. Moreover, the slaves were released from their apprenticeships. In 1838 *The Sun*, described as a Whig/Radical journal, commended Lord Rolle for having liberated his former slaves. It noted that to his 'immortal honour' he had 'voluntarily emancipated the numerous slaves on the estates left by his father'. [116]

# 5

# Captain John Stedman of Surinam, 1772 to 1777, and Tiverton, 1784 to 1797

The lives of one man and his teenage son who resided in Tiverton in the late 1700s raises questions on the reasons for individual attitudes towards slavery in the opening years of national and local moves towards abolition. In 1796 Captain John Stedman wrote one of the most revealing accounts of the conditions of men and women in slavery. He also wrote a personal journal of his daily life including in Devon which occasionally contradicts his printed account. It is because of these two sources that so much information can be gleaned from a man whose lover was a slave, had a son born into slavery but who himself also owned slaves and was against abolition.

While in his twenties Stedman volunteered for a Dutch force to subdue an insurrection amongst slaves in Surinam. He was there from 1772 to 1777. Stedman wrote a two-volume account of his experiences in the small South American country. It was published nineteen years later and amongst the subscribers were at least 30 Devonians including Sir Thomas Dyke Acland of Killerton.[117]

Stedman concluded it was not surprising the slaves revolted given the cruel punishments meted out by their owners[118] and yet he was not in favour of freeing slaves: in his account Stedman wrote that for the British to free the slaves would put the country at a financial disadvantage with other countries. Twenty years after he arrived in Surinam, in 1792, he had not changed his opinion: he refused that year

'A Surinam Planter in his Morning Dress' (John Gabriel Stedman, *Narrative of a five years' expedition against the revolted Negroes of Surinam, in Guiana, on the Wild Coast of South America, from the year 1772 to 1777*, II).

to sign Tiverton's petition against the slave trade. Stedman rewrote his original journals over the course of some seven to eight years.[119] His account would have been of greater public interest in 1796 given the heightened awareness of slavery compared to the 1770s. Stedman received an initial payment of £500 for his writing, a considerable sum at the time.[120]

Something of his character is revealed in a passage written by Tiverton's town clerk in 1793. He noted:

> 'The whole town seems now in a very quiet state, but there was a most violent comical bustle this day at Mr Dennys's, where Colonel Stedman and the Young Jacobin Mr Hogg were invited to dine. Mr Hogg is a violent Dissenter with strong Jacobin notions. He now happened to say something improper about the army whereupon the Colonel took fire and began to abuse the young gentleman and treat him in a way that frightened him. He left the room, but the Colonel ran after him, brought him back, made him sit down, and sit and drink, and Mr Dennys and his company were on the whole not displeased with the Colonel's behaviour'.[121]

One historian has assessed Stedman as being a 'spendthrift, incessant drinker and a gambler' as well as 'a lover of no mean character' who was comparable to Don Juan and Casanova. Stedman had loose connections with Tiverton. His father was Scottish and his mother Dutch. His residence in the town is probably the result of trade connections between Tiverton and Holland. Stedman moved to the mid Devon town in 1785 and died there eleven years later. Of as great of interest to Devonian historians is the curious history of his son who spent his teenage years in Devon.[122]

Stedman's account is greatly taken up with military action and descriptions of Surinam's natural history but he also frequently wrote of inhumane punishments given to the slaves. He warned his readers:

> 'as to the shocking cruelties that here are so frequently exposed, let it suffice to say, that to deter others from similar inhuman practices, and teach them virtue, was my sole and only motive; while, on the other hand, it must be observed that Liberty, nay even too much lenity, when *suddenly* granted to illiterate

Engraving, based on a drawing by John Stedman, entitled 'A female Negro slave, with a weight chained to her ankle' (John Gabriel Stedman, *Narrative of a five years' expedition against the revolted Negroes of Surinam, in Guiana, on the Wild Coast of South America, from the year 1772 to 1777*, London, 1806, I)

'A Negro hung alive by the ribs to a gallows' (John Gabriel Stedman, *Narrative of a five years' expedition against the revolted Negroes of Surinam, in Guiana, on the Wild Coast of South America, from the year 1772 to 1777*, I).

and unprincipled men, must be to *all* parties dangerous, if not pernicious.'[123]

Many of these descriptions are harrowing and he observed 'I have seen the most cruel tortures inflicted, for submitting to the desire of a husband, or for refusing the same to a libidinous master, and more frequently a rascally overseer: nay, even on the most innocent, from the false accusations of a lustful woman, prompted alone by jealousy . . .'[124] In one instance he noted 'before leaving Paramaribo, I must remark, that during my stay there no less than nine Negroes had each a leg cut off, for running away from their masters'. In this particular instance, four of the men died immediately while a fifth committed suicide by tearing off his bandages so he could bleed to death. Stedman also wrote 'others are seen deprived of an arm, and this is the forfeit for daring to raise it against an European'.[125] One of the most disturbing stories involved a young woman.

> 'the first object which attracted my compassion during a visit to a neighbouring estate, was a beautiful Sambo girl of about eighteen, tied up by both arms to a tree, as naked as she came into the world, and lacerated in such a shocking manner by the whips of two Negro-drivers, that she was from her neck to her ankles literally dried over with blood. It was after she had received two hundred lashes that I perceived her, with her head hanging downwards, a most affecting spectacle. When, turning to the overseer, I implored that these might be immediately unbound, since she had undergone the whole of so severe a punishment; but the short answer which I obtained was, that to prevent all strangers from interfering with his government, he had made an unalterable rule, in that case, always to double the punishment, which he instantaneously began to put in execution: I endeavoured to stop him, but in vain, he declaring the delay should not alter his determination, but make him take vengeance with double interest. Thus I had no remedy but to run to my boat and leave the detestable monster, like a beast of prey, to enjoy his bloody feast, till he was glutted.'[126]

Her crime had been to refuse the overseer's sexual advances.

Stedman's own position was contradictory given he himself owned

'Flagellation of a Female Sambo Slave' (John Gabriel Stedman, *Narrative of a five years' expedition against the revolted Negroes of Surinam, in Guiana, on the Wild Coast of South America, from the year 1772 to 1777*, I).

slaves as well as a sugar plantation.[127] In spite of the extraordinary cruelty he witnessed, and it must be said he was also guilty of administering harsh punishment, Stedman agreed with slavery. He wrote that he loved African Negroes but did not want abolition of the slave trade for at least four years otherwise it would be the financial ruin of both the white and black races.[128]

Stedman defined the various racial distinctions between white and black. He noted a Mulattos as being a person who is half black, a Quadroon was one quarter black and a Sambo as being three quarters black. Another definition for a Sambo was a person of various degrees of mixed ancestry.

Stedman's journey to Surinam took 63 days and when the ship arrived the Governor treated the 500 men to a reception. The waitresses intrigued Stedman. He noted 'the company were attended by a considerable number of extremely handsome Negro and Mulatto maids, all naked from the waist upwards, according to the customs of the country'.[129] Later that night he was shocked at the forwardness of the first slave who greeted him. Stedman wrote in his journal:

'I set out in search of the house of Mr Lokens, the hospitable gentleman who had so obligingly invited me to make it my own. I soon discovered the place but my reception was so ludicrous that I cannot forbear relating the particulars. On knocking at the door, it was opened by a young female Negro, of a masculine appearance, whose whole dress consisted of a single petticoat, and who held a lighted tobacco pipe in one hand, and a burning candle in the other.'

He had a drink but then:

'Tired with the employments of the day, I longed for some rest, and made a signal to my attendant that I wanted to sleep: but my motion was strangely misconstrued; for she immediately seized me by the neck and imprinted on my lips a most ardent kiss. Heartily provoked at this unexpected and (from one of her colour) unwelcome salutation, I disentangled myself from her embraces, and angrily flung into the apartment allotted for my place of rest. But here I was again pursued by my black tormentor, who, in opposition to all I could say, insisted upon pulling off my

'The Execution of Breaking on the Rack' (John Gabriel Stedman, *Narrative of a five years' expedition against the revolted Negroes of Surinam, in Guiana, on the Wild Coast of South America, from the year 1772 to 1777*, II).

'Female Quadroon Slave of Surinam' (John Gabriel Stedman, *Narrative of a five years' expedition against the revolted Negroes of Surinam, in Guiana, on the Wild Coast of South America, from the year 1772 to 1777*, I).

shoes and stockings, and in a moment disencumbered me of that part of my apparel. I was extremely chagrined at her conduct; though this is an office commonly performed by the slaves in Surinam, to all ranks and sexes without exception. Nor ought anyone to conceive that this apparently extraordinary conduct resulted from any peculiarity of disposition in the girl; her behaviour was only such as would have been practised by the generality of female Negro slaves, and what will be found, by all you visit the West India settlements, to be characteristic of the whole dark sisterhood.'

This was a version concocted for his readers whereas in his private journal he admitted 'go to sleep at Mr Lolkens, who was in the country. I – one of his Negro maids'.[130] Not long afterwards Stedman had another sexual offer which he noted in his published account:

'On the morning of the 22nd, an elderly Negro woman, with a black girl about fourteen, entering my apartment, it would be difficult to express my astonishment when she gravely presented me her daughter, to become what she was pleased to term my wife. I had so little gallantry, however, as to reject the offer with a loud laugh; but at the same time accompanied the refusal with a small but welcome present, with which they appeared perfectly satisfied, and departed with every possible demonstration of gratitude and respect. The girls here who voluntarily enter into these connections are sometimes mulattoes, sometimes Indians and often Negroes. They all exult in the circumstance of living with a European, whom, in general, they serve with the utmost tenderness and fidelity, and tacitly reprove those numerous fair ones who break through ties more sacred and solemn. Young women of this description cannot indeed be married or connected in any other way, as most of them are born or trained up in a state of slavery; and so little is the practice condemned, that, while they continue faithful and constant to the partner by whom they are chosen, they are countenanced and encouraged by their nearest relations and friends, who call this a lawful marriage; nay, even the clergy avail themselves of this custom without restraint; witness the Reverend Mr S-dh-s, Mr T-ll-t, etc. Many of the sable-coloured beauties will, however,

Engraving entitled 'Joanna'. In August 1790 Stedman hired a young woman named Betty Moon to be his 'anatomator', presumably a live model, for his drawings. (John Gabriel Stedman, *Narrative of a five years' expedition against the revolted Negroes of Surinam, in Guiana, on the Wild Coast of South America, from the year 1772 to 1777*, I).

follow their penchant without any restraint whatever, refusing, with contempt, the golden bribes of some, while on others they bestow their favours for a dram or a broken tobacco pipe if not for nothing.'[131]

There is also a different version in his journal which is revealing. Stedman wrote on February 22nd 'a Negro woman offers me the use of her daughter while here for a certain sum. We don't agree about the price.'[132] Afterwards Stedman met Joanna whom he described as 'the beautiful mulatto maid' and a 'charming young woman'. They met at the house of a Mr Demelly where Stedman took his breakfast. The teenager was 'a favourite' of his host's wife. At great length Stedman noted her in his book as being:

'Rather taller than the middle size, she was possessed of the most elegant shape that nature can exhibit, moving her well-formed limbs with more than common gracefulness. Her face was full of native modesty, and the most distinguished sweetness; her eyes, as black as ebony, were large and full of expression, bespeaking the goodness of her heart; her cheeks through which glowed, in spite of the darkness of her complexion, a beautiful tinge of vermilion, when gazed upon. Her nose was perfectly well formed, rather small; her lips a little more prominent, which, when she spoke, discovered two regular rows of teeth, as white as mountain snow; her hair was a dark brown inclining to black, forming a beautiful globe of small ringlets, ornamented with flowers and gold spangles. Round her neck, her arms, and her ankles, she wore gold chains, rings and medals; while a shawl of Indian muslin, the end of which was negligently thrown over her polished shoulders, gracefully covered part of her lovely bosom: a petticoat of rich chintz alone completed her apparel. Bare-headed and bare-footed, she shone with double lustre, as she carried in her delicate hand a beaver hat, the crown trimmed round with silver. The figure and appearance of this charming creature could not but attract my particular attention, as they did indeed that of all who beheld her ...'[133]

After surveying at least two other women, Stedman had found the one he wanted. Joanna was fifteen years old and Stedman twenty-nine.

'Rural Retreat – The Cottage' showing the young Stedman family (John Gabriel Stedman, *Narrative of a five years' expedition against the revolted Negroes of Surinam, in Guiana, on the Wild Coast of South America, from the year 1772 to 1777*, II).

She was the daughter of Mr Kruythoff, a Dutch planter, and Cery, a slave who was the property of Mr 'DB'. Joanna's father had offered one thousand pounds sterling to buy her freedom and those of her four siblings but Mr D. B. refused and Kruythoff had, according to Stedman, died of a broken heart shortly afterwards. Joanna remained a slave.[134] Stedman's private journal has a much briefer, and less effusive, mention of her merely as 'a mulatto girl'.[135] Stedman had specific meanings for terms which are used differently today. A mulatto was a specific term: it referred to the offspring of a union between a white and black person (one half black), a 'sambo' had a mulatto and a black for parents (three quarters black), and a 'quadroon' one mulatto and one white parent (one quarter black). In these situations it was only permitted for white men to be intimate with other races. White women who had sex with slaves were, Stedman wrote, 'detested' thereafter and the slave was executed without mercy. Interestingly, he noted this as the biased law of Dutch men.[136]

According to Stedman, Joanna offered herself to Stedman with an eloquent speech.

> 'I am born a low contemptible slave. Were you to treat me with too much attention, you must degrade yourself with all your friends and relations; while the purchase of my freedom you will find expensive, difficult and apparently impossible. Yet though a slave, I have a soul, I hope, not inferior to that of an European, and blush not to avow the regard I retain for you, who have distinguished me so much above all others of my unhappy birth. You have, Sir, pitied me; and now, independent of every other thought, I shall have pride in throwing myself at your feet, till fate shall part us, or my conduct become such as to give you cause to banish me from your presence.'[137]

Shortly afterwards their union was formalised. Stedman wrote to his readers that he visited Mr Demelly with whom Joanna was domiciled.

> 'However strange it may appear to many readers, they, with a smile, wished me joy of what, with their usual good humour, they were pleased to call my conquest; which, one of the ladies in company assured me, while it was perhaps censured by some, was applauded by many, but she believed in her heart *envied*

*Investment: Plantations and Trade*

'Group of Negroes, as imported to be sold for slaves' (John Gabriel Stedman, *Narrative of a five years' expedition against the revolted Negroes of Surinam, in Guiana, on the Wild Coast of South America, from the year 1772 to 1777*, I).

'Family of Negro Slaves from Loango' (John Gabriel Stedman, *Narrative of a five years' expedition against the revolted Negroes of Surinam, in Guiana, on the Wild Coast of South America, from the year 1772 to 1777*, II).

by all. A decent wedding, at which many of our respectable friends made their appearance, and at which I was as happy as any bridegroom ever was, concluded the ceremony; with which I shall beg leave to conclude a chapter, which, methinks I hear many readers whisper, had better never had a beginning.'[138]

The ceremony does not appear to have been legally recognised and Joanna remained a slave through their five-year relationship although he tried to buy her freedom on several occasions. On one occasion his fellow officers chided him for being overly concerned with her welfare and of the son she later bore him.[139] At another time he brought home his superior officer and noted 'I let him see my house and told him of my girl in such a way that, by God! he was obliged to approve both and behaved civilly.'[140]

In his printed account Stedman was at great pains to represent Joanna as the great love of his life however his journal recorded details of yet another conquest, described only as 'B-e', with whom he also had intimate relations at this time. On April 7th 1772 he noted 'a discovery concerning B-e', on the 11th 'Joanna, her mother and Quaco's mother come to close a bargain with me. We put it off for reasons I gave them', on the 12th 'B- and Joanna both breakfast with me. I call myself Mister', the following day 'B-e sleeps with me' and finally on May 8th he notes his wedding to Joanna. A month later he recorded, enigmatically, 'I dine with Joanna, with whom I resolve to lie no more for certain good reasons'. It is unclear whether his resolve was to cease sexual relations or refrain from telling untruths. He continued to describe her as his wife but nineteen months after the wedding he wrote 'Joanna a good-for-nothing', on the following day noted 'she makes me an odd discovery which makes me think' then the third day 'I hire her from her master, for 10 bits a week, and set her to doings for myself'.[141]

Stedman returned to Europe in 1777 and according to the printed account Joanna refused to sail with him because she had some standing in Surinam but would be a burden to him in England. His journal noted that not long his arrival he frequented brothels with at least one unhappy result. Stedman received at least one letter from 'the lovely Joanna' but he made no mention of writing to her. A few years later, in 1783, Stedman heard she was dead. Nine months earlier he had married Adriana Wierts Van Coehorn, on 2 February 1782, in Maestricht. One historian has described his Dutch bride as 'arrogant, highly-strung, nervous and hysterical'. If this is a correct assessment then perhaps her behaviour resulted from knowing of Joanna; if her husband's first marriage was legal then his second was not. The second Mrs Stedman was then only eighteen years old and the groom was twice her age.[142]

On November 27 1774 Stedman's son by Joanna was born and after her death the boy, then nine years old, was sent to him. A cousin wrote at this time:

> 'I am sorry for the melancholy end of the poor mulatto girl. It's a great loss for the poor boy. You do well to bring him home and give him some schooling and then let him do for himself, and know what the world is.'[143]

Stedman had managed to buy his son's freedom before leaving Surinam. Johnny Stedman arrived in Holland in 1784 and his father appears to have been devoted to him. His journal has many references to the boy and he was very public with him when they moved to England the following year ('We both dined, and Johnny, with Mrs Macaulay and so to the Royal Circus to see the riders', 'Johnny and I go to Wapping, at Pond's. Johnny & I dined with Mrs Hall'.[144] In 1785 they moved to Hensleigh House in Tiverton. Stedman wrote Johnny was successfully educated in Devon, joined the Royal Navy as a midshipman but was then drowned in action off Jamaica. The young Stedman had formed an attachment with a local woman, Miss Hobson of Halberton but it does not appear they married. Hannah Cowley, the Tiverton playwright, composed a poem on his loss as did John Stedman including the lines:

> No more they olive beauties on the waves,
> Shall be the scorn of such European slaves,
> Whose optics, blind to merit, ne'er could spy
> That sterling worth could bloom beneath a western sky.

The poem was printed in the *Weekly Entertainer* in 1795.[145]

At least occasionally there was bad feeling between Johnny and his stepmother. It would have been natural for her to have resented him. She was only ten years older than her stepson and Stedman noted arguments. For example, on Stedman's 42nd birthday, when his wife was 21 and Johnny 11, he noted:

'This evening some words happened between Mama and Johnny about his learning, he being today one year at Tiverton School. She said *'well, what have you learnt in that time?'* which he being affronted at, answered, *'so much in one year as you'd have done in two'*, when she struck him a black eye which made high words between she and I, and she was exceedingly ill all night. April 5. Johnny now begged her pardon to no purpose and he went crying to school. She and I again fell out about this and neither of us took any dinner till in the evening the boy came home and all was reconciled.'[146]

Stedman's name did live on amongst his slaves. Included among them was a young boy named Quaco whom he took from Surinam to Holland where he was given to the Countess of Rosendaal. Quaco was baptised and given a new name, Stedman. Years later, in 1792, Stedman recorded in his journal 'poor Quaco turned adrift by Rosendaal whom I upbraid for cruelty by a letter'.[147]

Captain Stedman died at the age of 52 in March 1797, a year after his book was published. He was, according to the town clerk, 'a brave, vigorous, extraordinary man, a little whimsical, who had he lived might have been further useful to society. Before his death tis said he desired to be buried in Bickleigh Churchyard near the famous Bampfylde Moore Carew, the old King of the Beggars. He was buried there on 6 March at midnight.'[148] It was pointed out by subsequent writers that this did not happen.[149] Stedman's obituary in the *Gentleman's Magazine* noted his 'attachment' with a beautiful Negro girl of 15' but it made no mention of his Dutch wife other than noting he had a widow.[150] Years before it had noted the death of Johnny: in 1793 Francis Gloyns, Johnny's teacher in Tiverton, wrote to the periodical about the youth's death and enclosed the following letter[151] Stedman had written to his son in 1787. The letter was intended to be given to Johnny upon his father's death. The advice on how to treat all men and the reference to Johnny's mother are particularly noteworthy.

My Dear John,

As the last good I can do for you in this world I join to the little trifles I have left you, the few lines which I beg of you often to read, for my sake, who always loved you so tenderly. Above all things, fear God as the Supreme Author of all good. Love

Him in your heart and be religious, but detest every tincture of hypocrisy. Regard your neighbours, that is all mankind, whatever nation, profession or faith, while they are honest, and be every so, yourself, it is the best policy in the end, depend upon it. Guard yourself against idleness, it is the root of every evil to which bad company gives the finishing stroke. Love economy without avarice, and be ever thyself thy best friend. Fly from the excesses of debauchery which will rot thy body, while they are a cancer to thy mind. To keep both sound, follow my words. Be never behind-hand

    With thy correspondence
    With thy lawful creditor
    With thy daily occupation
    Or with thy conscience
  And thy soul shall enjoy peace.

With air, exercise, diet and proper recreation, thy body shall possess health and vigour.

Dear John, should fortune frown, which depend upon it, sometimes it will do, look around on thousands more wretched than thyself, who perhaps less deserve to be so, and be content. Contentment is better than gold. Wish not for death, it is a sin, but scorn to fear it, and be prepared to meet it every hour since come it must, while the good mind smiles at its sting and defies its point. Beware of passion or cruelty, but rejoice in being good-natured, not only to Man, but to the whole creation without exception. Scorn to hurt them but for they food, and thy defence. To be cruel is the portion of a coward, while to be brave, and humane, goes hand in hand, and pleases God.

Obey with pleasure those set over thee, since without knowing how to be obedient no one ever knew how to command.

Now, my dear boy, love Mrs Stedman, and her little children, from your heart if you ever had a love for your dead father who requested it. She has most tenderly proved a help to thy infant state, while thou art a brother to her helpless little ones. Prove also a parent and a guardian by your kind conduct. Let your good sense keep peace and harmony in my dear family, then shall the blessings of Almighty God overspread you, and them, and we, together with your dear mother, my beloved Joanna, have a chance once more to meet wherein the presence of our

'Europe supported by Africa & America' (John Gabriel Stedman, *Narrative of a five years' expedition against the revolted Negroes of Surinam, in Guiana, on the Wild Coast of South America, from the year 1772 to 1777*, II).

> Heavenly Benefactor, our joy and happiness shall be eternal & complete, which is the ardent wish, the sincere prayer, and the only hope of your once loving father, who, my dear child, when you read this, shall be no more, and rests with a heartfelt affection to eternity. Yours ... John G. Stedman, Hensley House, in the county of Devon, January 14th 1787

Stedman had also included in the packet Johnny's freedom papers as well as other official Surinam documents and letters from naval captains regarding Johnny's service record.[152] While it is difficult to understand his feelings and actions regarding slavery in Surinam, Stedman gave every appearance of a deep, sincere and enduring love for his son Johnny. His work as a soldier suppressing the Surinam revolt helped continued the institution of slavery, as did his personal participation in the trade through the purchase and ownership of slaves for his own plantation. His ambivalence on the abolition of slavery coincided with his apparent deep love for a woman born into slavery and his own fathering of a son likewise born a slave. Nevertheless, when he retired to Devon Stedman brought with him a son to whom he appeared to be devoted.

# 6

# Slaves on a Nevis Island plantation belonging to Mary Scarborough of Colyton, 1821

Another slave account[153] survives for the island of St Nevis which was praised for its beauty by Henry Nelson Coleridge of Ottery St Mary but he criticised the inhabitants for their burial practices. He wrote 'when a white man and a black man are both stone dead I doubt if one be much better than the other, but grant that the white carcass is worth the most. Lord bless you, my white friends, you need not be so much afraid of lying side by side with the blackest slave you have! A time will come when one angel or another will pick you up as clean as ever you lay down, and separate you from Quaco as far as you shall wish!'[154] The name Quaco as a slave appears in several places in following documents but not in this particular plantation account. The document lists a considerable number of slaves and illustrates a connection between Devon and one of the main slaving centres in the country, Bristol. The account concerns the property of Mary Scarborough of Colyton, the widow of William Scarborough, a merchant who had dwelled in Nevis. He later moved to Bristol and subsequently died at Lyme Regis in 1809. His widow Mary inherited a share in a plantation in the parish of St Thomas on Nevis Island, which in 1823 she signed over to her father William Shepherd of Seaton and her brother John.

The Scarborough family had plantation interests in the island since at least 1779. This included the 74 slaves who are listed below. As with Captain Stedman's writings, the following document noted the colour of the slaves including Black, Sambo and Mulatto as well as 'Muslee' for two young female children. It also recorded their names, place of origin and age.

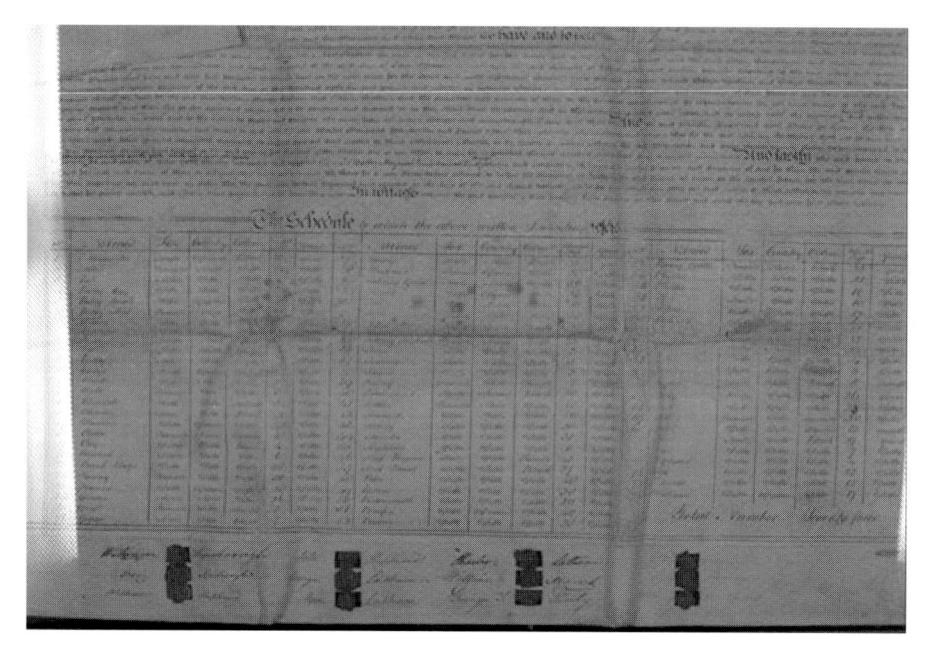

Slaves at St Nevis, 1821 (Devon Record Office, 337badd3/1/8/2)

**Schedule of slaves**

| No. | Names | Sex | Country | Colour | Reputed age | Years |
|---|---|---|---|---|---|---|
| 1. | Alexander | Male | African | Black | 30 | years |
| 2. | Abba | Female | Nevis | ditto | 14 | ditto |
| 3. | Bob | Male | ditto | ditto | 46 | ditto |
| 4. | Billy boy | ditto | ditto | ditto | 30 | ditto |
| 5. | Billy bush | ditto | African | ditto | 26 | ditto |
| 6. | Betsy Lees | Female | Nevis | ditto | 30 | ditto |
| 7. | Bessey | ditto | ditto | ditto | 32 | ditto |
| 8. | Bridget | ditto | African | ditto | 3 | ditto |
| 9. | Bess | ditto | Nevis | ditto | 32 | ditto |
| 10. | Bell | ditto | ditto | ditto | 7 | ditto |
| 11. | Billy | Male | ditto | ditto | 6 | ditto |
| 12. | Cudgo | ditto | African | ditto | 48 | ditto |
| 13. | Clarke | ditto | Nevis | ditto | 25 | ditto |
| 14. | Catto | Female | ditto | ditto | 50 | ditto |
| 15. | Charlotte | ditto | ditto | Mulatto | 34 | ditto |

*Investment: Plantations and Trade*

| | | | | | | |
|---|---|---|---|---|---|---|
| 16. | Charles | Male | ditto | Black | 4 | ditto |
| 17. | Daniell | ditto | African | ditto | 43 | ditto |
| 18. | Eletia | Female | Nevis | Sambo | 18 | ditto |
| 19. | Eley | ditto | ditto | Black | 4 | ditto |
| 20. | Edward | Male | ditto | ditto | 6 | ditto |
| 21. | Frank Bags | ditto | ditto | ditto | 38 | ditto |
| 22. | Fanny | Female | ditto | ditto | 50 | ditto |
| 23. | Frances | ditto | African | ditto | 28 | ditto |
| 24. | Glasgo | Male | Nevis | ditto | 26 | ditto |
| 25. | Grace | Female | ditto | Muslee | 3 | ditto |
| 26. | George | Male | ditto | Black | 7 | ditto |
| 27. | George | Male | Nevis | Black | 3 | ditto |
| 28. | Hannah | Female | African | ditto | 28 | ditto |
| 29. | Johney Gold | Male | Nevis | ditto | 36 | ditto |
| 30. | Jacob | ditto | African | ditto | 38 | ditto |
| 31. | Joe | ditto | Nevis | ditto | 18 | ditto |
| 32. | Job | ditto | ditto | ditto | 20 | ditto |
| 33. | John Pere | ditto | ditto | Sambo | 2 | ditto |
| 34. | James | ditto | African | Black | 30 | ditto |
| 35. | Jenney Mitchield | Female | Nevis | ditto | 32 | ditto |
| 36. | Jane | ditto | ditto | ditto | 3 | ditto |
| 37. | Jimmy | Male | ditto | ditto | 5 | ditto |
| 38. | James | Ditto | ditto | ditto | 2 | ditto |
| 39. | Kilsey | Female | ditto | Sambo | 5 | ditto |
| 40. | Lieutenant | Male | African | Black | 28 | ditto |
| 41. | Lettice | Female | Nevis | ditto | 50 | ditto |
| 42. | Mariah | ditto | ditto | ditto | 50 | ditto |
| 43. | Molly | ditto | ditto | ditto | 20 | ditto |
| 44. | Mimba | ditto | ditto | ditto | 31 | ditto |
| 45. | Matilda | ditto | ditto | ditto | 6 | ditto |
| 46. | Ned Byam | Male | ditto | Sambo | 43 | ditto |
| 47. | Ned Priest | ditto | ditto | Black | 27 | ditto |
| 48. | Peter | ditto | ditto | ditto | 48 | ditto |
| 49. | Pallas | ditto | ditto | ditto | 38 | ditto |
| 50. | Portsmouth | ditto | ditto | ditto | 20 | ditto |
| 51. | Pompy | ditto | African | ditto | 40 | ditto |
| 52. | Priam | ditto | ditto | ditto | 28 | ditto |
| 53. | Penny Cottle | Female | Nevis | ditto | 23 | ditto |
| 54. | Phillis | ditto | ditto | ditto | 21 | ditto |
| 55. | Phillis | ditto | ditto | ditto | 10 | ditto |
| 56. | Peter | Male | ditto | ditto | 10 | ditto |
| 57. | Robert | ditto | ditto | ditto | 17 | ditto |
| 58. | Richard | ditto | ditto | ditto | 20 | ditto |
| 59. | Rodney | ditto | ditto | ditto | 32 | ditto |

| | | | | | | |
|---|---|---|---|---|---|---|
| 60. | Richard | Female | African | ditto | 32 | ditto |
| 61. | R[damaged] | ditto | Nevis | ditto | 34 | ditto |
| 62. | Ruth | ditto | ditto | ditto | 4 | ditto |
| 63. | R[damaged] | ditto | ditto | Sambo | 3 | ditto |
| 64. | Rogers | Male | ditto | Black | 5 | months |
| 65. | Sentry | ditto | ditto | ditto | 26 | years |
| 66. | Seah | ditto | ditto | ditto | 28 | ditto |
| 67. | Suckey | Female | ditto | Mulatto | 30 | ditto |
| 68. | Sally | ditto | ditto | Muslee | 10 | months |
| 69. | Setris | Male | ditto | Black | 9 | years |
| 70. | Sam | ditto | ditto | ditto | 7 | ditto |
| 71. | Sheppard | ditto | ditto | ditto | 4 | ditto |
| 72. | Titus | ditto | ditto | ditto | 23 | ditto |
| 73. | Thomas | ditto | ditto | ditto | 10 | ditto |
| 74. | William | ditto | African | ditto | 17 | ditto |

Total Number     Seventy Four

# 7

# The account book of John Harrison, agent and attorney of Oldbury Plantation, Jamaica, 1831

A very detailed account[155] survives for a Jamaican plantation owned by Robert and James Sutton, John James Ronaldson, London merchants, and James Swaby, Esquire. The book has been dismembered and appears to have been kept by John Harrison in his capacity of manager. There are also sheets concerned with the Manchester Parish Workhouse in Jamaica for the 1830s along with school accounts kept by E. Harrison, almost certainly a relation of John Harrison, for the mid 1840s to the early 1850s. There are botanical specimens included in the volume. These appear to be English. The Devon connection of the document has not been ascertained. It may have been that James Swaby or John Harrison were Devonians. The volume itself came to the record office from a waste paper dealer in Exeter in 1949 and had presumably been discarded by its previous owner.[156]

The following is taken from a short run of lists of the slaves who were at the plantation. It noted them by their 'old' name and the new names which they had taken. Their colour differences were not recorded but such personal details as their fitness, occupation and age. One of the reasons for the list was the noting of an allocation of osnaburgs (a kind of coarse linen), penistones (a coarse woollen cloth), scissors, hats, knives, handkerchiefs, thimbles, thread and needles.

Slaves at Oldbury, Jamaica (Devon Record Office, 49/14)

*Investment: Plantations and Trade*

List of slaves on Old Bury Plantation served with clothing this 21st May 1831.

| Old names | new names | age | occupation | condition | |
|---|---|---|---|---|---|
| | | | Osnaburgs penistone hat knives handkerchiefs | | |
| Anthony | James Miller | 41 | Head driver | able | 12 7 1 1 1 |
| Blagrove | Blagrove McNally | 34 | former driver | able | 10 6 1 1 1 |
| Harry | James Green | 46 | Barber | able | 10 6 1 1 1 |
| Vernon | Henry McNally | 46 | carpenter | able | 10 6 1 1 1 |
| James | James Walker | 61 | house cook | weakly | 10 6 1 1 1 |
| Patrick | Thomas Heath | 41 | cooper | able | 10 6 1 1 1 |
| Oxford | George Green | 41 | pen keeper | able | 10 6 1 1 1 |
| Billy | William Smith | 61 | watchman | healthy | 8 4 1 1 1 |
| Charles | Mo Griffith | 66 | field & sawyer | healthy | 8 4 1 1 1 |
| Isaac | Thomas Pitter | 46 | ditto & ditto | able | 8 4 1 1 1 |
| Duckworth | Thomas Bridges | 41 | ditto & cooper | able | 8 4 1 1 1 |
| Quasky | Henry Robertson | 56 | ditto | weakly | 8 4 1 1 1 |
| Green Week | George Walker | 41 | ditto & carpenter | able | 8 4 1 1 1 |
| Nugent | Henry Dickson | 41 | ditto & carpenter | able | 8 4 1 1 1 |
| John | Richard McNally | 41 | field | able | 8 4 1 1 1 |
| Nottingham | Richard Powell | 36 | ditto & sawyer | able | 8 4 1 1 1 |
| Harry | Henry Green | 46 | ditto & ditto | able | 8 4 1 1 1 |
| Dick | Robert McNally | 61 | ditto | weakly | 8 4 1 1 1 |
| Cuffee | Mo. McKanzie | 46 | ditto | weakly | 8 4 1 1 1 |
| Sidney | George Graham | 41 | ditto | able | 8 4 1 1 1 |
| Smith | Robert Smith | 45 | ditto | able | 8 4 1 1 1 |
| Aberdeen | Wilken Harvey | 33 | ditto | able | 8 4 1 1 1 |
| July | James Griffith | 36 | ditto | able | 8 4 1 1 1 |
| Davy | Edward Richards | 30 | ditto | able | 8 4 1 1 1 |
| Sam | William Pearl | 31 | ditto | weakly | 8 4 1 1 1 |
| Bagond | James Griffith | 29 | ditto | able | 8 4 1 1 1 |
| Louis | Louis Vasall | 25 | ditto | able | 8 4 1 1 1 |
| Archy | Donald McLean | 49 | ditto | able | 8 4 1 1 1 |
| Sancho | Mo Ricketts | 25 | ditto | able | 8 4 1 1 1 |
| George | George Morgan | 22 | ditto | weakly | 8 4 1 1 1 |
| Hazard | McKenzie Green | 20 | ditto | able | 8 4 1 1 1 |
| James | James Greig | 29 | ditto | able | 8 4 1 1 1 |
| Will | Charles Philpotts | 23 | domestic | able | 8 4 1 1 1 |
| Johnny | Johnny Rochester | 23 | field | able | 8 4 1 1 1 |
| Cesar | Bob Roberts | 21 | ditto | able | 8 4 1 1 1 |
| Adam | James Rodin | 23 | ditto | able | 8 4 1 1 1 |
| Kent | Alexander Walker | 61 | watchman | weakly | 7 3½ 1 1 1 |

| | | | | | |
|---|---|---|---|---|---|
| Frank | Frank Francis | 61 | ditto | weakly | 7 3½ 1 1 1 |
| Cupid | Cupid | 61 | absconded | weakly | 7 3½ 1 1 1 |

**Children - males**

| | | | | | |
|---|---|---|---|---|---|
| Forester | James Forester | 61 | watchman | weakly | 10 7 3½ 1 1 1 6 |
| Maestro | Timothy Greens | 66 | ditto | ditto | 8 7 ditto |
| Joe | Joe Rochester | 15 | domestic | healthy | ditto |
| Linn | Linn Hawthorn | 15 | field | ditto | ditto |
| Stephen | Thomas Hall | 15 | domestic | ditto | 8 8 4 1 1 1 6 |
| Henry | Henry Poucee | 14 | field | ditto | 8 7 3½ 1 1 1 6 |
| Edward | Edward Wright | 14 | ditto | ditto | ditto |
| Charles | Charles Branch | 14 | ditto | sickly | ditto |
| Jimmy | Jimmy Rochester | 14 | ditto | ditto | ditto |
| Yarmouth | Richard Green | 13 | ditto | healthy | ditto |
| Pophams | Home Pophams | 12 | ditto | ditto | ditto |
| Nicholas | Nicholas Wright | 12 | ditto | ditto | ditto |
| Arthur | Arthur Heath | 11 | ditto | ditto | ditto |
| Frederick | Frederick Blagrove | 9 | ditto | ditto | ditto |
| Rodney | Rodney Heath | 9 | ditto | ditto | ditto |
| Michael | Michael Walker | 8 | ditto | sickly | ditto |
| Duncan | Duncan | 7 | ditto | healthy | ditto |
| Pompey | Mo Macilland | 5 | ditto | ditto | ditto |
| Edward | Joseph Blagrove | 5 | ditto | ditto | ditto |
| Francis | Francis Roche | 5 | ditto | ditto | ditto |
| Washington | Robert Daly | 4 | child | ditto | 6 5 2½ 1 0 1 4 |
| Alexander | Alexander Walker | 4 | ditto | ditto | ditto |
| Richard | Richard Dickson | 3 | ditto | ditto | ditto |
| Thomas | Bridges | 3 | ditto | ditto | ditto |
| Dover | George Brooks | 3 | ditto | ditto | ditto |
| Colin | Colin Griffiths | 3 | ditto | ditto | ditto |
| Robert | Robert Wright | 2 | ditto | ditto | ditto |
| Jonas | Thomas Jones | 2 | ditto | ditto | ditto |
| William | William Blagrove | 1 | ditto | ditto | ditto |

**Females**
Scissors osnaburgs penistone hat handkerchiefs knives thimbles thread needles

| | | | | | |
|---|---|---|---|---|---|
| Sarah or Grace | Sarah Walker | 46 | Doctress | able | 1 10 6 1 1 1 1 10 6 |
| Margaret | Margaret White | 57 | driveress | weakly | ditto |
| Jubba | Bessy Walker | 71 | midwife | weakly | ditto |
| Ellin | Elenor Francis | 31 | domestic | weakly | ditto |
| Queen | Queen Anne | 46 | washerwoman | able | ditto |

*Investment: Plantations and Trade*

| | | | | | |
|---|---|---|---|---|---|
| Sylvia | Sylvia Foster | 63 | field | weakly | 1 8 4 1 1 1 1 8 6 |
| Queen | [Ari]anna Griffith | 51 | ditto | ditto | ditto |
| Empress | Kath Wright | 51 | ditto | ditto | ditto |
| Delia | Nichola Wright | 51 | ditto | healthy | ditto |
| Beatrice | Bessy Miller | 46 | ditto | able | ditto |
| Jula | Bessy Rowe | 41 | domestic | able | ditto |
| Rachel | Isabella Brooks | 58 | field | weakly | ditto |
| Tamar | Elizabeth Green | 41 | ditto | able | ditto |
| Molly | Francis Walker | 36 | ditto | ditto | ditto |
| Sarah | Rebecca Heath | 33 | ditto | ditto | ditto |
| Lady | Maria Green | 39 | ditto | ditto | ditto |
| Nancy | Louisa Green | 31 | ditto | weakly | ditto |
| Sally | Sally Rochester | 29 | ditto | able | ditto |
| Sally | Camilla Green | 29 | ditto | weakly | ditto |
| Leah | Marian Cohen | 26 | ditto | able | ditto |
| Caroline | Marian Sinclair | 26 | ditto | weakly | ditto |
| Anne | Anne Smith | 28 | ditto | able | ditto |
| Lucky | Lucky Rowe | 31 | ditto | ditto | ditto |
| Ceuba | Rose Walker | 31 | ditto | ditto | ditto |
| Quashiba | Mary Walker | 25 | domestic | ditto | ditto |
| Worry | Molly Richards | 28 | field | ditto | ditto |
| Ruthy | Cath Daly | 28 | field | ditto | ditto |
| Hagard | Bill Richards | 26 | ditto | ditto | ditto |
| Sappy | Mary Ruddock | 28 | ditto | ditto | ditto |
| Jenny | Jane Palmer | 26 | ditto | ditto | ditto |
| Owana | Susan Richards | 23 | ditto | ditto | |
| Nanny | Nanny | 23 | ditto | ditto | ditto |
| Harriet | Harriet Powell | 19 | ditto | ditto | ditto |
| Fanny | Fran Rochester | 21 | ditto | ditto | ditto |
| Prue | Bessy Richards | 61 | ditto | weakly | ditto |

**FEMALES**

| | | | | | |
|---|---|---|---|---|---|
| Holly | Mary Brown | 57 | field | weakly | 8 4 8 1 1 1 1 1 6 |
| Patience | Felicia Green | 66 | field | weakly | ditto |
| Patricia | Susan Green | 56 | field | weakly | ditto |
| Countess | Maria Griffith | 56 | nurse | weakly | ditto |
| Sappho | Lavenia Walker | 71 | field | weakly | ditto |
| Daphne | Henrietta Green | 61 | ditto | ditto | ditto |
| Peggy | Ancilla Green | 68 | ditto | ditto | ditto |
| Lettuce | Clarissa Green | 23 | ditto | ditto | ditto |
| Patty | Sophia Sinclair | 21 | ditto | ditto | ditto |
| Dido | Dido James | 22 | ditto | ditto | ditto |
| Emma | Emma Powell | 16 | ditto | ditto | ditto |
| Milly | Marian Walker | 14 | ditto | ditto | ditto |

| | | | | | |
|---|---|---|---|---|---|
| Charity | Judith Green | 18 | ditto | ditto | ditto |
| Diana | Judith Walker | 76 | invalid | weakly | 73½6011106 |
| Kitty | Kitty Walker | 56 | ditto | ditto | ditto |
| Billa | Amelia Walker | 76 | ditto | ditto | ditto |
| Susan | Susan Wallis | 13 | field | healthy | 6 ditto |
| Chloe | Chloe Griffith | 13 | ditto | ditto | ditto |
| Rosanna | Rosanna Eaton | 12 | domestic | ditto | ditto |
| Nancia | Charlotte Wright | 10 | field | ditto | ditto |
| Olive | Olive Green | 9 | ditto | ditto | ditto |
| Janette | Janette Bridges | 9 | ditto | ditto | ditto |
| Johanna | Johanna Griffith | 9 | ditto | ditto | ditto |
| Bully | Bully Wright | 9 | ditto | ditto | ditto |
| Amelia | Amelia Bridges | 5 | ditto | ditto | ditto |
| Ceclia | Cecilia Griffith | 5 | ditto | ditto | ditto |
| Christiana | Christiana | 5 | ditto | ditto | ditto |
| Eve | Eve Roberts | 5 | ditto | ditto | ditto |
| Alicia | Alicia Green | 4 | ditto | ditto | 5 2½ ditto |
| Rosan | Rosan Jones | 4 | ditto | ditto | 6 3½ ditto |
| Angelina | Blagrove | 3 | ditto | ditto | 5 2½ 4 ditto |
| Dorothy | Green | 2 | child | ditto | ditto |
| Johanna | Johanna | 2 | child | ditto | ditto |
| Maggy | Charlotte Robertson | 2 | child | ditto | ditto |
| Margery | Margery | 1 | ditto | ditto | ditto |
| Felicia | Felicia | 1 | ditto | ditto | ditto |
| Nelly | Nelly | 1 | ditto | ditto | 5 – 4 - - - 1 – 6 |
| Belinda | Belinda | 1 | ditto | ditto | ditto |
| Grace | Grace | 1 | ditto | ditto | ditto |

# 8

# The Topsham sugar factory and Samuel Buttell of Plymouth, 1684 to 1742

For a short while, sometime after 1684 to not later than 1742, a sugar factory was run outside Exeter, on the east bank of the river Exe near the port of Topsham. The main building still stands and is now known as the Retreat. In about 1833 Nicholas Brand, a local man then about 80 years old, recalled the business from his boyhood. Robert Orme of nearby Clyst St George had converted the complex into a residence but could not afford it and sold the building to Sir Alexander Hamilton. Brand further wrote:

> 'This sugar house was built by Hodges and Buttell, the ancestor of the present Buttell. Hodges supplied the funds, Buttell the working partner. Hodges died and ended the concern. In the war ending in 1762 2,000 French prisoners were kept there. When very young I went into it and saw thousands of old sugar pots and at the edge of the rock saw the skeleton of the Crane House by which the hogsheads were hoisted out of the lighters.'

Another of his writings has further details.

> 'Sir Alexander added another storey and as it is now. The building was a Sugar House, built and carried on with success by Buthill [sic] and Hodges until one of the partners died. When

I knew it, it was a huge square building, unoccupied and out of repair. On going into the under floor I saw thousands of broken sugar pots. The rock had been dug down to an area and close to the river a skeleton of a crane house remained by which the sugar hogsheads were hoisted from the lighters and rolled into the sugar house.'[157]

Samuel Buttell purchased the site in 1684 and by 1707 had built 'a convenient house with the necessary utensils for the refining of sugar'. The sugar would be refined at the sugar house from the thicker brown sugar. Buttell was a Plymouth 'sugar baker' and had an estate in North or South Carolina. He appears to have been a Quaker by 1687: in April that year he was brought before the mayor of Plymouth for refusing to remove his hat during prayers at an Anglican funeral service. Buttell was described as a sugar baker. He appears to have continued to live in Plymouth into the early eighteenth century and died in around 1718. The factory then passed to his two sons, Benjamin and John, and in 1725 they sold a half share to Nathaniel Hodges and his son George. Seventeen years later, in 1743, the building was described as 'for several years void for want of a tenant'.[158] Another local man described the Retreat a generation before Nicholas Brand had recalled his boyhood memories in about 1833. In 1794 the Reverend John Swete, who lived across the river Exe, wrote that it:

'Appeared to great advantage a very short distance beyond the northern extremity of the town situated on the very of the river. Having landed, I rode to the Retreat where I breakfasted. This, now a most excellent house, was about thirty years ago a Sugar House – with the materials Mr Orme erected for himself a mansion, which by the addition of an attic storey has received vast improvements from the hands of the present possessor. The gardens, offices, greenhouse and greater part of the beautiful shrubberies have been raised by him and there are few more elegant and comfortable seats in the county.'[159]

Swete's lack of curiosity in the factory was partly due to his main concern being describing the Picturesque in Devon but he was well placed to provide informed comment on the factory given he himself

*Investment: Plantations and Trade*

was an owner of sugar plantations in the West Indies (see above, pages 95 to 105).

Sugar imports appear regularly in the county's port books with some molasses coming via Newfoundland ships in the autumn months as well as directly from the West Indies. In 1688 for instance, the *Susan and Abigail* brought molasses and muscovado sugar from St Christopher's as did the *New York* and the *Regard* from Barbados and St Christopher's.[160] At the time Exeter's sugar factory was lying derelict a new one was in operation in Plymouth: in about 1750 a new enterprise was underway near Sutton Pool on Exeter Road. It was replaced by a Victorian sugar factory that continued through the nineteenth century.[161]

# PART THREE

# ABOLITION AND EMANCIPATION

Throughout Devon there were a great number of men and women who campaigned for the end of slavery through agitation to influence events in Parliament: the two Devon committees of abolitionists, organised at Exeter and Plymouth, were among the most active in the country. Abolition meetings are known to have been held in such places as Ashburton, Chagford, Crediton, Exeter, Honiton, Ilfracombe, Moretonhampstead, Plymouth, Stonehouse, Tavistock, Tiverton and Topsham. There were others as well: petitions were sent from places where no record of meetings has yet been found. Even so, two Devonians supported slavery in Parliament. William Devyanes, M.P. for Barnstaple and formerly a chairman of the East India Company, and who had lived in Africa for some time, said Africans would kill their prisoners if the Europeans did not buy them for slaves. His point was they were better in slavery than dead. Possibly the apparent lack of abolition agitation in Barnstaple was connected to his influence. Sir Charles Pole, Member for Plymouth, claimed the 'immediate abolition of the slave trade would be the most barbarous proceeding even to the Negro himself'.[162]

No other opposition to abolition has been found in the records and it might be that local support for abolition arose from lesser commercial interests than in the prime slaving ports of London, Bristol and Liverpool. The Nonconformists, particularly the Quakers and the Unitarians, appear to have taken the lead in abolition and after a few years the Anglicans joined them.

The national process to end slavery was incremental and lengthy. Abolition was first formally proposed in 1788 but it took until 1807, 19 years later, for Parliament to enact legislation. Even so, this was a first step: abolition was not the end of slavery but only of the transportation of slaves from Africa. Full emancipation did not take place until 1838 and even then there was a transitional period whereby slaves were legally required to continue working for their owners for several years.

The fifty years of campaigning for abolition and emancipation had four periods of heightened activity. These were from 1787 to 1792, 1804 to 1807, in 1814 and from 1822 to 1834. This took the form of public meetings to rally public opinion, the setting up of petitions to national government and the lobbying of political figures. It has been argued that abolitionists used petitioning more effectively than other political movements. The method in attracting signatures was straightforward: after the wording was agreed blank sheets were distributed in public places and advertised in local newspapers and billposters. Abolition became highly respectable and across the country public venues were put at abolitionists' disposal through the support of the churches and local government. Petitioning could be highly efficient: as will be seen in the following pages, one such Devon abolition petition attracted some 10,000 signatures in only a few days. The petition papers were subsequently collected and presented by a sympathetic M. P. to the House of Commons or to the House of Lords by a Peer.[163]

A range of documents and several newspaper reports are used in the following pages to illustrate the stages of development in gaining universal freedom for the slaves. These cover more than a century.

# 1

# The petition of William Castillo, formerly of Plymouth, 1758

The legal status of Africans in England was investigated by the Admiralty Board in 1758 in a case concerning William Castillo, a man who had been baptised in Plymouth six years earlier and who claimed his freedom. In December 1758 Castillo petitioned William Pitt and the Prime Minister sent the petition to the Admiralty Board which then instructed Portsmouth's harbourmaster to investigate.[164] The petition[165] laid out Castillo's dilemma:

> 'May it please your honour,
> The most humbly petition of William Castillo, that your honours' petitioner was born in the island of Barbados and brought over to England by James Jones, master of His Majesty's Ship the *Northumberland* in the year 1752 and was christened in the parish church of St Andrews, Plymouth by the Reverend Mr Mudge which I most humbly conceive entitles me to the privilege of a free subject instead of which I was pressed by the order of the said Jones, and put onboard the *Hunter* tender at the Tower and sent from thence in a post chaise in irons to Portsmouth. And am now onboard his Majesty's ship the *Neptune* at Spithead, with a collar on my neck on day and in irons at night in order to be sent onboard the first ship bound to Barbados to be sold. Most humbly beg that your honours would be so good

William Castillo's petition, 1758 (National Archives, ADM1/927)

of your great goodness to assist me to claim the privilege of a free subject which I most humbly conceive I am entitled to by the laws of this land being very willing to serve onboard his Majesty's ship which I am aboard, of [obscured] if your honours would take my case under our honours' consideration and let me claim your honours' protection from being sent onboard to be sold as a slave having a wife and two children in London and your honours' most humbly petitioner as in duty bound shall ever pray.'

Plymouth in 1733 (Westcountry Studies Library, SC1982)

Castillo was baptised under the name 'William Castalio' on 31 December 1755 in St Andrews' Church in Plymouth. He was noted as being 'a Negro about 22 years old'.[166] According to his owner, James Jones, the later changing of his name was an act of independence or defiance. The previous year, 1751, the two men had met in Boston in New England. Jones testified that he had bought Castillo at his own request and they agreed Castillo would repay the costs through seven years of service. Jones also stated that he had spent a further ten to twelve pounds in paying for violin lessons in London. Five years into their agreement Castillo left Jones and it was another two years later that Jones caught up with his slave. On Christmas Day 1758 the Admiralty Board made its decision that 'the laws of this country admit of no badges of slavery' and asked for information on how Castillo was recorded on the navy's labour books. It subsequently transpired that Castillo was listed as an able seaman and therefore, because he was paid for his labour and not acknowledged as a slave, then he was considered a free man.[167] There were a number of other black men baptised in Plymouth in the eighteenth century.[168]

## 2

# William 'Bull' Davy of Exeter and the trial of James Somerset, 1772

One of the great legal cases to question the legality of slavery in England involved William Day, a former Exeter man. His nickname, 'Bull Davy', is said to have been taken from his manners. Davy's fame as an advocate and quick wit in court contributed to a considerable number of anecdotes being attributed to him. This was partly due to his rising to being a Serjeant-in-law, the position awarded to certain barristers practicing in the Common Law courts which gave them precedence over other barristers.

His origins have also become the stuff of legend. Many writers have suggested he came from Exeter and one wrote he lived in a house along the top of South Street in what was formerly known as Bell Hill. Various writers have suggested he, or sometimes his father William, was a druggist, grocer and chemist. The turning point in his life appears to have been Davy's failure in business: his subsequent insolvency was the reason for his turning to a career in law. One historian alluded to this in 1852:

> Being once on the Western Circuit he cross-examined an old country-woman very rigorously respecting a circumstance that had happened within her observation some years before. 'And pray, good woman', said the Serjeant, 'How is it that you should be so particular as to remember that this affair happened

on a market day?' 'Why, sir', replied the woman, 'by a very remarkable token, that all the cry of the city went that Mr Davy, the druggist, had that morning shut up shop and run away.' 'I think, brother', said the Judge, 'that you want no further proof of the witness' memory'.[169]

Harry Hems, the well-known Victorian sculptor of Exeter, wrote that Davy acquired his 'taste' for the law after being served with a process from the Court of Common Pleas. A jest with the sheriff's officer that parchment was as edible as mutton supposedly resulted in the Court imprisoning him in Fleet Prison for contempt. After a period of quiet contemplation Davy began to study law.[170] Another Victorian writer suggested it was Exeter's Member of Parliament who urged Davy upon his release from gaol to 'devote his acute and comprehensive mind to the study of law. By indefatigable industry and zeal he made rapid progress in his new profession and soon acquired a fame & practice.'[171]

It was this curious individual who played a key role in the long process of emancipation for Britain's slaves. The slavery case took place from December 1771 to June 1772 in London. Davy argued for the freedom of James Somerset who was confined in irons on the *Ann & Mary* in the Thames. Somerset had been brought to England in 1769 by his owner Charles Stewart, then discarded because of his ill health and subsequently retaken upon becoming fit. He was being transported by his master to Jamaica when the court intervened on the instigation of several third parties. Somerset subsequently won his case with the decision that slavery could not be maintained under English law: the laws of Jamaica could not apply to England and James Somerset could not be sent to the West Indies against his will. This was due in part to Davy's work[172] who argued during the trial 'no man can be a slave, being once in England, the very air he breathed made him a free man, that he has a right to be governed by the laws of the land'.[173] His choice of wording in the trial distinguished his argument. He also said:

'I hope, my lord, the air does not blow worse since. Now what of it, if slavery may be acknowledged in lands unluckier than England? What, indeed, if slavery was legitimate under the laws of Barbados or the colonies of America where a new species of tyranny had been created entirely by Colony government? Why should such laws, made by bodies other than Parliament, have any more influence, power or authority in this country than the laws of Japan?'[174]

Part of his argument during the trial on May 14th 1772 was that:[175]

'To punish not even a criminal for offences against the laws of another country; to set free a galley-slave, who is a slave by his crime; and make a slave of a Negro, who is one, by his complexion; is a cruelty and absurdity that I trust will never take place here: such as if promulgated, would make England a disgrace to all nations under earth: for the reducing a man, guiltless of any offence against the laws, to the condition of slavery, the worst and most abject state, Mr Dunning has mentioned, what he is pleased to term philosophical and moral grounds, I think, or something to that effect, of slavery: and would not by any means have us think disrespectfully of those nations, whom we mistakenly call barbarians, merely for carrying on that trade: for my part, we may be warranted, I believe, in affirming the morality or propriety of the practice does not enter their heads; they make slaves of whom they think fit. For the air of England; I think, however, it has been gradually purifying ever since the reign of Elizabeth. Mr Dunning seems to have discovered so much, as he finds it changes a slave into a servant; tho' unhappily, he does not think it efficacy enough to prevent that pestilent disease reviving, the instant the poor man is obliged to quit (voluntarily quits, and legally, it seems we ought to say) this happy country. However, it has been asserted, and is now repeated by me, this air is too pure for a slave to breathe in. I trust I shall not quit this court without certain convictions of the truth of that assertion.'

Davy died in 1780. Part of his legacy is having uttered one of the most stirring phrases in the history of British abolition.

# 3

# An American Black Loyalist at Marystow, 1786

Several thousand black loyalists fled the North American Colonies after the American Revolution and came to Britain. One of them was James York who, upon his arrival in Cornwall, became masterless when his owner died. York moved around the country and for a while was employed at Sydenham in the West Devon parish of Marystow. While in London he was baptised, possibly to reinforce his state of freedom, but was still forced to beg as he was often unemployed. As a vagrant York was questioned by a magistrate and the following document reveals his experiences in England after his arrival.[176]

> 'The Examination of a Black who appears by a Certificate to be of the name of James York taken on oath before me John Prideaux Esquire, one of his Majesty's Justices of the Peace in & for the said County the first Day of May in the Twenty Sixth year of the reign of our Sovereign Lord George the Third, who on his oath sayeth, that he was a servant in Charles Town, South Carolina with Colonel Faulcon, & that he came to England in the *William & Mary* Transport & landed at St Ives in Cornwall. On the Passage over the said Colonel Faulcon died and was buried at St Ives, that he served a Mr Cox at St Ives about two months; from thence he went in a wagon to London, when he came there was advised to be baptized, & it appears by the copy

of the register that he was baptised in the parish of St James: in the liberty of Westminster & county of Middlesex. That he went from London to the West of England & came to Devon, in the parish of Marystow & begged there at the house of Arthur Tremayne Esquire upon which the said Arthur Tremayne Esquire took him into his service & that he lived with the said Arthur Tremayne Esquire about three quarters of a year & had meat, drink, clothes & a guinea for his service. He went from thence to Camelford in Cornwall & lived with William Mitchell about six months but had nothing for his service but meat & drink which was in the last summer. Since which time he has been wandering from place to place & supports himself by begging,

Taken & signed and sworn before me the 1st day of May 1786.
John Prideaux

The mark of James York'

# 4

# Expatriation and Equiano at Plymouth, 1787

At the time James York was in West Devon the town of Plymouth was the scene for an extraordinary scheme to resettle other former black slaves to Africa. In the mid 1780s the British government was faced with dealing with the hundreds of American blacks like York who had come to England following the loss of the New World colonies as well as others who had come from the East Indies. Most of them were living in dire poverty in London. A scheme was devised to resettle them outside of England and among the places considered were Nova Scotia and the Bahamas. Eventually it was decided to send them from Plymouth to Sierra Leone.

Equiano, a prominent former slave, was one of those who became involved. He already had some first-hand knowledge of Devon; in 1777 he had spent 'some little time at Plymouth and Exeter among some pious friends'. Nine years later he returned as one of the Navy Board administrators for the project but quickly became embroiled in financial mismanagement. He was dismissed five months later in March 1787.

Equiano's role in this endeavour, which later ended disastrously, appears to have been as a whistle-blower. Twelve years later he would become widely known for *The Interesting Narrative of the Life of Olaudah Equiano or Gustavas Vassa, the African*. His autobiography has been hugely influential since its publication although only lately have parts of it been questioned. In it Equiano related his compelling memories of his African boyhood but documents have recently been found in which he had recorded, before he wrote his autobiography, he was born in the United States. The chapters on his early childhood, becoming enslaved and the horrors of the Atlantic crossing now have to read with a reminder of the unreliability of autobiographies: by their very nature such works not only lack objectivity but comprise those elements which the writer wants readers to share. Part of the appeal of Equiano's book to the Georgian public, as now, was his life journey from a small African village to his becoming cultivated and civilised man. Equiano's experiences in the Sierra Leone project are more widely documented and a more reliable understanding of it can be had from the greater number of sources.[177]

Equiano himself wrote:

'On my return to London in August I was very agreeably surprised to find that the benevolence of government had adopted the plan of some philanthropic individuals to send the Africans from hence to their native quarter; and that some vessels were then engaged to carry them to Sierra Leone; an act which redounded to the honour of all concerned in its promotion, and filled me with prayers and much rejoicing. There was then in the city a select committee of gentlemen for the black poor, to some of whom I had the honour of being known; and, as soon as they heard of my arrival they sent for me to the committee. When I came there they informed me of the intention of government; and as they seemed to think me qualified to superintend part of the undertaking, they asked me to go with the black poor to Africa. I pointed out to them many objections to my going; and particularly I expressed some difficulties on the account of the slave dealers as I would certainly oppose their traffic in the human species by every means in my power.'

It was shortly after this that he received his warrant and he travelled to Plymouth. Equiano later lodged a petition against his dismissal and the government awarded him eighteen pounds for his wages of four months in Devon. This was he concluded 'more than a free Negro would have had in the western colonies!!!'[178]

# 5

# The correspondence of Henry Addington, First Viscount Sidmouth, 1788 to 1824

Henry Addington was at the heart of government with his role as Speaker of the House of Commons from 1789 to 1801 and later Chancellor of the Exchequer, Home Secretary and President of the Council. He was a Devon man with the family home at Upottery in East Devon. Included amongst his vast surviving correspondence are letters noting political debates on slavery. The issue would become of great concern to Addington and the correspondence has examples of the arguments made concerning slavery and the political pressures applied to him. In February 1788 one friend, George Huntingford, later bishop of Gloucester and Hereford, wrote:

> 'Dr Lawrence (our Winchester acquaintance) called on me. He talked much on Mr [Edmund] Burke's ideas respecting the slave trade. I found by him that Mr B. foresaw the total ruin of the West India Islands if the Trade were at once prohibited. He is for a better regulation of the ships, which carry on that commerce (in my opinion infamously) he would lay the captains under some restrictions, and punish them with rigour for wanton severity or brutal inhumanity to the slaves; and when these wretches are purchased at the West India Islands, he would have them instructed in religion, and be suffered to purchase their freedom, when by industry they could acquire a sufficient

sum for that purpose. For their religious instruction he would erect more churches and to enable them in time to accumulate the price of their ransom, he would enact that the property of a slave should be as sacred as that of a free man.

The point on which Mr B. and the advocates for what is in agitation materially differ is the leading question – will the planters be enabled to carry on their works without an annual supply of new slaves? Many West India merchants have cursed the very name of slavery – and at this time Bryan Edwards is writing a history of Jamaica, in the preface of which he strongly censures Great Britain for suffering it to exist. Now is a question, where party & politics are not concerned, but where the interests of merchants is most materially affected, I cannot conceive any quixotical notions of liberty would induce those very people to decry slavery who would most sensibly feel the bad consequences if any such were to ensue from the abolition of it.

I see petitions are set on foot, unnecessary surely to a House of Commons which I should suppose has not ten advocates for the slave trade. It were better to point out methods by which to cure the evil. It will be difficult. I would not destroy mankind because there are moral and natural evils, nor the islands because they have existed by slavery, but I should be as much at a loss how to rectify one as the other system.'[179]

Huntingford was an intimate of Addington and in 1802 compiled an account of his political administration. In regard to slavery he wrote 'as a Good Whig I wish every human being as free as civil society can allow, but from experience & observation of the consequences which ensue from hasty innovations & from consideration of national welfare, I should be extremely deliberate in bringing about a change, much very much to be wished for but doubtful as to practicability'. Huntingford provided further advice on slavery.

'. . . I should conceive they would be actuated to work by the same principles which operate in our peasantry, ie necessity, and great encouragement to be laborious. It has been found too that industry has increased where a small degree of civilization has been introduced, let the free-born children be taught their

*Abolition and Emancipation*

duties to God & Man as our children are. Why should they not derive the same benefits from this education which our children do? The Legislator may moreover enact laws for compelling every person of certain descriptions to work so many hours – as you are the givers of freedom, you may give it on what terms you please. I am sure it will be a blessing to this country . . .'[180]

The following year, in 1789, Huntingford wrote expressing hope that France and Spain would also refrain from slavery but noted 'if our enemies continue that trade, and if by that trade they may be enabled to endanger the welfare of this country very materially, the law of self-preservation, that first principle of nature, will justify us in continuing even against our wishes a system in that case absolutely necessary.'[181] The following year Huntingford again wrote on slavery. He pointed out to Addington a recent pamphlet which noted medieval Bristol had slaves. Huntingford concluded with his favourite quote from the new publication: 'let all children of slaves born in a Christian country be free, and let them be educated at the public expense as in the Foundling Hospital and the Workhouses'.[182]

A secret proposal, from about this time, also survives in the Addington papers for bringing another 'race of cultivators' to the West Indies. It was suggested that Chinese settlers could be taken to Trinidad in order to lessen the proportion of blacks in the islands. They would be 'kept distinct from the Negroes and who from interest would be inseparably attached to the European proprietors'.[183] Addington's views on this proposal have not been determined but not long afterwards Indian workers were sent to some of the islands.

In 1817 Addington received a report from a correspondent in Demerara who commended the planters for the extreme care with which they treated their slaves. His letter is fulsome in his praise.[184]

Finally, in 1824 another letter was sent from Nassau in the Bahamas which further acquainted Addington with the state of slavery. The correspondent, Colonel A. Murray, used a variety of arguments against emancipation. One of these was the fear white settlers in British colonies in the West Indies would be overwhelmed by the black population and 'the women compelled to submit' to their 'brutal lusts'. It was Murray's view that freedom was not in a slave's best interests: his long letter deplored the owners who had given freedom to their slaves because they had become 'the laziest & most worthless of beings'.

Murray denounced the people of Haiti who had established their own state: his opinion was they had degenerated to the savage state they had been in Africa. Rumours of British emancipation had, in Murray's opinion, made life difficult for the plantation owners by fuelling the hopes of the slaves. He particularly blamed female slaves, like women of the 'lower classes in England', for leading insurrections. They were, in his view, 'the most numerous class of evil disposed' and shared a loose sense of morals.[185]

# 6

# Abolition from 1787 to 1792: Exeter, Plymouth, Tiverton, Kingsbridge, Topsham, Bradninch, Cullompton, Totnes, Dartmouth, Bere Alston, Crediton, Ashburton, Moretonhampstead and Honiton

The first formal moves to end slavery came in 1787 with the establishment of the Society for the Abolition of the Slave Trade. Provincial liaison committees were subsequently established including two in Devon.[186] In one historian's view these abolitionists demonstrated 'energy, enthusiasm and considerable ingenuity'.[187] The local committees' purpose was to galvanise local support and in mid July 1787 two of the Society's members in London wrote to Francis Fox for Plymouth, Walter Prideaux for Dartmouth and Joel Cadbury for Exeter with the hope of encouraging help.[188]

The first moves in Devon appear to have been from Exeter and Plymouth. According to Thomas Clarkson, the leading Abolitionist who was a member of the Society's committee, the Society received a letter of help from Samuel Milford of Exeter shortly it was formed.[189] Clarkson also recalled a letter from 'the Reverend James Manning of Exeter in which he stated himself to be authorised by the dissenting ministers of Devon and Cornwall to express their high approbation of the conduct of the committee and to offer their services in the promotion of this great work of humanity and religion'.[190] According to the minute book of the Society this was written on May 9th 1788.[191] Not long after Clarkson visited Exeter. He was then 28 years old, a tall and well-built man in his prime but although committed to the point of being obsessive he was also brusque and socially awkward.[192] Clarkson remembered 'having meetings with the late Mr Samuel Milford, the late Mr George Manning, the Reverend James Manning, Thomas Sparkes, and others a desire became manifest among them of establishing a committee there. This was afterwards effected; and Mr Milford, who, at a general meeting of the inhabitants of Exeter, on the 10th of June, on this great subject, had been called by those present to the chair, was appointed the chairman of it.' Three further letters were sent to the Society from Exeter; one was from Manning and the others were written by Samuel Milford who subsequently wrote more often than other provincial committee chairmen.[193] In July the Exeter committee had collected 50 guineas to support the Society.[194] Another meeting took place on 1 November 1788 and the *Exeter Flying Post* reported:

'Saturday last a meeting (more respectable than numerous) was held at the Guildhall of this city, convened by notice from the Right Worshipful the Mayor, in order to consider on some propositions which were to be laid before them for the abolishing the African Slave Trade. The Reverend Dr Clarkson, in a very able manner, entered into the business of the meeting: he showed, from the best authority, the enormous cruelties that were committed, proving also, that more sailors in the year 1786 lost their lives by that trade, than all the other fleets which sailed from England in the same year conjoined. Mr Robert Paul, junior, who had been in that trade upwards of 15 months, gave an account of what dreadful inhumanities he had been witness to during his continuance therein.'[195]

Exeter's list contained more than 250 names of supporters.[196] These abolitionists who subscribed to raising funds for the Society comprised Sir C. W. Bampfield, M.P. £10, John Baring, Esquire, M. P. £5 5s, Richard Hey Esquire £5 5s, Mr William Byrd of Uffculme £2 2s, Mr Richard Milward of Uffculme £1 1s, Mr Robert Fry of Culmstock £1 1s, Miss Sarah Fry of ditto 10s 6d, Mr Henry Trickey of Uffculme £1 1s, Mrs Elizabeth Were of Uffculme £1 1s, Miss M. Were of Uffculme £1 1s, Mr D. Henton of Uffculme 10s 6d, Mr W. Trickey of Uffculme 10s 6d, Mr

Thomas Milward of Torrington 10s 6d, Miss Ann Ellis of Uffculme 10s 6d, Mr Philip Jones of Barnstaple 5s, Mr J. Trickey of Uffculme £1 1s, R. T. 10s 6d, D. B. 10s 6d, Mr Joseph Pope 10s 6d, Revd Mr Hole £1 1s, Revd Mr Kitson £1 1s, Mr W. Kennaway Senior £1 1s, Mr Thomas Kennaway £1 1s, Mr George Herbert £1 1s, Mr William Holmes £2 2s, Miss Dunsford £1 1s, Miss William's £1 1s, Dr Okes, M. D. £1 1s, Miss Sheppards 10s 6d, Mr Samuel Churchill 10s 6d, J. B. 10s 6d, Mr R. Trewman 10s 6d, Mr Degeo 10s 6d, Mr A. Larkworthy 5s, Mr John Lewis 5s, Mr Williams 5s, Mr Worthy 5s, Mr Bowdidge 5s, Mrs Browne 10s 6d, Mr John Drew 10s 6d, Mr Floyd 10s 6d, Mr William Hussey £1 1s, Mrs Judgson £1 1s, Mr G. Waymouth £2 2s, Mrs Lewis 10s 6d, Mr Ogborn £1 1s, Mr Jervoise 10s 6d, Mr William Kemp 10s 6d, Mr Ellard 10s 6d, Miss Speke 10s 6d, Mrs Pitt 10s 6d, Mrs Hamilton £1 1s, Mr John Land £1 1s, A. B. 10s 6d, Mrs Burrow 10s 6d, Mrs Pinkstan 10s 6d, Messrs Harold & Land 10s 6d, Mr Arundel Philip £1 1s, Mr John Jerwood £2 2s, R. £1 1s, Messrs H. & D. Sweetland of Topsham £1 1s, A. T. of Newton 10s 6d, Mrs Pine £1 1s, Mr John Stoodley £1 1s, Mr George Short £1 1s, Revd Mr Francis 10s 6d, Mr Kemble £1 1s, Revd Micjah Towgood £1 1s, J. O. 10s 6d, Mr Granger £1 1s, Mr Harris 10s 6d, Mr Browne 10s 6d, Miss Milfords £1 11s 6d, Mrs Milford £1 1s, Mrs Clarke £1 1s, Miss Clarke 10s 6d, Mrs Hutton 5s, Mrs Gore 5s, Mrs Williams 5s, Mr Abraham Kennaway £1 1s, Mr Robert Kennaway 10s 6d, Mr Alexander Gard 5s, Mr Peter Hole £1 1s, Mrs Cook £1 1s, Mr Dawe 5s, Revd Mr Stooke 10s 6d, Mrs Towgood 10s 6d, L. Duval Esquire £1 1s, Mr Addicot £1 1s, Mr Richard Turner 10s 6d, Mrs J. Lee of Ebford £2 2s, Mr Dyer 5s, Mrs George Mannning £2 2s, Mr Luccraft £1 1s, Mr Grant 10s 6d, Mr John Shute £1 1s, Mr Bodley 5s, Mr Thomas Pearce £1 1s, Revd Mr Tozer £2 2s, Miss Tremletts £2 2s, Mr John Creswell £1 1s, Mr Henry Reed £1 1s, Mr John Rowe £1 1s, Mr Mountjoy 5s, Rev. M. Tarrant £1 1s, Mr Henry Tarrant £1 1s, Mr James Tremlett £1 1s, Mr J. D. Worthy £1 1s, Mr Francis Turner 10s 6d, Mr J. Glyde 5s, Mrs Bennet 10s 6d, Rev. Mr Churchill £1 1s, Mrs Churchill 10s 6d, Mrs Hill £1 1s, Mr Dugdale 5s, Mr Henry Melhuish 10s 6d, Mrs Hannah Cotter 10s 6d, Mrs Elizabeth Merivale 10s 6d, Mrs Bowbier 6s, Mr Nation £2 2s, T. R. And Co. £1 1s, Mrs Fownes £1 1s, Mr Stephen Shute of Cullompton £1 1s, Messrs Griffey 5s, Revd Mr Lockyer 10s 6d; Mr Joseph Ford £1 1s; Mr J. Pasmore 10s 6d; Mr Thomas Foot 5s; Mr Jonathan Worthy 10s 6d; Mr John Cousche 10s 6d; Mr W. Browne Junior of Cullompton 10s 6d; Mr W. Burd Evans of Ottery 10s 6d; Mr Samuel Morgan 10s 6d, Mr Tucker 10s 6d, Revd Mr Eddisford 5s 6d, Mr John

Morn 10s 6d, I. S. M. 10s 6d, Mr Powell 5s, T. D. 10s 6d, Mr Dale 10s 6d, Mr Clapp £1 1s, '*Humanus*' 10s 6d, Mr Joseph Hunt £1 1s, Mr Sharland 5s, Mr Humphrey Squire 5s, Mr John Luke 10s 6d, Mr John Stabback 5s, Mr George Stabback £1 1s, Mr Peckford 5s, Mr Henry Smith £1 1s, Mr Wilcox 5s, Mr Joseph Rowe 10s 6d, Mr T. Squire 10s 6d, Mr Richard Parnell 10s 6d, Mr S. F. Milford £1 1s, Mr J. Milford £1 1s, Mr Taylor £1 1s, Miss Densham 5s, Mr Cranch 5s, Mr J. Green, merchant £1 1s, Mr Shirley Woolmer 10s 6d, Miss Anna Tremlett £2 2s, Revd Mr Pering 10s 6d, Revd William Ellicombe £1 1s, Mrs Honyhood 10s 6d, Mr Robert Mole 6s, Robert Berber Esquire 10s 6d, Edward Harris Esquire 10s 6d, Mr Daniel Keene 10s 6d, Mr William Berry 10s 6d, Mr Blatchford 5s, Mr Thomas Heard 5s, Mr Thomas Templer 10s 6d, Mr John Tucker 5s, Mr L. M. Hallaren 10s 6d, Miss Bodleys 15s, Mr Samuel Symons 5s, Lieut. Humphrey West 7s 6d, Miss Walrond 10s 6d, Edward Chute Esquire £1 1s, Mr Abraham Tozer £1 1s, Mrs Morris £1 1s, Mooney Belfield £1 1s, Mr Joseph Clark £1 1s and Mr Anthony Tremlett.[197]

These were not merely Exeter people but they came from parishes outside the city, from East Devon and from the north of the county as far as Great Torrington and Barnstaple. More than half of the subscribers were manufacturers, merchants or shopkeepers. There were sixty women who made up more than twenty per cent of the subscribers including Mrs Pinkstan who ran a boarding school in St Sidwell's parish. Many of the subscribers were also Dissenters.[198]

This was at least the third public meeting on slavery. Earlier that year, in March 1788, yet another meeting had been held and a petition was sent to Parliament. It reportedly had one thousand signatures; this was some sixteen per cent of the adult population. The March meeting was preceded by the reprinting in the *Exeter Flying Post* of a poem written by William Shenstone in about 1738. The anonymous contributor sent it 'at a time when human sensations, in pity to the distresses of our unfortunate fellow-creatures in the West Indies, are making their way to the hearts of mankind'.[199] It included the four lines:

'For them our tusky elephant expires;
 For them we drain the mines' embowell'd gold:
 Where rove the brutal nation's wild desires.
 Our limbs are *purchas'd*, and our Lives are *sold*!'

*Abolition and Emancipation*

Clarkson's list of abolitionists reveals Milford worked with a group of Unitarians and Quakers. He himself was a Unitarian, worshiped at George's Meeting House in South Street and was also prominent in supporting Reform. He was a banker whose premises, the City Bank, were on the corner of Cathedral Yard and Martin's Lane. The building is now part of the Royal Clarence Hotel. Reverend James Manning, a Unitarian Minister also at George's Meeting, was presumably a relative of George Manning. Thomas Sparkes was a member of a leading Quaker family in Exeter; it was they who developed the northern outskirts and renamed it Pennsylvania. They were also bankers and the pound note of the General Bank featured an engraving of William Penn.[200] One of these men probably supplied Shenstone's poem to the local newspaper. By the June meeting of 1788 Milford had increased the number of his committee. He advertised those helping him. They comprised:

| | |
|---|---|
| Samuel Milford Esquire | Mr Thomas Sparkes |
| Richard Hall Clarke Esq. | Mr Thomas Hill |
| Joseph Sanders Esq. | Mr Samuel Cross |
| Mathew Lee Esq. | Mr Philip Moor |
| Thomas Huckle Lee Esq. | Mr George Manning |
| John Holmes Esq. | Mr William Tucker |
| Mr Samuel Fred. Milford | Mr Robert Cross |
| Mr John Milford | Mr John Bowring |
| Mr John Williams | Mr Jonathan Evans |
| Mr John Withers | Mr Jonathan Tucker |
| Mr Henry Waymouth | Mr Samuel Dunsford |
| Rev. Thomas Morgan | Mr Joseph Kingdon |
| Rev. James Manning | Mr Joseph Sparkes Dymond |
| Rev. Timothy Kenrick | Mr John Dymond |
| Mr R. S. Vidal | Mr Joseph Littlefear |

Many were Unitarians[201] or Quakers.[202] They held their meeting at the Royal Clarence Hotel which was situated adjoining Milford's bank.[203] Shortly before this Granville Sharp, another leading national abolitionist, wrote to Exeter for support and a meeting took place at the end of May at the hotel to publicly show the letter. Milford subsequently received another from Sharp which was advertised in the local press.[204]

Religion and politics also played their part in dividing local support: in 1788 Exeter's chamber of councillors, overwhelmingly Anglican in nature, refused to support the petition because they suspected the Presbyterians. On April 2nd Henry Ley, the city's town clerk, informed his brother 'Mr Moore brought the present petition about the slave trade to the meeting and therefore mine was not produced. The Chamber said they would not petition themselves because they thought it a Presbyterian trick'. There was a similar dispute later at Tiverton.[205]

There had also been another meeting in Exeter to enlist support among other men: on March 20 a county meeting was held at the courthouse at Rougemont Castle with the intention of writing to the county's Members of Parliament to instruct them on how to vote regarding abolition.[206]

Clarkson noted the second Devon group of Abolitionists was at Plymouth but the Society appears to have heard from them before the Exeter group had written: a letter was received from Digory Tonkin of Plymouth on February 28th 1788 'mentioning that a petition to Parliament had been signed by the inhabitants of that town'.[207] Once again, it was the Nonconformists who began the movement. Clarkson visited the port and 'laid the foundation of another committee. The late William Cookworthy, the late John Prideaux and James Fox, all of the Society of the Quakers, and Mr George Leach, Samuel Northcote and John Saunders, had a principal share in forming it. Sir William Elford was chosen chairman.'[208] Elford was like, Milford in Exeter, in banking but was also a friend of William Pitt and later became one of Plymouth's Members of Parliament. John Tingcombe, a business partner of Elford's, also became a leading local figure.[209]

They had met at the Guildhall in Plymouth on 25 February with Digory Tonkin as Chairman. Among their resolutions was that 'the buying and selling any of the human race is a violation of the natural and inalienable Rights of Mankind'.[210] Another meeting was held on November 3 at the Pope's Head. Subsequent publicity reveals the supporters in Plymouth; the committee members were John Tingcombe Esq. (who was treasurer), John Mudge M. D., Reverend John Gandy, Jonathan Elford Esq., Reverend John Bidlake, Charles Fox Esq., James Fox, Reverend Herbert Mends, Reverend Philip Gibbs, Philip Madge Esq., Francis Fox, Reverend John Collins, John Moore junior, Jonathan Tingcombe, Samuel Northcote Esq., Andrew Saunders Esq., George Leach Esq., William Cookworthy, John Saunders and John Prideaux.[211] It was on November 3rd that Elford wrote to the Society presumably to inform them of his success in Plymouth.[212] The Plymouth group would become successful in organising support in Cornwall.[213]

Clarkson also visited Tiverton in November 1788. He preached a sermon and noted 'the unhappy Africans were our fellow creatures, that they possessed the same hearts, the same passions and feelings with ourselves'. It was reported that Clarkson had a large audience. The following day two Church of England clergy met with a dissenting minister and two merchants. The five men solicited subscriptions for abolition with some success. It was claimed that shortly before Clarkson's visit the town's population had been 'averse or indifferent to the cause' but the reading of sermons, public discussions and Clarkson's sermon had changed their views.[214]

The Plymouth Abolitionists had the most national impact of all the Devon men. Clarkson later wrote that it was from there that Abolitionism received the greatest propaganda tool. He explained William Elford, chairman of the Plymouth committee, had:

> 'sent up for inspection an engraving of a plan and section of a slave ship, in which the bodies of the slaves were seen stowed in the proportion of rather less than one to a ton. This happy invention gave all those, who saw it, a much better idea than they could otherwise have had of the horrors of their transportation, and contributed greatly as will appear afterwards to impress the public in favour of our cause'.

The image of the *Brookes* effectively conveyed to the British the horrors of the passage across the Atlantic. The Plymouth Committee published it in a leaflet in 1788 and it was subsequently adapted, in the spring of 1789, and reprinted nationally. The Plymouth men were supplemented by Reverend John Bidlake, master of Plymouth Grammar School, who published a tract against slavery in January 1789.[215] He also wrote to the Society.[216] The following month yet another pamphlet was published in Plymouth against slavery[217] and Elford wrote in March to the Society presumably to inform them of local activities.[218]

Initially the Society was able to enlist popular support but the brutality of the French Revolution of 1789 subsequently altered the British political climate to the detriment of abolition. The public became apprehensive of radicalism and abolition was weakened as a movement. Even so, by April 1789 more than thirty-two pounds were

Tiverton Castle in 1769 (Westcountry Studies Library, SC2973)

raised in Exeter for the Society and the committees in Exeter and Plymouth remained active that year and in 1790 as well as 1791.[219] In July 1791 a meeting was held in Exeter to push for abolition of 'this barbarous traffic in human flesh'.[220] Then, in the following year, 1792, more than 500 petitions were sent from around the country to London[221] including at least 12 from Devon including Plymouth, Kingsbridge, Honiton, Crediton, Topsham, Bradninch, Cullompton, Tiverton, Totnes, Dartmouth and Bere Alston.[222] There were meetings at Crediton in February at the Angel Inn and in Ashburton. In both places a sermon was preached the day before the meetings.[223] On the 16th of March a meeting took place at the White Hart in Moretonhampstead where a 'great number' of local people reportedly signed the petition.[224] That same week a meeting was organised at Exeter's Guildhall with the Mayor as chairman. One local newspaper reported it was resolved:

'That it appears to this meeting that the trade to Africa for slaves is unjust, cruel and oppressive; subversive of every principle of morality and religion; utterly inconsistent with sound policy, and in the highest degree disgraceful to the nation.

That nothing short of a total abolition can in our opinion be applied as an effectual remedy for the enormous and unparalleled evils which this trade produce.

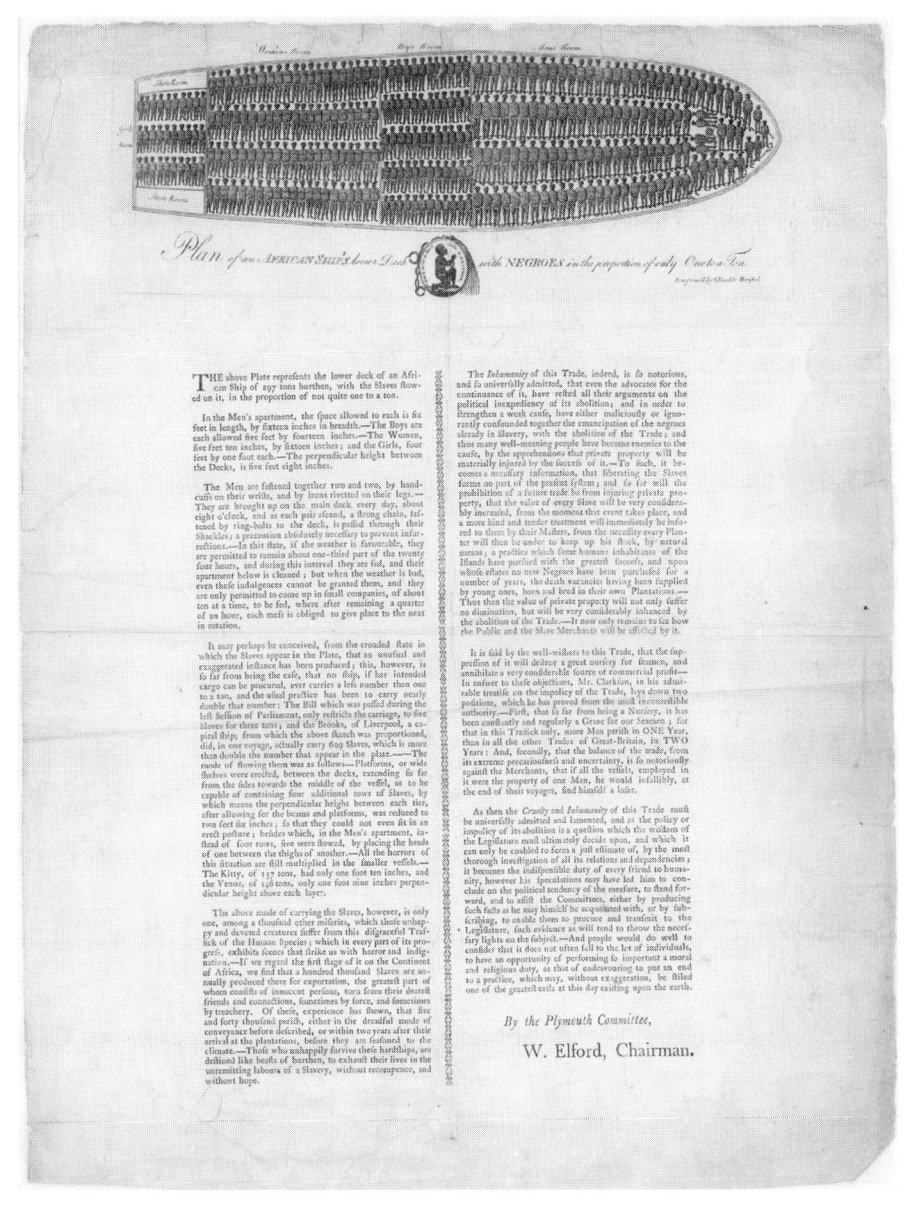

The Plymouth Abolitionists' masterstroke in propaganda: the 'Plan of an African Ship's Lower Deck', from which the *Brooks* of Liverpool was later redrawn, 1788 (Bristol Record Office, 17562/1)

That a petition for this purpose now produced, and unanimously approved, be forthwith signed, and presented to the honourable House of Commons; and that the members for this city be requested to present the same and to give it their most strenuous support.

That the thanks of this meeting be given to Reuben Phillips, esquire, the chairman, for his readiness in calling this meeting, and presiding therein; and that he be requested to transmit the petition when signed to the members of this city, to be by them presented to the house of Commons.'[225]

Another meeting took place in Honiton. One hundred people signed the resulting petition:

'the humble petition of the Portreeve and principal inhabitants of the borough of Honiton, in the county of Devon, showeth,

That it is with the deepest regret your petitioners behold the existence of that most horrible traffic in human flesh, the slave trade; which begun by avarice and completed by luxury; presents us this day with a more distressed scene of rapine, bloodshed, cruelty and oppression, than has ever at any period of history stained the annals of human events. They, therefore, impelled by the conviction of reason and conscience, most earnestly implore the Honourable House, speedily and effectually to put a stop to these evils, so derogatory to us as individuals, so disgraceful to us as a nation, and so totally repugnant to the mild, pure and benficient spirit of Christianity; being avowedly founded on violence and injustice, without the least plea in necessity or true policy, and utterly irreconcilable to any principle of morality or religion.'[226]

Tiverton also took part in abolition in 1792. Beavis Wood, the town clerk, wrote that year on 20 February:

'the time since Christmas has been very dull, and had not the men of humanity raised up the subject of the Slave Trade this town would have appeared as quiet almost as Rackenford Moor. But Mr Sampson, Mr Land and some others have prevailed on the mayor to call a meeting to consider again of a petition to

Parliament to abolish the Slave Trade. A committee is this day appointed to prepare such petition. Only 21 now attended. Of the Corporation there were present Mr Mayor, Mr [John] Pitman [curate of Pitt and Tidcombe Portions], Mr W[illiam] Besly [Presbyterian merchant and banker], Mr Tucker and myself. The remainder consisted of Mr Follett, Sampson, [Martin] Dunsford [merchant and historian of Tiverton], Sprague, Land and J[ohn] Wood [attorney]. The latter joined with me in supposing that the *sudden* abolition would not be safe or prudent. I did not attend the Committee, although appointed one of it, as I know the trim of the parties concerned, and that it would be difficult if not impossible to remove any impression or opinion they had taken. With much difficulty a petition was proposed, signed and sent to Mr Ryder.'[227]

On March 5th a letter was sent by Mr J. Sampson of Tiverton to the Society enclosing the petition and Walter Prideaux of Dartmouth wrote two weeks later with that port's petition.[228]

Local public pressure also took other forms. It was reported in April 1792 there were moves to boycott sugar. An *Exeter Gazette* reporter wrote:

> 'the foregoing the use of sugar, rum and cotton, is becoming very general throughout Devon and Cornwall, from the idea of its being manufactured by slaves. Children are now taught to believe, that eating sugar is an enormous crime; and the wearing of clothes contaminated in the dye by indigo from the West Indies is deemed unpardonable – Some of the Abolitionists are of opinion that if Parliament do not annihilate the slave trade soon, the consumption of sugar etc in England will experience such a decrease as must eventually be productive of serious consequences to the revenue.'[229]

At least four years earlier it was claimed in Devon that sugar consumption was immoral: during Clarkson's visit to Exeter it was said 'every cubic inch of sugar we consume costs a cubic inch of human blood'.[230] In Tiverton the boycott appears to have had local support by December 1791. John Stedman noted in his diary that month 'now the use of sugar is laid aside in Great Britain in order to enforce the abolition of the Slave Trade'.[231] Nationally the abolition campaign faltered in the mid to late 1790s although in Exeter an interesting pamphlet was printed in 1794.[232] It was not until the following decade that efforts were popularly revived.

# 7

# Abolition to Emancipation, 1807 to 1833: Ottery St Mary, Plymouth, Exeter, Topsham, Stonehouse, Moretonhampstead, Tavistock, Ashubrton and Chagford

Abolition efforts were revived in the early 1800s and legislation was finally passed in 1807. That February a meeting in Exeter supported abolition and the chairmanship passed from Samuel Milford to his son Samuel Frederick Milford. Gradually local Nonconformists relinquished their lead to clerics from the Church of England. In 1841 the main anti-slavery meeting in Exeter was prominently supported by the Dean of Exeter but by then other Anglicans had been actively working against slavery for a generation; as early as 1814 the Reverend Prebendary Oxnam was one of Exeter's most public supporters of emancipation as was the curate of St John's Church.[235]

The national debate to end the transportation of new African slaves was opposed on a number of grounds. It was argued by British commercial interests that slavery greatly increased prosperity while West Indian plantation owners stressed they needed new slaves because it was impossible to maintain their numbers through natural increase, slave labour kept their produce as economical as that produced by other European colonies and a decrease in slaves would hit production and in consequence profits.[236]

Abolition had been argued on moral grounds: it was unchristian. The movement coincided with another growing debate in Britain which meant abolitionists did not have to only discuss the humanitarian rights of Africans. Ending slavery became not just about the most extreme denial of rights but was linked with improvement and reform; part of a general acknowledgment of the unfair treatment of many others involving such issues as Catholic emancipation, poor relief, labour representation and electoral reform.

The abolitionists' struggle did not finish with the end to transporting slaves from Africa in 1807. It was hoped legislation would lead to amelioration, that is, the improvement of slaves' lives, but it became apparent this was not happening. The consequence was a gradual realisation that only emancipation was acceptable: after their initial victory in achieving abolition in 1807 the abolitionists' efforts became fixed on winning full freedom for slaves. That year the Society for the Abolition of the Slave Trade was superseded by a new body, the African Institution, but it took seven years, until 1814, for sufficient public feeling to resurface and give the issue a high profile. The impetus was the end of war with France which it was feared would trigger a resumption of slave trading. In addition to Britain the countries of Denmark, Holland, Sweden and the United States had withdrawn from transporting slaves and a change of French government made it possible for slaving to restart. In 1814 hundreds of petitions were sent to London including from several places in Devon. One was Ottery St Mary. Although undated it clearly was written at the time of the (first) end of the Napoleonic war. The petition was addressed to both Houses of Parliament.[237]

> 'The Humble Petition of the undersigned inhabitants of Ottery Saint Mary in the County of Devon showeth
> 
> That your Petitioners have seen with the deepest regret and disappointment, that in the late Treaty of Peace with France no provision has been made for the immediate Abolition of the African Slave Trade – a Trade avowedly repugnant to every moral & religious principle – but that, on the contrary,

the consequence will be its revival, on a large scale, and to an indefinite extent.

That it appears to your Petitioners, that this revival is attended with circumstance of peculiar aggravation; great and populous Colonies, in which during the last seven years, the importation of Slaves, has been strictly prohibited, and as even been made highly penal, having been freely ceded to France, not only without any stipulation for the continuance of that prohibition, but with the declared purpose, on the part of that country of commencing a new Slave Trade for their supply; and thus a system of robbery and murder, which had for many years been practically extinct is now to be revived at the very moment when France has been manifestly and signally favoured by Divine Providence! And the restoration to that country of the blessings of Peace is to be the signal for bringing all the evils and miseries of a continued warfare on the unoffending inhabitants of the African Continent.

That the revival of the French Slave Trade, and the unconditional restoration to France of her African Forts and Factories, have excited the peculiar regret of your Petitioners, by disappointing the hopes they had been led to indulge of the improvement and civilization of that large district in which those possessions are situated, and in which the Slave Trade having been nearly suppressed, the consequent introduction of cultivation and a legitimate commerce had begun to make some compensation to Africa for the miseries formerly inflicted.

That it appears to your Petitioners, that the fair and legitimate commerce with Africa which since the Abolition of the Slave Trade by Great Britain had materially increased, and was rapidly enlarging itself to an extant which promised important advantages to both countries is exposed to immediate injury, and to eventual destruction, by the revival of that inhuman traffic which had for so many ages retained that ill-fated coast in a state of barbarism and desolation.

That your Petitioners cannot but lament that the recognition in the Treaty of the radical injustice of the African Slave Trade, should be followed by a provision for its revival: and though that provision is accompanied by the declaration of an intention to abolish the Trade in Slaves after Five Years, yet they cannot conceal from themselves that rapacious and extensive interest will be created, which at the end of the specified term will present new and alarming obstacles to the fulfilment of the declared intention.

Your Petitioners therefore, deeply impressed with the necessity of immediately adopting such measures in Parliament as may be best calculated to prevent all the before-mentioned evils, as well as the evasion or infraction of the Abolition Laws of Great Britain by the clandestine importation of Slaves from the French colonies into our own, or by the employment of British Capital in this nefarious traffic, humbly pray your Lordships to take the premises into your serious consideration, and to adopt such measures thereupon as your Lordships wisdom may seem meet.

And your Petitioners will very pray etc. etc. etc.

[signed] Sir J. Kennaway Baronet, Richard Kennaway Esquire, George Smith Vicar, James Coleridge Esquire Deputy Lieut., George Coleridge clerk, John Warren clerk, Charles Hodge surgeon, George Whitlock D., Thomas Glanville solicitor, Richard Houlditch clerk, John Wreford, Charles Huddy, Benjamin Saunders, Peter Horsey, Joseph Wheaton, William Norrington, Peter Wheaton, William Coles, William Palmer, S. Harrop, James Norrington, Abraham Harding, Benjamin Leatt, Henry Ware, Joseph Horsey, Joseph Wheaton, Walter Pulman, Edward Anstice, William Row Junior, William Leatt, Thomas Stocker, James Manley, Charles Norrington, Thomas Jones, James Leatt, Charles Salter, Jos. Lathrope, Nathaniel Rowland, William Row, Josias Walker, John Salter, Thomas Bankes, Richard Seaward, Roger Salter, Abraham Salter, Jn Denning, James Burrow, John Burgoin, Richard Coles, Jn Ellis, William Haris, Thomas Harvey, John Reid, Nicholas Bole, Christopher Bond, T. Seaward, Richard Salter, Thomas Pulman, Thomas Salter, John M-ell, Jos. Mitchell, James Sheppard, Richard Sheppard, William Baker, George Passmore, John Whicker, William Blackmore, James Walker, James Sorrell, T. Toby, Nathaniel Sanford, Richard Windover, William Godfrey, John Thorne, John Windover, [?], William Livermore, J. Combes, Charles Webb, Samuel Evans'

A small collection of papers, comprising letters and bill posters, have survived for Plymouth which show that for the years 1814 to 1828 there was continual pressure applied in the port for closing the trade.[238] The first document in the collection illustrates moves made in Plymouth in 1814.

> 'To Henry Woollcombe Esquire, Mayor of Plymouth
> Sir, We the undersigned request you will be pleased to call a meeting of the inhabitants of Plymouth to consider the propriety of petitioning '[the Houses of Parliament' crossed through] ['the Prince Regent' inserted] that ['they' crossed through] ['he' inserted] will adopt such measures as to ['their' crossed through] ['his' inserted] wisdom may seem meet if possible to prevent the renewal of the horrors of the slave trade, as well as the evasion or infraction of the abolition laws of Great Britain by the clandestine importation of slaves from French Guinea into our own, or by the employment of British Capital in this nefarious traffic,
> [signed] William Elford, Jn Tincombc, Jos. Whiteford, Thomas Cleather, George Eastlake, Joseph Pridham, W. Woollcombe, William Prideaux, Joseph Treffry, [?] Remmell, William Eastlake, William Langmead, Joseph Clotworthy, Robert Fuge, Richard Derry, Benjamin Balkwill'[239]

This was sent before 30 June 1814 for on that day a billposter was printed advertising a meeting. It was similar in wording.[240] It read:

> 'Having received a Requisition, signed by many respectable Individuals, for convening a MEETING of the INHABITANTS of PLYMOUTH, to consider of the Propriety of presenting a PETITION to *His Royal Highness* the PRINCE REGENT, praying that he will be pleased to adopt such Measures, as to his Wisdom may seem meet, to prevent, if possible, the Renewal of the Horrors of the SLAVE TRADE, as well as the evasion or Infraction of the *Abolition Laws of Great Britain*, by the clandestine Importation of Slaves from the French Colonies, into the Colonies of this Country, or by the Employment of British Capital, in this nefarious Traffic.
> I do in Pursuance of such Requisition, hereby request a

General Meeting of the Inhabitants of this Town and Borough, at the Guildhall thereof, on MONDAY next, the Fourth Day of July Instant, at Twelve o'clock at Noon, for the above Purpose.
HEN. WOOLLCOMBE, MAYOR'

The meeting was duly held on the 4th and another billposter was printed.[241] It was 'a very numerous and respectable meeting of the mayor and inhabitants' and convened for the purposes stated in the earlier poster. Eight resolutions were passed. These were:

'That a humble ADDRESS and PETITION be presented to his Royal Highness the PRINCE REGENT, expressing the deep and heart-felt Regret of this Meeting, at that Article in the Treaty of Peace lately concluded between his Royal Highness and the King of France, which authorises that Country for several ensuing years, to carry on the SLAVE TRADE, to a most afflicting and alarming Extent. That as the Meeting have partaken in the Joy and Exultation which the Abolition of that most criminal Measure diffused throughout this Country, they cannot but experience a proportionable Degree of Disappointment, at thus appearing to confederate in the Revival of it; and therefore most humbly, most earnestly, and most confidently expressing the Hopes of the Meeting, that His Royal Highness will be graciously pleased to impress on the Minds of his Negotiators, at the ensuing Congress, his Royal Will and Pleasure, supported as it will be by the united Wishes and Prayers of the whole Country, that they shall continue to use their utmost Endeavours, in Conjunction with those of the other Allied Nations, to put and immediate and universal Termination to so dreadful a Calamity, and thus to avert that Divine Vengeance, which the Meeting cannot but apprehend must fall on all those who shall either carry on or be wanting in their utmost Expectations, to prevent, the Continuance of so odious and detestable a Traffic.'

The second Resolution was:

'That the ADDRESS and PETITION produced and read to this Meeting by Sir William Elford, Baronet, Recorder, be approved and adopted, and that the same be forthwith engrossed, and do lie on the Guildhall Table, for the Signature of the Inhabitants, until Noon of Monday next, the Eleventh Day of July Instant.'

This was followed by resolutions that the city's Members of Parliament should present the address and petition to the Prince Regent, that the meeting acknowledges its gratitude to Sir William Elford for his assistance as well as to the mayor for his help, and that the Resolutions should be printed as handbills and appear in the *Courier*, *Morning Chronicle* and the Sherborne, Plymouth and Plymouth-Dock newspapers. It subsequently cost the council five pounds to have the resolutions printed in one national paper. The meeting also agreed that:

'The thanks of this meeting be given to William Wilberforce, Esquire, M.P., for his great and most honourable Exertions in promoting the total Abolition of the *Slave Trade*, and that the Mayor be desired to communicate to him, the high Sense this Meeting entertains of his Conduct, on an Occasion which involves the best Feelings of Human Nature, and to request him to continue to use his Vigilance, so as still to contribute to the immediate and universal Abolition of that inhuman Traffic, and to promote the Observance of the existing Laws on that Subject, or the Enactment of others more effectual for that Purpose.'

There were also similar meetings held in that summer of 1814 at the Guildhall and Rougemont Castle in Exeter as well as in Topsham. Reverend James Carrington chaired a meeting in Topsham at the vestry on 4 July. Two petitions were left at the Globe and Salutation Inns for local residents to sign.[242] A petition formed at the Exeter Guildhall meeting was later reported to have attracted the signatures of between 9,500 and 10,000 people in only three days. A number of speakers addressed the meetings among whom was Sir Thomas Dyke Acland of nearby Killerton. He was at the Castle and reportedly said he 'was sure there could not be in a meeting of the county of Devon one dastardly soul who would wish for the promulgation of the Slave Trade a single day'.[243] It was during July, shortly after the Exeter and Plymouth meetings that the Duke of Wellington complained of the public 'degree of frenzy' about abolition. Across Britain some 800 petitions were formed and signed by three quarters of a million people. These meetings were the result of concerns that the overthrow of Napoleon would be followed by a renewal of the French transporting slaves to the Americas. Despite the crucial help of the British in bringing him to the throne, Louis XVIII failed to immediately abolish trafficking. It took another six months before an international treaty was signed to end the trade.[244]

Even so, slavery continued and abolitionists were disappointed with the lack of an improvement in the living conditions of slaves. Public pressure was reactivated nine years later with the establishment of yet another body, the Anti-Slavery Society (its' full name was the Society for the Mitigation and Gradual Abolition of Slavery throughout the British Dominions).[245] Public pressure was reapplied with more than two hundred petitions sent from around the country including from Exeter, Plymouth and Stonehouse.[246] On April 2nd 1823 one man wrote to Joseph Whiteford.[247]

> 'The Mayor has requested me to deliver the requisition to yourself with many compliments on your worth & to it with much pleasure although you have some oddities. I first proposed Wednesday next, subsequently Thursday, as there might be many county gents in town. It has however since occurred to me that a market day might keep many Quakers form the meeting particularly the grainy men. Therefore possibly Wednesday or Friday next week might be preferable. Will you get the bills out as early as possible, send me a few. I wish to keep the requisition which the mayor has promised to return to me, if these be no *sine qua non* [nothing essential] to the contrary.
> 
> Wishing your wife better health, believe me to be yours truly,
> 
> JW
> 
> I will endeavour to see you before the meeting.
> 
> L[?] has refused an answer to our resolutions which me doubt T[?] will lend you. I only read them in the street.
> 
> Do read a pamphlet on Negro Slavery left in Library table. I have not looked at it when the requisition was drawn, [Mr Fowell] Buxton Mohon is on 22 April.'

*Abolition and Emancipation*

Chagford in 1811 (Westcountry Studies Library, SC0327)

sewing circles.[267] Public concern over slavery continued through the Victorian period: there was a meeting in Exeter of the Anti-Slavery Society as late as 1882.[268]

Legislation was finally passed on 29 August 1833[269] and Chagford was so excited that in August 1837 the village continued to celebrate the anniversary: a 'transparent painting' depicting emancipation was exhibited at the Three Crowns.[270]

# 8

# The freedom of four Africans at Plymouth in the early 1800s

On three occasions Plymouth Abolitionists were called upon to intercede in cases where the legal status of Africans was questioned. The first was in 1811 when Henry Woollcombe received a letter from William Allen, a London Quaker of whom one historian noted he 'was associated in one way or another with almost every philanthropic endeavour of the day'. Allen was then 41 years old, a lecturer in chemistry at Guy's Hospital, a Fellow of the Royal Society and was on the Executive Committee of the African Civilization Society.[271]

> '24th of 7th month, 1811
> Esteemed friend,
> I am convinced from our short acquaintance that I shall be doing thee a pleasure by giving thee an opportunity for exerting the benevolence of thy disposition and therefore feel no hesitation in applying to thee in the following occasion.
> Our government, in order to promote the view of the African Institution in the civilization of Africa has granted a license to Paul Cuffe master of the brig *Traveller*, a man of colour and citizen of the United States, to proceed from Sierra Leone to this country with the privileges of a British subject. On entering the port of Liverpool Aaron Richards, a black man aged about 21 years old, whom he had taken on board at Sierra Leone,

*Abolition and Emancipation*

# BOROUGH OF Plymouth.

GUILDHALL, *April* 4, 1823.

HAVING received a Requisition signed by Sixty respectable Individuals, for convening a "MEETING of the Inhabitants of this Town and Neighbourhood, to consider and determine on the propriety of petitioning Parliament for the gradual abolition of Slavery, throughout the Colonies and Dominions of the united Empire; and to express their hopes that His Majesty's Government would take steps to induce the other Governments of Europe to complete the ABOLITION of the SLAVE TRADE":—

I do therefore hereby request a GENERAL MEETING of the INHABITANTS of this Town and Neighbourhood, at the Guildhall thereof, on WEDNESDAY, the NINTH Day of APRIL Instant, by Twelve o'Clock at Noon, for the purposes expressed in the said Requisition.

*W. A. WELSFORD,*
MAYOR.

HAVILAND, Printer, Frankfort-Place, PLYMOUTH.

Poster to advertise abolition meeting in Plymouth, 1823
(Plymouth & West Devon Record Office, 1/669/20)

Two days later, on April 4 1823, a billposter appeared under the name of W. A. Welsford, Mayor.[248] It noted:

> 'Having received a requisition signed by Sixty respectable Inhabitants, for convenience a "MEETING of the Inhabitants of this Town and Neighbourhood, to consider and determine on the propriety of petitioning Parliament for the gradual abolition of Slavery, throughout the Colonies and Dominions of the united Empire; and to express their hopes that His Majesty's Government would take steps to induce the other Governments of Europe to complete the ABOLITION of the SLAVE TRADE":
>
> I do therefore hereby request a GENERAL MEETING of the INHABITANTS of this Town and Neighbourhood, at the Guildhall thereof, on WEDNESDAY, the Ninth Day of April Instant, by Twelve o'clock at Noon, for the purposes expressed in the said Requisition. W. A. WELSFORD, MAYOR

A meeting was also held in Exeter in 1823.[249] The subsequent refusal at this time of the West Indian plantation owners to modest suggestions from the Government hardened the stance of abolitionists. For the next ten years there was continual pressure from them for the complete end of slavery.[250] On 16 February 1824, yet another public meeting was held at Plymouth Guildhall to petition Parliament. The wording was 'for the progressive amelioration of the condition of the Negroes in the Colonies, in accordance with the humane views expressed in His Majesty's Speech; and with the Resolutions of the House of Commons on the subject in the last Sessions'. It was convened on February 23 by Nicholas Lockyer, Mayor of the borough.[251] Not long afterwards one Plymouth man noted a meeting at the Athenaeum that '[William] Welsford [former mayor] has also made I am told an admirable speech at Devonport on the subject of the Antislavery measures. I have not yet read it, but it was to be seen in the *Devonport Telegraph*'.[252] Exeter also had a meeting a week later at the Guildhall,[253] there was one at Moretonhampstead in the School Room chaired by the Portreeve[254] and others were held in Tavistock and Ashburton.[255] Two years later, on 21 February 1826, yet another Plymouth meeting was held. A bill poster was printed on the 4th with a requisition from 34 notable residents made on the 10th.[256] It was published with the authority of

Ashburton in about 1845 (Westcountry Studies Library, SC0012)

W. H. Hawker, the mayor that year, and Henry Woollcombe chaired the meeting.[257] Meetings also took place in Exeter, where Mr Cropper of Liverpool spoke, and in Tavistock.[258] The Exeter meeting is curious given the mayor attended but did not take the chair. It was explained that 'though not joining all the opinions of the requisitionists, [he] had afforded them with the use of the Guildhall for the purpose'.[259]

In 1828 political agitation continued in Plymouth. Yet another petition was drawn up and sent to London. This address in late March to the House of Lords stated that as slavery was 'incompatible with the Christian Religion' it pressed for the 'gradual improvement and emancipation of the Negro Population in Our Colonies'.[260] It went on to state:

> 'That your Petitioners are severely disappointed at the pertinacious resistance to these resolutions by the Colonial Legislators.
>
> That your Petitioners would gladly make pecuniary sacrifices to satisfy the reasonable claims of Proprietors for the gradual Abolition of Slavery but feel the strongest objection to restrictive duties in favour of Slave Produce calculated to aggravate that condition to injure free labourers in other of our colonies and to confine the commercial resources of the Country.'

A similar petition was drawn up for the House of Commons.[261] Two months later yet another meeting was held in the Guildhall, on May 23rd 1828, and the following month the Earl of Morley, who resided at Saltram, presented the petition to the House of Lords.[262] Meetings continued across Devon including at the Public Rooms in Ilfracombe in August of 1830.[263] It would take several more years before the slaves were emancipated. In the meanwhile meetings continued including on 8 May 1832 when there was one of the Devon & Exeter Anti-Slavery Society in the Assembly Room at the Royal Clarence. Local clergy led discussions. In Exeter local groups formed to support national societies: meetings took place in July 1834 for the Society for the Abolition of Slavery,[264] in 1840 for the British Foreign Anti Slavery Society[265] and in 1841 for the Society for the Extinction of the Slave Trade & for the Cultivation of Africa.[266] These were mostly held to form auxiliary societies. By the 1850s it appears men had deserted the cause in Exeter and left women to organise the movement through charity drives and was pressed, put on board the *Intelligent* gun brig and sent to the *Salvador Mundi* of Plymouth. We have however made such interest at the Admiralty that an order is sent down for his discharge but as the young man is a perfect stranger and probably unfurnished with the means of travelling I shall be obliged by thy inquiring whether Frank Fox is at present at Plymouth, if so, he will receive a letter by this post from Thomas Clarkson and I need not trouble thee any further but if Frank Fox is absent I shall be obliged by thy finding out the young man and putting him in the way of getting to Liverpool as soon as possible. For the brig *Traveller* will probably sail in about two weeks from this time. I will pay to thy order in London any money that thou mayest advance in this account, I remain, thy sincere friend.'

Three years later, in 1814, there were concerns in Plymouth over the welfare of two African children sold into slavery and brought into port onboard a navy vessel which had seized their French ship as a prize. The children were to be transported by their owners, two Portuguese and Spanish merchants, to Gibraltar when the mayor intervened. An official letter was sent seeking advice with their plight.[272]


Guildhall, Plymouth
April 11 1814

My Lord
   Having information from some very respectable Inhabitants of this Town that two African Children who were onboard *L'Etoile*, French frigate, lately captured by HMS *Helms* have been landed within this borough and were about to be taken to Lisbon by a Portuguese captain who claimed them, I thought it right to cause the Captain and Children to appear before me which they have this day.
   Upon examination I find that the Captain, whose name is Ignacio Joze Ninues, was late Master of the Portuguese Brigatine *Oceano* captured by the French Frigate's *La Sultane* and *L Elorte* which was sunk after the Capture, received these Children on board at Balua from a merchant called Jose

African Children, who were on board L'Etoile french Frigate lately Captured by H.M.S. Helms have been landed within this Borough, and were about to be taken to Lisbon by a Portugueze Captain who claimed them — I thought it right to cause the Captain and Children to appear before me which they have this day — Upon examination I find that the Captain whose name is Ignacio Joze Ninues, was late Master of the Portugueze Brigantine Oceano Captured by the French Frigates La Sultane and L'Etoile which was sunk after the Capture, received those Children on board at Bahia from a Merchant called Jose Antonio Roiz Vianna resident there, and they were to have been delivered to a Jew Merchant at Gibralter called Moize Levy and that both Vianna and Levy were part owners of the Brigantine, but were to pay the Captain £20 Sterling for the passage of the Children. The Captain says that the Children are called Antonia and Francisca that one is about the age of 9 Years and the other about 11 he says he does not know from whence they came but supposes from the Eastern Coast of Africa. From these circumstances it appears to be that the Children have been sold as Slaves, and are still in that Condition. I have therefore deemed it prudent to detain them here, and to give your Lordship this Information as I am led to understand that the African institution have made some provision for Cases of this description — I have promised to give the Captain a Certificate of the cause of detention of those Children and shall be obliged by your Lordships reply, as to what may be determined on relative to their disposal —

J. W.

Letter regarding two African children
(Plymouth & West Devon Record Office, W669)

Antonio Rouz Vianna [who is] resident there and they were to have been delivered to a Jew Merchant at Gibraltar called Moize Levy and that both Vianna and Levy were part owners of the Brigantine but were to pay the Captain £20 sterling for the passage of the Children. The Captain says that the Children are called Antonia and Francesca, that one is about the age of 9 years and the other about 11. He says he does not know from whence they came but supposes from the Eastern coast of Africa. From these circumstances it appears to be that the Children have been sold as Slaves and are still in that condition. I have therefore deemed it prudent to detain them here, and to give your Lordship this Information as I am led to understand that the African Institution have made some provision for cases of this description – I have promised to give the Captain a Certificate of the cause of detention of these children and shall be obliged by your Lordship's reply, as to what may be determined or relative to their disposal, JW

Some nine years or so later there was another dispute over the freedom of a former female slave. John Prideaux, a leading figure amongst Plymouth abolitionists, sought help. He was suspicious the woman had not willingly given up her freedom.[273]

'I have just received my reply from the Anti-Slavery Society in London, written in the midst of a public meeting & therefore without legal references but otherwise fully confirmatory of the sentiments I ventured to express in the Guildhall. I copy the part relating to her case:

"The case of the female Negro is plain, having reached the shores of England she is <u>free</u> <u>absolutely</u>. If she is on board ship and not permitted to come on shore, to appear before a magistrate, the magistrate may visit the ship, & give a certificate of her having been to Plymouth, or those who detain her may be compelled to give her up by a writ of *Habeas Corpus*. The Certificate is merely necessary as evidence of her having been in England, as she is free without it but it may be proper to take into account of her late owners, the estate she was on, the estate she goes to, with a description of her person & any particular mark upon her, her name & any other particulars, that if she be reduced into slavery again she may be identified as having been in England."

Now although this is not written in a legal shape exactly, yet since it was dated 'Freeman's Hall in the Public meeting' for the purpose of petitioning Parliament against slavery, there can be [no] doubt that my letter was handed to Messrs Brougham, [Stephen] Lushington & other characters of legal celebrity who would not fail to be present on such an occasion. The reply is from the Secretary, Richard Mathews Esq., who says he writes in a great hurry – tomorrow I expect to hear further on the subject from Earl Bathurst.

But in the meanwhile, we are thrown to leeward, I will not say out-manoeuvred (whatever I may think). The day after the Colonel's appearance at the Hall, in came the woman, bag & baggage, to all appearances, for us to provide for. We accepted the charge, & told the sergeant who brought her, to say that she was now at our cost, & the colonel need give himself no further trouble. But she said she had a word to say before the Sergeant's departure & this was that 'she had been thinking more about it, since she saw me before, & would rather not have a certificate'. I asked her what had induced her to change her mind. 'She had thought more about it and believed it best for her to remain as she is'. This, of course, settled the business – we had no business to extract from her an unwilling confession of what had been said to her. But since she assured me, the time before, that 'she had been thinking of this ever since she came here, but had had no one to speak to, but persons who have her inconsistent accounts, & that she thought it best do nothing till she could learn what was the right step to take'. It is pretty clear that her own reflections could not have changed her opinion.

However, she has certainly been kindly treated for a slave, & taught, so far as concerns the common business of life & even Christianity (but she can neither write nor read) and if she is content in slavery, after freedom has been given her, it does not seem our business to interfere unless we are sure that unfair advantage has been taken of her.'

The subsequent history of this woman has not been found.

# 9

# A Plymouth missionary's view of South African slavery in 1815

In 1815 Frederick Hooper, an aspiring Congregationalist missionary, travelled to South Africa where he observed the state of slavery in a short account of his experiences. He was particularly interested in the expressions of Christianity amongst the white settlers in regards to their treatment of Africans. Hooper was from Plymouth and aged twenty-five when he visited Africa.[274]

> 'The Advocates of Slavery say the African tribes of Blacks are heathen, their practices, their customs, their habits are as bad or worse than those of ancient idolaters. They certainly do not varnish over their crimes with the name of sanctity and religious worship, and exhibit the depraved passions of man in their true character; but, does the Slave Dealer make them slaves to correct their vices, reform their habits, model their society, and by religious instruction lay a foundation for their present and eternal happiness? No.
> 
> No, their cupidity impels them to take them from the lands where they were born and transport them to distant regions, to do the work of brutes, and, all they show, by their conduct, they think of, is to gratify their avarice and keep the slaves in ignorance.
> 
> And, when persons come out as instructors, it is but grudgingly

they consent to their attendance at the Place of Public Worship, reading, still more grudgingly, and those who consent to the latter, except in very rare instances, forbid writing.

In Cape Town, Cape of Good Hope, as has been mentioned, persons belonging to a Missionary Society formed there persons even who are natives of the place are engaged in the religious instruction of the slaves, yet notwithstanding, of the thousands of slaves belonging to people in this town, seldom more than fifty receive religious instruction, and in the instruction of these, the sombre complexion of their rather hobbling zeal, throws a damp on the sanguine spirits of Europeans, and emanates like a dim light, amid the obscurity which surrounds them. And, their lazy exertions are palliated by the expressions, it is useless, it is vain, to try to beat anything into their heads – they remain the stupid and obstinate creatures still. The fact is, they are degraded, they are of little consideration in society, are excluded from the places of worship, where the White People are assembled, have little sometimes nothing to gain by their exertions; are entirely dependent on their masters & mistresses; are their property, and dare go nowhere without their leave and public security prevents them from being allowed to be out after dark. A slave is always considered a heathen or Mohammedan by their White Owners, even if able to give the fullest testimony of his conversion and faith in Christ, except by a few pious persons, and even these refuse him baptism. Thus the slave is still an outcast . . .'

## 10

## 'The Ballad of the Negro' in a Marystow cottage in 1828

An unusual pen and wash drawing of a cottage in Devon in 1828 was made by George Wightwick, a Plymouth architect. He wrote a caption which has a curious reference to slavery: in his 'Devonshire Interior, Number 2' at a time of great public interest in the emancipation of slaves.

> 'The principal object is Miss Damart, with her funny little 'puds' of feet, and the huge oval scuttle bonnet of the period, 1828. <u>Facts</u> should speak for themselves, and the observer, will observe that there is not one touch of imagination in the picture. I spoke of the 'youngest child', i.e. the youngest of the mother who was seen at the pasty in the last picture. The child in the cradle is her grandchild: ask no more. The little boy nursing it is also – equivocal: the Devonshire customs are speculative. The peasantry scorn regularity, as may be seen by the *Ballad of the Negro*, which is by no means 'square' with the horizontal of the joists above, or with the perpendicular of the chimney piece. The fire opening illustrates the fallacy of supposing that an arch cannot exist without a keystone. William Jacobson said 'he would come if it rained cats and dogs' but, as before mentioned, he came <u>not</u>. You anticipate his excuse, he came not because it

did not 'rain cats and dogs', a wretched joke! 1828! And I write this, in October, 1858! Thirty years ago! These sketches were all taken within the year first set down. George Wightwick, 13th October 1858.'

'The Negro Ballad' in a Marystow cottage
(Westcountry Studies Library, P&D09454)

## 11

## Devon slave owners in the mid 1830s

It is not yet possible to compile a list of all Devonians who owned slaves in the seventeenth, eighteenth and nineteenth centuries because the evidence is patchy and disparate. However, comprehensive records exist relating to the mid 1830s when the Emancipation Bill was passed: within this collection are details of the £10,000,000 given to owners for the loss of their slaves. They show that one of Devon's great county families, the Rolles of Stevenstone, owned slaves (see pages 106 to 111) in contrast to the Earls of Devon at Powderham, the Earls of Morley at Saltram, the Dukes of Somerset at Stover, the Dukes of Bedford at Endsleigh and the Earls Fortescue at Castle Hill. Fewer than one hundred Devon residents received compensation. They included some who acted as agents rather than as owners, including Henry Phillpotts, Bishop of Exeter, who received financial compensation in his capacity as an executor. Perhaps not surprisingly, a considerable number were West Indians who had retired to Devon's seaside resorts. Slave owners born outside the county outnumbered those who were native born. Some had built or rebuilt substantial properties before compensation money was given so it could be reasonably assumed that income from slave plantations contributed to the building costs. One residence which may have been constructed in part or completely with existing money from West Indian plantations is Follaton House at Totnes. George Stanley Cary, part of the Cary family of Torre Abbey, was born in London and inherited properties in St Kitts and St Croix. He rebuilt Follaton in 1826, nearly a decade before he received his emancipation compensation.[275]

The Devon-born slave owners included Sir William Templer Pole of

Shute House near Colyton. He inherited two plantations in St Kitts from his maternal grandfather in Essex. Likewise, George Pearse of Bradninch was another absentee owner: his plantations in Jamaica were acquired through his wife, the daughter of a West Indian planter who lived at Lower Duryard in Exeter. In contrast, Thomas Rossiter emigrated to Jamaica only to return to his native Tiverton in his middle years while George Cole had a similar history regarding Dawlish and Trinidad. Both men owned slave plantations.

Some individuals owned only a single slave, such as West Indian born Martha Moody who retired to Exeter or Reverend Hinds Howell who was born in Barbados but later became the cleric at Bridestowe and Shobrooke. They received between £35 and £38 (£2,373.05 - £2,576.45) in compensation. In contrast, the most significant slave owner in Devon was Thomas Daniel Junior. He was the fourth generation of his family to be born in Barbados but as a child had emigrated to England. Daniel had extensive land holdings in the West Indies but it was his shrewd business acumen and domination of Bristol's local government that earned him the title 'the king of Bristol'. He was given more than £135,000 in compensation, the equivalent of £9,153,180 today, and with this money he purchased the Stoodleigh estate near Tiverton. It became his third home.[276] William Hudson Heaven, another Bristollian, purchased the island of Lundy shortly after receiving his compensation money and there he built Millcombe House, now a Landmark Trust property.

Henry and Thomas Porter, two brothers from Demerara, purchased substantial properties near Exeter before they received compensation for the loss of their slaves. The former lived at Winslade House in Clyst St Mary from 1821 until his death in 1858. The latter came to Devon at the same time and resided at Rockbeare House which had an estate of some 900 acres. It was said at the time that 'his equipage of four horses was one of the most dashing and when he came forth *en grande tenue* [in full dress] the country folk rubbed their eyes.' In 1833 the men received £55,256 2s 8d or £3,746,437.67 in today's money. However, Thomas Porter's fortunes failed him: twenty years later one journalist commented 'Mr Porter, the generous squire, became an impoverished man. He had to put down his equipage, abandon his large house, for his West Indian property has melted away like a tropical mist.' Porter moved to a smaller property in Lympstone and five years later died one day after his wife had passed away.[277] The history of Porter's 385 former slaves living in Demerara, now Guyana, has not been written.

## 12

# John Scott of Lympstone and Emancipation at Trinidad, 1837

In 1837 and 1838 John Scott, a Devon man, served in Trinidad as a Special Magistrate. Scott later lived along the Exe Estuary at Lympstone. By 1848 he was friendly with Elihu Burritt and met him on his lecture tour of Devon at Exeter[278] where he was speaking on the League of Universal Brotherhood. Scott had been appointed by the Colonial Office as a Special Magistrate; they were required by the Emancipation Act to ensure that measures regarding the rights and living and working conditions of the slaves, renamed apprentices, were fairly enforced. Scott very quickly became embroiled in local politics and in the struggle between the interests of the plantation owners and the rights of the black workers. He was on the island on the evening in which the slaves were finally granted their freedom and his account provides fascinating insights.[279] Immediately after emancipation Scott met with the island's Royal Governor who promptly discharged him from his duties. He earlier had an indication his services might not be needed when he noted he:

> 'received the copy of a circular sent by Lord Glevely to the Special Magistrates informing them that Government would not bind itself to provide them with situations at the expiration of the apprenticeships in 1840. That after 1838 when the non-praedial are free there probably will be a diminution in the

Lympstone in 1827 (Westcountry Studies Library, SC1480)

number of the magistrates which will take place at the expense of those whose appointments are of the most recent date. Well, I care little about it, come what will, I am prepared to meet it.'

Scott returned to England where he was informed the Governor lacked authority to remove Scott from his position. Moreover, the Governor had employed compliant islanders who were subsequently fired by the Colonial Office. Scott appears to have then returned to Trinidad and afterwards sailed back to Exeter. He was married and living near Exeter at Lympstone by 1842.

During his two years on the island Scott oversaw justice in his part of Trinidad. In February 1837 he noted:

'Tuesday February 13. . . . [I] received a circular from the governor informing me that in my capacity as Special Magistrate I was to visit all the estates in my district, call up the apprentices, and ascertain by communication with them whether from the

Wednesday August 1st 1838 — South Naparima, Trinidad

This day will be justly celebrated in after times not only throughout the West Indies but throughout the whole British Empire, and I hope throughout the whole World — as the day on which the remaining dregs of Slavery was swept from off the British Dominions; and I trust the death blow is given to that detestable system, Slavery, all over the universe.

During the past night I was disturbed by continued Thunder, Lightning and rain of the true Tropical sort — Tremendous — Rose between 6 and 7 o'Clock — Thunder & Lightning passed and the rain abating. 8 o'Clock the rain has ceased, and it looks as if we should have a fine day — All is Tranquil, not a negro stirring abroad as yet. No set of people could have behaved more orderly than the negros have since the announcement was made that they were all to be made Free on this day. I have had numbers here since the announcement, which is only a week since, to express their gratitude for the boon, and they promised to be orderly, and work well for themselves, as they had done for their Employers. I have no doubt but they will. A negro drum in the distance and the report of a few guns, are the only demonstrations of Joy I have heard at this time. Took breakfast at 9 o'Clock — The liberated apprentices came from the different Estates in great numbers, Scores of them stopped at my house, and expressed their gratitude for their Freedom, and thanked me for the Kindness I had shewn them, and the good I had done them during their apprenticeship

after

John Scott's journal (Devon Record Office, Z19/36/19)

nature of their employment from 1832 to 1833 they had been wrongly classed or not, thinking it would have a bad effect, especially as the government had signified their intention to appoint commissioners for that purpose.'

Scott suggested that the Governor's administration of the island was muddled and noted that he shortly afterwards rescinded this particular order. His own personal attitudes towards slavery were revealed in another passage two months later regarding the 'apprentices', the slaves who were being given their freedom over a period of time.

'received this day the *Trinidad Standard* containing a new bill for the future regulation of the apprentices. One clause in it has afforded me much satisfaction viz. that men after the 1st of September next are not to be flogged for offences committed for which free men may not be punished in a like manner. This I think is a very wise piece of legislation, as it will prevent many a captious little personages, just popped into power, exercising their love of tyranny, by threatening good men (from any pique they feel towards them) to have them flogged and then teasing and tormenting the magistrate by exercising their loquacious powers in order to prove that these poor devils deserve it, and if the magistrate happens to differ from these little Great Personages, they travel all over the country saying the magistrate has been the cause of the ruin of the estate, and the continued disobedience of the apprentices by not giving them justice back. I am sick of the whole system, pray God the time was arrived when the Slave will be wholly free. But this clause will free us from some of our vexatious trouble, because when imprisonment will be the only punishment complaints will be fewer as the employers will not like to lose the apprentices' time, and I have no doubt but the apprentice will feel the degradation of imprisonment and avoid the crimes which will render it necessary to be resorted to.'

The apprentices were unhappy with future arrangements for them. A few days later, on April 28, he continued to list them and explain the responsibilities to their owners.

'Went with Mr C. Campbell to Golconda Estate, revised the registered list of apprentices, called them all up and explained the law to them. They grumbled at having to serve 2 years longer than the House Servants, had a long talk with them, and returned home.'

At the end of his journal he wrote an extraordinary account of the key moment.

'Trinidad Wednesday August 1st 1838, South Naparind
This day will be justly celebrated in after times not only throughout the West Indies but throughout the whole British Empire and I hope throughout the whole world as the day on which the remaining dregs of Slavery was swept from off the British Dominions, and I hope the death blow is given to that detestable system, Slavery, all over the Universe.

During the past night, I was disturbed by continued Thunder, Lightning and rain of the true Tropical sort – <u>Tremendous</u>. Rose between 6 and 7 o'clock – thunder and lightning passed and the rain abating, 8 o'clock the rain has ceased, and it looks as if we should have a fine day – all is tranquil, not a Negro stirring abroad as yet. No set of people could have behaved more orderly than the Negroes have since the announcement was made that they were all to be made Free this day. I have had numbers here since the announcement, which is only a week since, to express their gratitude, for the boon, and they promised to be orderly, and work well for themselves, as they had done for their employers. I have no doubt but they will. A Negro drum in the distance and the report of a few guns, are the only demonstrations of joy I have heard at this time. I took breakfast at 9 o'clock – the liberated apprentices came from the different estates in great numbers, scores of them stopped at my house, and expressed their gratitude for their freedom, and thanked me for the kindness I had shown them, and the good I had done them during their apprenticeship. After breakfast I went to the Roman Catholic Chapel where some hundred of the Liberated Apprentices were congregated to hear the Reverend Mr Cahill preach. He addressed them in a plain and forcible style, stating to them the great boon of liberty bestowed on them by the British

Nation, and exhorting them to habits of industry, honesty and sobriety – assuring them the more they cultivated those habits the happier they would be here and hereafter, and that if they departed from them they must inevitably become miserable. The Reverend Gentleman's discourse appeared to make a deep impression on their minds. He desired them to go after Divine Service was over quietly and orderly to their estates, which they did, for in a few hours after, not an estate apprentice was to be seen in San Ferdinando, all was peace and quietness. I was there all day and I did not see or hear of a single breach of the peace. But on the contrary the liberated apprentices appeared religiously impressed with gratitude to god for his merciful kindness to them.

I never in the whole course of my life received so many thanks and blessings as I have received this day from the grateful Negroes. Oh! How I wish for some of my Emancipating Friends from dear old England to have been with me to share in my feelings. Me thinks, I am repaid for all my toils, and all my three long years of labour, and sacrifice. What is to be my future lot, and the part destined for me to perform in the Drama of Human Life I know not. But this I do know, that if I am destined by the great and glorious change, to live without any salary for the next two years, I can never regret the change, nor would I did I had the power, again enslave the Negro by the anomalous name of apprentices for the whole of my lost salary.

Thus ends the glorious 1st of August 1838 which I hope I shall ever on the return of it commemorate as a Holy Day.

Tomorrow I intend going to Port of Spain to see the Governor and shall then determine whether I shall remain any longer here in this Island or return immediately to England.'

Scott noted, with some satisfaction, that the governor died shortly after being suspected of corruption. Scott himself will be remembered in a different light.

# 13

# Dahlia Graham of Senegal, the West Indies and Exeter Workhouse, 1854

In 1854 an Exeter man visited the city's workhouse, a grand late seventeenth-century building which formerly stood on Heavitree Road. He wrote of it for *The Western Luminary and Family Newspaper for Devon, Cornwall, Somerset and Dorset* as part of a series on the state of the poor. This unknown writer, who used the *nom de plume* 'A White Slave', observed the public was fascinated about the poor in novels and thought they should be equally interested to learn about their real lives. His reports appeared after the trials of local people who were in bread riots the previous year.[280]

> 'The White Slave' toured the workhouse and saw the efforts made to make the inhabitants productive and the care taken of them. He approved of much of it except for married paupers not being allowed to remain together.

His most astonishing description is of Dahlia Graham, a woman of 93 whom he first sighted seated in a cane chair. He recounted her life history: she had been kidnapped from Africa as a child, sold into slavery, shipped to the Americas and then released with emancipation. In his opinion Miss Graham 'rejoiced' in her accommodation and in the care she received: she was 'somewhat eloquent', 'exceedingly happy' and 'very grateful'. Also, he suggested her life was better than had she

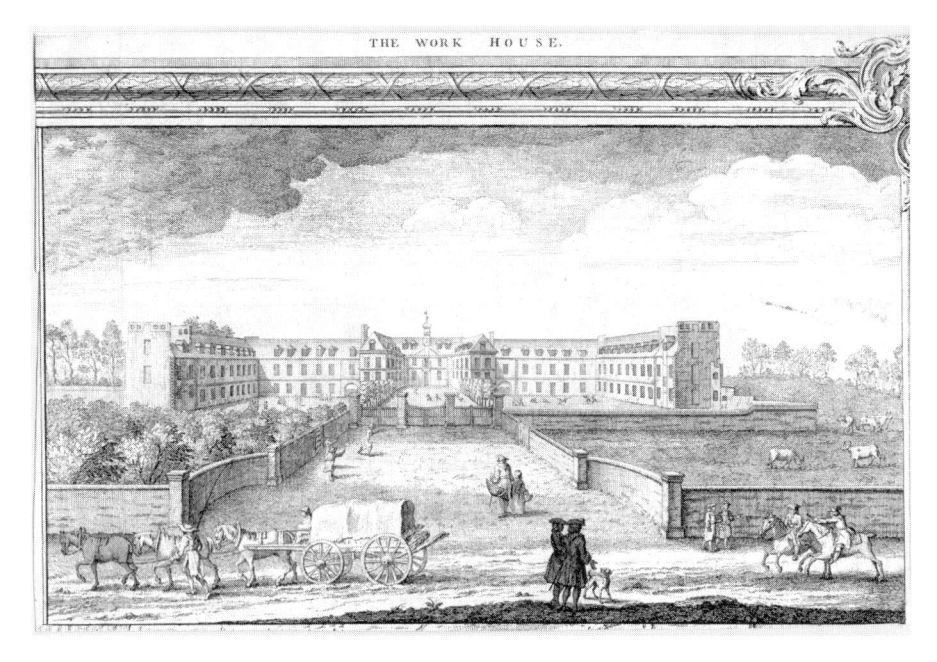

Exeter Workhouse in 1744 (Westcountry Studies Library, SC0999)

stayed in Africa. The census of 1851 listed Delia Graham as employed as a General Upper Servant in a house in Hill's Court Road, later called Pennsylvania Road. Another source, *The Exeter Journal and Almanack*,[281] shows the house was known as Rose Cottage.

Miss Graham was listed in the census as having been born in Senegal and the household head was Mrs Harriet Louisa Wardrobe (otherwise Wardrope), a widow aged 76. Presumably the Wardrobe family retained the former slave as a paid servant until sometime between 1851 and 1854 when, after a lifetime of service, she was sent to the workhouse. Mrs Wardrobe died shortly afterwards.

> 'The Aged-women's-ward (below) has 13 beds occupied now by 14 persons: at one end, separated by a petition, is the Day-ward for the same parties. At the moment we entered they had congregated round the fireplace, and their appearance was somewhat grotesque. We approached and observed one old lady seated in a cane-wrought chair with considerable ease and dignity. She saluted us blandly, and we soon observed that she was of African blood. A novel sight in our Union-house!

Around her head was bound a many-coloured kerchief, in that fantastic style that obtains in tropical climates. She was somewhat eloquent; exceedingly happy, and very grateful. She told us that her name was Dahlia Graham, given her by an English family, to whom she was sold by a slave-dealer in the West Indies, of that name. She was the eldest of four children, and was very young when placed in the bonds of captivity. From the hands of Mr Graham she passed to those of Mr Wardrobe, who was, when she was sold to him, a large plantation holder, but the policy of our governments towards the West India planters having beggared many, the Wardrobe family, have been sufferers, and Dahlia rejoices in her present happy position. Such are the mutations of sublunary things! Dahlia, kidnapped in Africa, endured the horrors of the middle passage, was sold into bondage in our colonies, and now at the patriarchal age of 93, she has a mansion to live in, gardens to live in, and the lieges of the Queen of England to minister to her wants! Fortunate Dahlia. How different an end to that which would, probably, have awaited her in her own country!'

Harriet Louisa Baillie was born in the United States and in 1812 married William Wardrobe, a Scot, in Georgia. Seven months later he died. Mrs Wardrobe continued to live in Savannah through the 1830s but by 1841 had taken part of her household across the Atlantic to live at Premier Place in Exeter. Presumably Miss Graham, who was not given a surname in the 1841 census but only listed as 'Delia', was given her freedom upon arrival in England. In contrast, her fellow slaves she had left behind in Georgia were bequeathed by Mrs Wardrobe to her brother in 1857.[281]

# 14

# Lord St Maur's diary of the American Civil War, 1861

A diary kept by Lord St Maur during the American Civil War is held in the Devon Record Office and illustrates attitudes towards slavery nearly a generation after it was illegal in the British Empire. The war was fought between the northern and southern states and one key issue was the continuation of slavery in the South.[282] The writer was Edmund Percy Seymour who was the second son of the 12th Duke of Somerset. He was born in 1841 and at the age of twenty visited America. In his diary he expresses his opinions of abolitionists and slaves. There were other Englishmen covering the war, such as William Howard Russell a war correspondent for *The Times* who published his account in two volumes,[283] but this writer recorded his thoughts in a small personal diary and then rewrote some of it for *Blackwood's Magazine*. The young lord wrote that when he returned to England 'I was Northern when I went over but came back a Southerner'.[284]

He wrote in his diary:

> 'The attempt to make England believe that this is a holy war for the freedom of the blacks, that as it is said Queen Victoria is now supporting slaves as Queen Elizabeth formerly introduced it, is one of those attempts at falsity. Almost all the majority of the respectable men in armies now in the field hate the abolitionists more than they do the southerners against whom

*Abolition and Emancipation*

they are fighting and rightly, for these men have been mainly instrumental in bringing this miserable war on the country and they display so great an ignorance on the subject on which they have been perpetually discoursing that they can arrive at no practical mode of dealing with the few thousand Negroes that have run away, far less with the four million now inhabiting the south, in Washington ...'

Lord St Maur died not long after he returned to England. It has been suggested this happened in 1869 in India when he was mauled and eaten by a tiger but his death occurred four years earlier, in 1865, after being wounded by a bear.[285]

## 15

## Slave entertainment in Devon, 1867

Throughout the nineteenth century, and continuing until nearly the end of the twentieth, entertainment based on slave culture was regularly performed in Devon, as in the rest of the country, by either travelling American blacks or white men in blackface. Performances took place in Exeter in 1867, shortly after the end of the American Civil War. A generation after the emancipation of slaves throughout the British Empire, slavery had become a popular form of entertainment not just to be enjoyed but relished. Sixteen former slaves performed in Exeter and an advertisement alerted local people of their arrival.[286]

'Royal Public Rooms
Friday, Saturday, Monday and Tuesday, June 7th, 8th, 10th and 11th
The Great American Slave Troupe
and Brass Band
from the United States.
Sixteen natural talented artistes
who, prior to June, 1865, were slaves in America, now on a tour through England, have appeared in the Theatre Royal, Liverpool; Free Trade Hall, Manchester; New Exchange Rooms, Birmingham; and most of the principal towns in England, giving THEIR OWN and the only true representation of NEGRO LIFE on
the plantations of America.
PLANTATION SCENES, SONGS AND DANCES.

> New and original burlesques, pleasing ballads,
> New, by American authors;
> comic ditties and banjo music,
> all given in that peculiar and mirth provoking manner
> characteristic of the Negro Race.
> Admission – 6d, 1s and 2s
> Doors open at a quarter-past seven, to commence at eight o'clock.
> W.H. Lee, advertising agent,
> Sam Hague, Manager.
> Carriages can be ordered at ten o'clock.'

On the day they appeared in Exeter one newspaper pre-empted their performance with a report.[287]

> 'A clever troupe of genuine Negro minstrels will give a series of entertainments at the Royal Public Rooms in this city, commencing this Friday evening. The talent of the company is highly spoken of by our Liverpool and Swansea contemporaries, at which places they have lately been performing. The troupe (who also form a brass band) is under the direction of Mr Sam Hague, whose success in the organisation of the minstrels justly supports the title given him of the 'Veteran Minstrel King'. We should state that all the Negroes prior to June 1865 were slaves in the Southern American state of Georgia and therefore the Exeter public will have an opportunity of witnessing a representation of the real life of the Negro on the plantations of America and the natural characters of humour with which the black race are said to be endowed.'

A subsequent review was even more enthusiastic.[288]

> **'American Slave Troupe**
> On Wednesday and Thursday evenings a party of Negro Minstrels, travelling under the above title, gave entertainments at the Athenaeum. The entertainments were far superior to anything of their kind which have lately been given in this town; for besides displaying considerable ability and genuine Negro humour on the part of many of the numerous company, it was perfectly unexceptionable in every sense. This troupe possessed

the advantage of being real unmistakable 'darkies', and though some of them had evidently deepened their line (a mistake in the way of taste we think) still they were genuine Negroes and not impostors in the shape of coloured white men. The troupe form an excellent brass band, and played through the streets during the afternoon of both days, making their appearance preceded by their manager, Mr Sam Hague, and one of the company bearing aloft the 'Star-spangled banner' of their native land, a compliment which would hardly be appreciated in America were an English Company to imitate it by parading the Union Jack through one of their towns to attract an audience. The company is a very numerous one and consists of some 16 or more persons. The programme necessarily included a good deal of vocal music, the singing was really good, and one or two of the solo singers had voices much above the average, 'Where are the friends of my youth?', 'Sweet Home' and 'Lilly Dale' were admirably rendered with much pathos. Between the pieces there was the usual cross fire of banter and repartee kept up between the 'bones' and tambourine man, both of whom were capital in their way, their by-play and facial contortions being comic in the extreme. Mr Day, who played a violin solo with great ability, responded to a well-merited encore, as did also Mr Wright after singing 'Sweet Home'. But one of the most wonderful performances of the evening was the 'Bone solo', for not only was the performer a thorough master of the 'bones' but a proficient in extraordinary feats of agility and strength. While keeping time on the bones he lifted a tumbler of water, placed it on his forehead, and balanced it there, while he knelt, laid down, and rose again, playing all the time in all manner of positions, then he took up a chair by the back in his teeth and went through the same performance of lying down with it still vigorously rattling the bones, after some other feats of agility he retired amidst deafening and well-merited applause. 'Scenes in the planter's kitchen' were much appreciated, and created great amusement. The whole entertainment was an excellent one, and gave great satisfaction to the audience. The attendance was only middling on Wednesday, the room being not more than half-full, but on Thursday there was a good house.'

# Conclusion

Several themes emerge from this collection of documents. Clearly the voyages of Sir John Hawkins are noteworthy in their importance not merely to Devon but to the history of English exploration and colonialism as well as to general Atlantic history. The audaciousness of Hawkins' actions, as his travels took in three continents, leaps out from his accounts. The difficulties he faced in slaving and then in trading with the Spanish no doubt made other mariners hesitate to follow his lead. Yet, what he achieved in the 1560s became outdated for the later sixteenth century: other Devon men found privateering to be more lucrative and less problematic. Hawkins' voyages proved to be an aberration and a more 'traditional' local activity took hold which continued to dominate Devon's maritime affairs in time of war: it may be that Devon's subsequent lack of interest in slavery in the seventeenth and eighteenth centuries was because of a continuing relish for privateering.

Hawkins's voyages are so well known that they have overshadowed other themes which hopefully the remaining documents help to bring out. These show a range of ways, most of which have not registered in the public consciousness, in which slavery impacted upon Devon, some of them unexpected. The enslaving of Devonians in North Africa is one. It is a reminder of how localised history can be: Devon was more harmed by the Barbary Corsairs than any other part of Britain and consequently it was a greater issue in the county than elsewhere. It was at this time that other parts of England were leading the way in enslaving Equatorial Africans. Several of the documents illustrate how individuals thought about slavery: the writings of Captain Stedman provide insights as to how people in the past lived with it and the account by Lieutenant Incledon-Webber of his voyage along the African coast shows his resentment at having to enforce Parliament's regulations which limited the number of slaves which could be transported per ship. When faced with the unhealthy conditions onboard the slave vessels his hostility was not to the slavers but to the Quakers for whom he blamed the new law. Other documents in this collection have shown what has been an under-appreciated history of abolitionism in Devon and no doubt more details will emerge of the roles of individuals from the various churches. The few plantation accounts which survive are important in their minute details. These are a startling reminder of the human face of slavery. Too often the documents are not concerned with this aspect of individual life but these particular records, which recorded people alongside animals as property, are a reminder of how humanity can be lost. Nonetheless, their real impact and worth will probably be realised on those islands in the West Indies and on the North American continent where the slavery took place.

It is unlikely that enough material will come forward to demonstrate Devon's economy was built on slavery. Doubtless there are other estates and houses which benefited from plantation investment and more information will emerge on other slaving voyages. Those that have been found to date appear to indicate a half-heartedness in the efforts that were made. No Devon merchant built a family fortune from these few voyages and some, like that of the *Daniel & Henry*, lost money. Where money was made was in importing plantation goods. Port books and customs accounts in any year for any Devon port show a small number of ships arrived with plantation goods. Even so, some men and women specialised in West Indian trades as well as in importing southern American goods, particularly rice and tobacco. Those that gained financially from these commodities, as either importer or consumer, were complicit in slavery in the same way as those today who buy imports of cheap goods produced in Asia or Africa from poor wages or by prison labour. The differences are negligible between a cup of eighteenth-century sugar and many items of clothing in Britain's shops today.

Nearly every other aspect of Devon's history which is written today makes easier reading. Even so, it is important to tackle uncomfortable subjects and this study shows some of the ways, some surprising, in which slavery has touched Devon's history. No doubt studies of other parts of Britain would show some similarities as well as differences. It would be naïve to suggest race does not matter today in Devon but these documents are a reminder of how much more so it once did. Race, alongside religion, gender and wealth, have shaped the county's history as in the rest of humanity. This collection of Devon documents shows their influence on our ancestors and, in turn, on us today. How they are interpreted, and what impact they might have, relies upon the reader.

I have expanded upon the theme of prejudice and hate in *Not One Of Us* (2018), a history of the separation of individuals from the rest of society in Exeter. These examples of other peoples' lives show how we were constantly challenged not just by our physical differences but also by new ideas and thinking. The course from exclusion to toleration, acceptance and inclusion has often been hesitant, uncertain and gradual but it has, in many instances, been successful though much remains to be done. What is clear is that one cannot be fully understood without examining the others. The legacy of the African slave trade remains uncomfortable, and divisive, but we are only now appreciating the complexities and course of that history. What is becoming clear is that Devon, as it now is, owes much to both the sufferings and the achievements of countless people who were enslaved, even though many of them will never have known that Devon existed, let alone the role their labour was to play in its development.

# Notes

1. Jeremy Black, *The Slave Trade* (2006), 132.
2. See the letters pages of the *Western Morning News* for the spring of 2007; *Western Morning News*, 1 December 2006.
3. *Express & Echo*, 14/6/2007.
4. www.foda.org.uk.
5. W. G. Hoskins, *Devon* (Newton Abbot, 1954).
6. Bernard Susser, *The Jews of South-West England* (Exeter, 1993); Helen Fry, *The Jews of North Devon* (Tiverton, 2006).
7. This was noted in a history of Devon published in 1986 in which the author wrote 'the county of the slaver Hawkins and the East India pilot John Davis has not attracted many coloured people': Robin Stanes, *A History of Devon* (Chichester, 1986), 121.
8. Devon Record Office, Winkleigh parish register, 24 December 1818. I am grateful to Joyce Totterdell for this reference.
9. Plymouth & West Devon Record Office, Charles Church parish register, 10 August 1783.
10. Ilfracombe Museum, Raparee Cove Box; *Western Morning News*, 25/2/1997, 26/2/1997, 2/3/1997, 8/4/1997, 29/1/2001, 8/2/2001, 19/5/2001; Mark Horton, 'Bones of Contention', *Nonesuch*, Autumn 1998, 40-1.
11. Ilfracombe Museum, Raparee Cove box, poster.
12. *Express & Echo*, 27 April 2001.
13. It was there sometime between 1688 and 1743: E. A. G. Clark, *The Ports of the Exe Estuary, 1660–1860* (Exeter, reprinted 1968), 68-70.
14. Lucy McKeith, *Local Black History; a beginning in Devon* (London, 2003), 7.

## Notes

15. See Joyce Youings, *Tuckers Hall Exeter* (Exeter, 1968).
16. Editors' introduction to Mike Duffy, Stephen Fisher, Basil Greenhill and Joyce Youings (eds), *The New Maritime History of Devon* (1992), I, 14.
17. Devon Record Office, Sidmouth parish register.
18. Devon Record Office, ECA, petitions to the chamber for relief, benefits, offices, etc, 4/1, 4/20, 4/14.
19. Devon Record Office, Chanter 862, 170 & 143.
20. Westcountry Studies Library, pxB/EXE/098.1/BLA U.
21. Todd Gray, *Devon Household Accounts, 1627-56*, II (Devon & Cornwall Record Society, NS 39, 1996), 33, 52, 65, 117, 173, 178, 206, 248, 297.
22. G. E. M. de Ste Croix, 'Slavery and other forms of unfree labour' in Leonie J. Archer, *Slavery and other forms of unfree labour* (1988), 21-3.
23. Devon Record Office, DQS/128/15.
24. Hugh Thomas, *The Slave Trade: The history of the Atlantic Slave Trade, 1440-1870* (1997), 471-4.
25. Thomas, *The Slave Trade*, 805.
26. Philip D. Curtin, *The Atlantic Slave Trade: A Census* (Madison, 1969), 5, 7.
27. This estimates that 2 slaves were transported for every ton of the ships listed and Drake's 2nd and 3rd voyages had the same number of slaves taken as his first. An average was taken for those Devon ten per centers which did not list their tonnage for those which did. It also excludes the French ships which left from Plymouth following the Seven Years' War.
28. Elizabeth Donnan (ed.), *Documents Illustrative Of the History of the Slave Trade to America* (New York, 1965), I, 14; Black, *Slave Trade*, 28.
29. The accounts were published as part of Richard Hakluyt's *The Principal Navigations, voyages & traffiques & discoveries of the English Nation made by sea or overland to the remote and farthest distant quarters of the earth at any time within the compass of these 1600 years*. The following notes are taken from the Everyman's Library edition; Harry Kelsey, *Sir Francis Drake* (New Haven, 1998), 25-39 & *Sir John Hawkins* (New Haven, 2003), 15, 19, 56, 66, 77.
30. North Devon Record Office, Barnstaple parish register. One copy of each entry was edited by Thomas Wainwright in his *Barnstaple Parish Register* (Exeter, 1903).
31. Todd Gray (ed.), *The Lost Chronicle of Barnstaple, 1586-1611* (Exeter, 1998).
32. J. F. Chanter, 'On Certain Documents Relating to the History of Lynton and Countisbury', *Transactions of the Devonshire Association* (XXXVIII, 1906), 240. I am grateful to the Friends of Devon's Archives for this reference.
33. Gray, *Lost Chronicle*, 68-9.

36. Gray, *Devon Household Accounts*, II, 297.
37. Todd Gray (ed.), *The Lost Chronicle of Barnstaple, 1586–1611* (Exeter, 1998), 21-3.
38. Todd Gray, 'Turkish Piracy and Early Stuart Devon', *Transactions of the Devonshire Association*, 121, 1989, 159-71.
39. Anon., *A Description of the Nature of Slavery Amongst The Moors & The Cruel Sufferings Of Those That Fall Into It* (1721), 20.
40. Thomas, *The Slave Trade*, 591.
41. National Archives, SP71/13/29.
42. National Archives, SP71/13/31.
43. Tattersfield, *The Forgotten Trade*, 15.
44. Tattersfield, *The Forgotten Trade*, 282.
45. Donnan, *Documents*, II, 31.
46. Tattersfield, *The Forgotten Trade*, 281, 426.
47. The information is taken from David Richardson (ed.), *Bristol, Africa and the Eighteenth Century Slave Trade to the Americas* (Bristol Record Society, 1986), XXXVIII, 1-2; Tattersfield, *The Forgotten Trade*, 227-76.
48. Tattersfield, *The Forgotten Trade*, 227-76.
49. David Richardson (ed.), *Bristol, Africa and the Eighteenth Century Slave Trade to the Americas* (Bristol Record Society, 1986), XXXVIII, xvi.
50. Tattersfield, *The Forgotten Trade*, 36.
51. Joyce Youings, *Tuckers Hall* (Exeter, 1968).
52. Devon Record Office, 3327Aadd/pz23; Tattersfield, *The Forgotten Trade*, 124.
53. Tattersfield, *The Forgotten Trade*, 36, 39, 184.
54. These have been described by Tattersfield on page 124.
55. James A. Rawley, *The Transatlantic Slave Trade; a history* (New York, 1981), 243 citing F. C. P. Naish, 'Extracts from a Slaver's Log', F. C. Prideaux Naish, 'Extracts from a slavery's log', *Mariner's Mirror*, vol. 6, no. 1 (1920), 9, 10.
56. Tattersfield, *The Forgotten Trade*, 120, 282, 306.
57. Tattersfield, *The Forgotten Trade*, 282-6.
58. Tattersfield, *The Forgotten Trade*, 183, 306-7.
59. Tattersfield, *The Forgotten Trade*, 286-7.
60. Tattersfield, *The Forgotten Trade*, 303.
61. Tattersfield, *The Forgotten Trade*, 290-3.
62. Donnan, *Documents*, II, 29-30.
63. D. J. Starkey, *British Privateering Enterprise in the Eighteenth Century* (Exeter, 1990), 89-90.
64. Topsham Museum.
65. *Journal of the Commissioners for Trade, 1750 to 1753* (1935), 22, 25.

66. Donnan, *Documents*, II, 507.
67. *Journal of the Commissioners for Trade, January 1759 to December 1763* (1935), 30.
68. James A. Rawley, *The Transatlantic Slave Trade* (1981), 242-3.
69. National Archives, BT 6/3/153.
70. National Archives, E190/1079/2.
71. Sheila Lambert (ed.), *House of Commons Sessional of the Eighteenth Century* (Wilmington, Delaware, 1975), vol. 67.
72. Starkey, *British Privateering*, 165.
73. North Devon Record Office, 3704M/O5. Lysons places the family at Yeotown in Goodleigh by 1822 but originally of Incldeon in Braunton since the reign of Edward III: Daniel & Samuel Lysons, *Magna Brittania: Devon* (1822), clxviii.
74. Johnson U. J. Asieqbu, *Slavery and the Politics of Liberation, 1787–1861* (1969), 8. According to Captain John Taylor of the *Myler* he signed a treaty on 22 August 1788.
75. British Library, Add Ms 18989.
76. North Devon Record Office, 3704M/06.
77. The Chairman of the Committee of the Relief of the Black Poor: Asieqbu, *Slavery and the Politics of Abolition*, 54.
78. Plymouth & West Devon Record Office, 710/582.
79. Plymouth & West Devon Record Office, 216/1 (2).
80. Black, *The Slave Trade*, 113.
81. *Exeter Flying Post*, 31/7/1845.
82. *Exeter Flying Post*, 7/7/1845.
83. *Exeter Flying Post*, 18/12/1845.
84. Alison Grant, 'Bermuda Adventurer: John Delbridge of Barnstaple, 1564 –1639', *Bermuda Journal of Archaeology and Maritime History*, Vol. 3 (1991), 1-17.
85. See Devon Record Office, 1508M.
86. For example, see the Willoughby family of East Devon: Todd Gray (ed.), *Devon Household Accounts, 1627-59* (Devon & Cornwall Record Society, NS 38, 1995), I, xlii.
87. Todd Gray, 'Devon's fisheries and Early-Stuart New England' in Mike Duffy *et al* (eds), *The New Maritime History of Devon* (1992) I, 139-44; Devon Record Office, Z8/1/5a-b.
88. Devon Record Office, ECA, Letters 373-6 & 603.
89. One example of ongoing research concerns the Davy family and its early-nineteenth century plantation at Topsham, Jamaica. This is currently being investigated by volunteers at Topsham Museum.
90. Devon Record Office, 5139B/F/1.
91. W. B. Pollard, 'William Pollard of Devon and the West Indies and some of

his descendants', *Journal of the Barbados Museum History Society*, 1958, 54-74.
92. Plymouth & West Devon Record Office, 874.
93. Devon Record Office, 281M/T885&886. The will of James Lyde of Staunton Drew, Somerset, 1731, notes he had a share in a plantation near the Potomoc River in Virginia with 'negroes'.
94. K. G. Davies, *The Royal African Company* (1957), 38.
95. Richard A. Preston, *Gorges of Plymouth Fort* (Toronto, 1953).
96. Devon Record Office, Withycombe Raleigh parish register.
97. Thomas, *The Slave Trade*, 201; Davies, *The Royal African Company*, 1-44, 89-91, 128.
98. *Journal of the House of Commons*, vol. 16, 240.
99. *Journal of the House of Commons*, vol. 16, 259.
100. *Journal of the House of Commons*, vol. 16, 260.
101. Elizabeth Donnan (ed.), *Documents Illustrative Of the History of the Slave Trade to America* (New York, 1965), Vol. II, 97.
102. Davies, *The Royal African Company*, 93, 166.
103. Elizabeth Donnan (ed.), *Documents Illustrative Of the History of the Slave Trade to America* (New York, 1965), Vol. II, 140-1.
104. Davies, *The Royal African Company*, 44-6, 179.
105. Youings, *Tuckers Hall*, 86-8.
106. Youings, *Tuckers Hall*, 104-108, 167; David Seward, 'The Devonshire Cloth Industry in the Early Seventeenth Century', in Roger Burt (ed.), *Industry & Society in the South West (Exeter Papers in Economic History*, Exeter, 1970), 29-49.
107. Youings, *Tuckers Hall*, 86-7; Davies, *The Royal African Company*, 165-79, 352.
108. Tattersfield, *The Forgotten Trade*, 369-74.
109. Devon Record Office, 337B/1/435 (46/5).
110. Henry Nelson Coleridge, *Six Months in the West Indies in 1825* (1826), 109-110.
111. Todd Gray (ed.), *Travels in Georgian Devon* (Tiverton, 1997), I, xi.
112. Devon Record Office, Z19/40/10a. He was pursuing the legal case before the Privy Council in 1793.
113. Devon Record Office, 388M/E2. There are several other accounts and letters in this small collection.
114. Robert Legg, *A Pioneer in Xanadu* (Whitchurch, Hants, 1997).
115. National Archives, T77/15/194-5.
116. Legg, *Xanadu*, 131.
117. John Gabriel Stedman, *Narrative of a five years' expedition against the revolted Negroes of Surinam, in Guiana, on the Wild Coast of South America, from the year 1772 to 1777* (London, 1806), two volumes.

118. Stedman, *Narrative*, II, 321.
119. Stanbury Thompson, *The Journal of John Gabriel Stedman, 1744–1797; soldier and author* (1962), 339, 395.
120. Thompson, *Journal*, 337.
121. John Bourne (ed.), *Georgian Tiverton; the political memoranda of Beavis Wood, 1768*-98 (Devon & Cornwall Record Society, NS 29, 1986), 139.
122. Thompson, *Journal*, vi.
123. Stedman, *Narrative*, I, v.
124. Stedman, *Narrative*, I, 211.
125. Stedman, *Narrative*, I, 314-315.
126. Stedman, *Narrative*, 339-40.
127. Stedman, *Narrative*, II, 224.
128. Stedman, *Narrative*, I, 211.
129. Stedman, *Narrative*, I, 23.
130. Thompson, *Journal*, 119.
131. Stedman, *Narrative*, I, 29-30.
132. Thompson, *Journal*, 121.
133. Stedman, *Narrative*, I, 93-5.
134. Stedman, *Narrative*, I, 93.
135. Thompson, *Journal*, 122.
136. Stedman, *Narrative*, I, 103, 310.
137. Stedman, *Narrative*, I, 111-112.
138. Stedman, *Narrative*, I, 113.
139. Stedman, *Narrative*, I, 373.
140. Thompson, *Journal*, 151.
141. Thompson, *Journal*, 123-4, 143.
142. Thompson, *Journal*, 203, 221.
143. Thompson, *Journal*, 237.
144. Thompson, *Journal*, 241, 243, 242.
145. Thompson, *Journal*, 375-6.
146. Thompson, *Journal*, 276-7.
147. Stedman, *Narrative*, II, 416; Thompson, *Journal*, 341.
148. Bourne, *Georgian Tiverton*, 150, 170.
149. Thompson, *Journal*, 399.
150. Thompson, *Journal*, 398.
151. Thompson, *Journal*, 369.
152. Thompson, *Journal*, 307-309.
153. Devon Record Office, 337Badd3/1/8/2.
154. Coleridge, *Six Months*, 194-5.
155. Devon Record Office, 49/14.
156. The volume was purchased on 5 May 1949 from Messrs. Pearse & Sons of Exeter.

157. Devon Record Office, Z19/21/38/4.
158. E. A. G. Clark, *The Ports of the Exe Estuary, 1660-1860* (Exeter, 1968), 69; Aileen Fox, 'The Retreat, Topsham', *Devon Archaeology Society Proceedings*, No. 39, 1991, 131; Plymouth & West Devon Record Office, W327, fo.86r; Plymouth & West Devon Record Office, 407/3/11/2 & W192/1, p.15.
159. Todd Gray (ed.), *Travels in Georgian Devon* (Tiverton, 1998), II, 80.
160. National Archives, E190/965/11.
161. Llewellynn Jewitt, *A History of Plymouth* (Plymouth and London, 1873), 637-8; R. N. Worth, *History of Plymouth* (Plymouth, 1890), 321-2.
162. Thomas, *The Slave Trade*, 549, 555.
163. James Walvin, 'The Public Campaign in England against Slavery, 1787–1834', 63-5, in David Eltis and James Walvin (eds), *The Abolition of the Atlantic Slave Trade* (Madison, 1981).
164. Vincent Carretta, *Equiano, the African* (Athens, Georgia, 2005), 86-8.
165. National Archives, ADM 1/927.
166. Plymouth & West Devon Record Office, St Andrew's parish register.
167. Carretta, *Equiano*, 86-8.
168. 'Peter Hope, a black boy privately baptised during his sickness', buried on 19 June 1800 at St Andrew's: Plymouth & West Devon Record Office, Bishop's Transcripts Reel 27; William Cousins, a black lad about 18 or 19 years of age, a native of Maryland in America' baptised on 24 May 1779, 'George Handerson, a black lad about 12 years of age brought from Jamaica by Philip Couch' baptised 8 June 1781, 'Peter Vinson from the coast of Guinea about 22 years of age a black' baptised 14 August 1783, 'James Oliver from the coast of Guinea about 21 years of age a black' baptised 14 August 1783, 'George Thompson from St Kits about 24 years of age a black' baptised 1 September 1783, 'William Day a black man and a native of the coast of Guinea' baptised 21 April 1784, 'John William, a black lad a native of George Town America' baptised 20 August 1797: Plymouth & West Devon Record Office, East Stonehouse baptism register. I would like to thank Janet Henwood for these references.
169. Westcountry Studies Library, Davy family folder, citing William Henry Grimmer, *Anecdotes of the Bench and Bar* (1852), 40.
170. Westcountry Studies Library, Davy family folder, Harry Hems' article.
171. Westcountry Studies Library, Davy family folder, sheet on William Davy taken from W. R. Crabbe's scrap book.
172. Michael Craton, James Walvin and David Wright (eds), *Slavery, Abolition and Emancipation* (1976), 169-70; Donnan, *Documents*, II, liii.
173. *Dictionary of National Biography*.
174. Simon Schama, *Rough Crossings* (2005), 67-8.
175. *Somerset v. Stewart*, (1772) Lofft 1.

## Notes

176. Devon Record Office, DQS/Box 1786. I am grateful to Gill Selley for this reference.
177. Vincent Carretta, *Equiano The African* (Athens, Georgia, 2005).
178. Paul Edwards (ed.), *Equiano's Travels* (1967), 164-9.
179. Devon Record Office, 152M/C1784/F54.
180. Devon Record Office, 152M/C1784/F55.
181. Devon Record Office, 152M/C1784/OZ28.
182. Devon Record Office, 152M/C1790/OZ21.
183. Devon Record Office, 152M/1803/OL16.
184. Devon Record Office, 152M/C1817/OC2.
185. Devon Record Office, 152M/C1824/OC6. I am grateful to Bonhams for allowing me to see these documents which temporarily are in their care. Photocopies were supplied of the preceding documents. It was not possible to see other letters which are also of interest. These would, no doubt, provided further information on Addington's knowledge of the slave trade: C1792/OZ1 & F18-27; C1796/OC2; C1799/OC9; C1800/OC4; C1805/OF2; C1813/OF3; C1815/OF23.
186. The only account of abolition in Devon was written by J. R. Oldfield, *Popular Politics and British Anti-Slavery; the mobilisation of public opinion against the slave trade, 1787-1807* (Manchester, 1995), 97-101 and 107-108.
187. Oldfield, *Popular*, 100.
188. British Library, Add Ms 21254, 9.
189. Thomas Clarkson, *The History of the Rise, Progress and Accomplishment of the Abolition of the African Slave Trade by the British Parliament* (1808), I, 494.
190. Clarkson, *History*, I, 495.
191. British Library, Add Ms 21255, 20.
192. Oldfield, *Popular*, 70.
193. British Library, Add Ms 21255, 23, 27. It was on June 10th that Clarkson was asked to travel throughout the country to encourage support. See 21255, 43, 45, 50, 69, 88, 104, 114, 137 and 21256, 11, 29, 36, 90.
194. British Library, Add. Ms 21255, 43.
195. *Exeter Flying Post*, 6/11/1788. Clarkson had been in Poole on September 21st and Falmouth on October 18th: British Library, Add. Ms 21255, 59 & 64.
196. Oldfield, *Popular*, 130-1.
197. *The Sherborne Mercury*, 24/11/1788. The subscription list included a number of anonymous donations and from Tiverton the sum of £41 6s.
198. Oldfield, *Popular*, 129-38.
199. *Exeter Flying Post*, 14/2/1788, 20/3/1788, 27/3/1788, 21/2/1788; Oldfield, *Popular*, 114.

200. Allan Brockett, Nonconformity In Exeter (Exeter, 1962), 140; Robert Newton, *Eighteenth-Century Exeter* (Exeter, 1984), 126; Todd Gray, *The Essence of Exeter* (Exeter, 2005), 11.
201. 15 of these men were listed at George's Meeting comprising Samuel Milford, Mathew Lee, Samuel F. Milford, John Milford, John Williams, John Withers, James Manning, Timothy Kenrick, Thomas Hill, Philip Moor, William Tucker, John Bowring, Jonathan Tucker, Samuel Dunsford, Joseph Littlefear: Devon Record Office, 36930/M4.
202. The Quakers included Saunders, Thomas Sparkes, Samuel Cross and John Dymond: Oldfield, *Popular*, 98.
203. *Exeter Flying Post*, 12/6/1788. These include John Bowring, Rev. Timothy Kenrick, Mathew Lee, George Manning, Rev. James Manning, Rev. Thomas Morgan, William Tucker and John Withers. Quakers include John Dymond, Joseph Sanders. Richard Clarke was Milford's partner in the City Bank: Arthur Allan Brockett, 'Nonconformity in Exeter, 1650-1875', University of Exeter MA thesis, 1960, 488; Newton, *Eighteenth Century Exeter*, 66, 165.
204. *Exeter Flying Post*, 29/5/1788 & 26/6/1788.
205. Oldfield, *Popular*, 107, 108; Devon Record Office, 63/2/11/2.
206. *Exeter Flying Post*, 27/3/1788. See also 21/2/1788.
207. British Library, Add Ms 21255, 3.
208. Clarkson, *History*, II, 7. Other Quakers who were active were Charles Fox and John Mudge: Plymouth & West Devon Record Office, 1176/7 & 1444/17/1.
209. Oldfield, *Popular*, 99.
210. *Exeter Flying Post*, 13/3/1788.
211. *Exeter Flying Post*, 20/11/1788. These men subscribed to funds as subsequently did John Cooban, Lydia Fox, Elizabeth Fox, Philip Cookworthy, Philip Yeoland, Lovall Fox, Reverend Humphrey Julian and William Clarke of Stonehouse. Walter Prideaux of Modbury and George Prideaux of Kingsbridge became corresponding members.
212. British Library, Add Ms 21255, 66.
213. Oldfield, *Popular*, 99-100.
214. *Exeter Flying Post*, 13/11/1788.
215. Clarkson, *History*, II, 28-9. Clarkson later wrote 'the committee at Plymouth had been the first to suggest the idea but that in London had now improved it...': p.111; Bidlake's sermon was preached at Stonehouse Chapel on 28 December 1788: *Exeter Flying Post*, 29/1/1789; the Society discussed it throughout the spring and early summer months: British Library, Add Ms 21255.
216. British Library, Add Ms 21255, 88 & 91.
217. Herbert Mends, *The Injustice and Cruelty in the slave trade considered*,

*in a sermon preached in Plymouth on Lord's Day, February 22 1789* (Plymouth, 1789).
218. British Library, Add Ms 21255, 88.
219. British Library, Add Ms 21255, 104, 119, 137 & 21256, 11, 26, 29, 36, 43.
220. *Exeter Flying Post*, 28/7/1791.
221. Walvin, 'the public campaign', 66.
222. They appeared before the House of Commons from 'the inhabitants of the town and neighbourhood of Plymouth' on 15 February, from the 'gentlemen, clergy and freeholders residing in and near the town of Kingsbridge' on 5 March, from 'the portreeve and principal inhabitants of the borough of Honiton' on 8 March, from 'the principal inhabitants of the town and neighbourhood of Crediton' and the 'inhabitants of the town and parish of Topsham' on 10 March, from the 'mayor, recorder, minister, capital burgesses and principal inhabitants of the borough of Bradninch' and the 'gentlemen, clergy and principal inhabitants of the town and neighbourhood' of Cullompton on 15 March, from 'the mayor, clergy and other respectable inhabitants of Tiverton' on 19 March, from 'the inhabitants of the town and neighbourhood of Moretonhampstead' and 'the principal inhabitants of the borough of Totnes' on 26 March, from 'the mayor, burgesses, merchants, freeholders and inhabitants of the borough of Clifton, Dartmouth and Hardness' on 2 April and the 'inhabitants of the borough of Bere Alston and neighbourhood' on 25 April: *Journal of the House of Commons* (1792), 382, 472, 510, 532, 552, 565, 589, 637, 732.
223. *Exeter Flying Post*, 1/3/1792, 16/2/1792, 1/3/1792.
224. *Exeter Gazette*, 22/3/1792.
225. *Exeter Gazette*, 15/3/1792.
226. *Exeter Gazette*, 19/3/1792.
227. John Bourne (ed.), *Georgian Tiverton* (Devon & Cornwall Record Society, NS Vol. 29, 1986), 126, 170.
228. British Library, Add Ms 21256, 48 & 91.
229. *Exeter Gazette*, 5/4/1792.
230. *Exeter Flying Post*, 6/11/1788.
231. Stedman, *Journal*, 336.
232. Anon., *Selico, an African tale* (Exeter, 1794). The profits were given to the campaign against slavery. Milford wrote to the Society on December 31 1793: British Library, Add Ms 21256, 90.
233. *Exeter Flying Post*, 12/2/1807.
234. *Exeter Flying Post*, 6/5/1841.
235. *Exeter Flying Post*, 7/7/1814.
236. Dale H. Porter, *The abolition of the slave trade in England, 1784-1807* (1970).

237. Devon Record Office, 1262M/L50.
238. Plymouth & West Devon Record Office, 1/669/1-18.
239. Plymouth & West Devon Record Office, 1/669/5.
240. Plymouth & West Devon Record Office, 1/669/1&2.
241. Plymouth & West Devon Record Office, 1/669/4 & 12.
242. *Exeter Flying Post*, 7/7/1814. The committee comprised Reverend Carrington, Rev. John Follett, James Patch Esq., Mr John Palmer, Mr Robert Cross, Mr Richard Harrison, Mr Gilbert Mudge, Mr Thomas L. Brown, Mr Francis Trobridge and Mr H. Hellett.
243. *Woolmer's Gazette*, 2 & 14 July, 6 August 1814; *Exeter Flying Post*, 7/7/1814.
244. Thomas, *The Slave Trade*, 583-5.
245. Howard Temperley, *British Antislavery, 1833–1870* (1972), 9-10.
246. *The Debate on Abolition of Slavery*, 1823 (1968), xxxvii-xxxix.
247. Plymouth & West Devon Record Office, 1/669/6.
248. Plymouth & West Devon Record Office, 1/669/20.
249. *Exeter Flying Post*, 8/5/1823.
250. Temperley, *British Antislavery, 1833–1870*, 11,
251. Plymouth & West Devon Record Office, 1/669/19.
252. Plymouth & West Devon Record Office, 710/597.
253. *Exeter Flying Post*, 26/2/1824 & 4/3/1824.
254. *Exeter Flying Post*, 26/2/1824. It took place on February 23.
255. *Exeter Flying Post*, 4/3/1824.
256. Plymouth & West Devon Record Office, 1/669/8.
257. The individuals were John Hatchard, Robert Lampen, Septimus Courtney, Joseph Garton, J. S. Tozer, James Coffin, I. Symes, John Thickness, Joseph Hingston, Walter Prideaux, Joseph Treffry, Edward Blackmore, William Seabrook, David Derry, W. P. Davies, Samuel Rowe, John Prideaux, Henry Woollcombe, Joseph Pridham, William Prance, George Corydon, A. Tozer, R. N., William Jacobson, Thomas F. Jessop, George Eastlake, I, H. Luscombe, Joseph Whiteford, I. Y. Fownes, Joseph W. Fox, Samuel Nicholson, I. H. Macaulay, Samuel Williams and J. C. Cookworthy: Plymouth & West Devon Record Office, 1/669/8. Woollcombe noted in his diary 'meeting to abolish slavery in West Indies': Plymouth & West Devon Record Office, 710/397.
258. *Exeter Flying Post*, 9/2/1826.
259. *Exeter Flying Post*, 2/3/1826.
260. Plymouth & West Devon Record Office, 1/669/16.
261. Plymouth & West Devon Record Office, 1/669/17.
262. Plymouth & West Devon Record Office, 1/669/3, 9, 10, 11, 13, 15 & 18.
263. *Exeter Flying Post*, 9/9/1830.
264. *Exeter Flying Post*, 10/7/1834.

265. *Exeter Flying Post*, 8/10/1840.
266. *Exeter Flying Post*, 6/5/1841.
267. Howard Temperley, *British antislavery, 1833-1870* (1972), 229.
268. *Exeter Flying Post*, 22/2/1882.
269. *Trewman's Exeter Flying Post; or Plymouth and Cornish Advertiser*, 10 May 1832; *The Western Times*, 12 May 1832; *Woolmer's Exeter & Plymouth Gazette*, 12 May 1832.
270. *Exeter Flying Post*, 11/8/1837.
271. Plymouth & West Devon Record Office, 710/439; Temperley, *British antislavery, 1833-1870*, 69, 72, 55.
272. Plymouth & West Devon Record Office, W669.
273. Plymouth & West Devon Record Office, W362/88/2.
274. Plymouth & West Devon Record Office, 993/15.
275. The compensation documents are now available at <http://www.ucl.ack.uk>. I am grateful to Peter Wingfield-Digby for pointing out that Phillpotts was an executor and not an owner.
276. Kenneth Morgan, 'Bristol West India Merchants in the Eighteenth Century', *Trans. Royal Historical Society*, Vol. 3 (1993), 185-208.
277. *Western Times*, 31 Jan. 1852; *London Evening Standard*, 6 May 1857.
278. He was also in Exeter in 1864: Todd Gray (ed.), *Exeter: The Travellers' Tales* (Exeter, 2000), 130-7.
279. Devon Record Office, Z19/36/19.
280. These reports have been republished in full: Todd Gray (ed.), *The Victorian Under Class of Exeter* (Exeter, 2001).
281. *The Exeter Journal and Almanack* (Exeter, 1851). Mrs Wardrobe was not listed as living in Exeter in the volume for 1850; Ancestry.com. *Savannah, Georgia, Land Tax and Property Records, 1809-1938* [database on-line]. Provo, UT, USA: Ancestry.com Operations, Inc., 2012
282. Devon Record Office, 867b/Z36.
283. William Howard Russell, *My diary, north and south* (1863), two volumes.
284. R. A. Warren in the journal of the Confederate Historical Society (Summer, 1986), 21.
285. R. A. Warren in the journal of the Confederate Historical Society (Summer, 1986), 21.
286. *Woolmer's Exeter Gazette*, 7/6/1867.
287. *The Devon Weekly Times*, 7/6/1867.
288. *Tiverton Gazette and East Devon Herald*, 11/6/1867. I am grateful to the members of the Friends of Devon's Archives for this reference.

# Index

Abolition 149-214; African Institution 178, 193; African Civilization Committee 190; bicentenary 4; Anti-Slavery Society 184, 193; British Foreign Anti Slavery Society 188; Cornwall 165; Devon & Exeter Anti-Slavery Society 188; petitions 114, 150, 178-88; League of Universal Brotherhood 201; Society for the Abolition of the Slave Trade 165-6, 178, 188; Society for the Extinction of the Slave Trade and for the Cultivation of Africa 188
Acland, Thomas Dyke 112, 183
Adams, Edward 37; Mathew 36
Addicot, Mr 167
Addington, Henry 161-4
Admiralty Board 151-3
Africa 5, 7, 10, 15, 42, 46-9, 57-73, 193, 207; Accra 63, 70; Algeria 31; Anamabo 62-3, 65; Angola 57, 70, 71; Benin 65; Cabinda 67-9, 70; alabar 42, 51; Cape St Mary 59; Cape Verde 21, 40, 42, 43, 50; Congo 70; Freedom colony 57, 59; Gambia 26, 42, 50, 51, 59; Ghana 7; Grand Topo 63; Guinea 20, 26, 42, 51, 64, 66, 224 n.168; James Island 59, 60; Libya 31; Loango 67; Madagascar 40; Mayumba 67; Melimba 68; Morocco 31-9; Mozambique 74-6; Nigeria 51; North 25; Principe 67; Reparation Movement 6; St Thomas 65-7; Senegal 26, 40, 54, 57; Sierra Leone 20, 21, 159-60, 190; South Africa 12, 40, 195-6; Timba 67; Tunisia 31; Whydah 63, 64-5; Zaire 70
Allen, Robert 98; William 190-1
Alves, Manuel Josi 80
Americas, the 17
Anne, Queen 142
Anstice, Edward 180
Antonio, Jove 81; Manuel 81
Appledore 28
Archaic words 58
Arrows 44
Arthur, Henry 42
Ashborne 38
Ashburton 39, 90, 149, 172, 186-7
Asia 92
Assencion 72
Augery, Henry 38

## Index

Australia 25
Ayer, Mrs 26-7
Ayres, Thomas 33

Bagshot, Jo: 37
Bahamas 111, 159, 163
Baker, Jo: 36; William 180
Balkwill, Benjamin 181
*Ballard of the Negro*, 197-8
Baltic 5, 43, 91
Bampfeild, Edward 37; Sir C. W. 166
Bankes, Thomas 180
Barbados 200
Baring, John 166
Barnes, Edward 36
Barnstaple 26-7, 29, 38, 39, 52, 57, 106, 149, 167
Barons, George 41-2, 51, 52
Barret, Richard 35
Bartlett, Joseph 35
Bartram, John 35
Basins 44
Bate, Humphrey 36
Bath, Countess of 29
Bedford, Ann 35
Belfield, Mooney 168
Bell, William 107
Benbow, John 199-200
Benion, William 36
Bennet, Mrs 167
Berber, Robert 168
Bere Alston 172
Berry, William 168
Besly, William 175
Beson, Richard 35
Bickleigh 131
Bicton 106
Bideford 30, 51
Bidlake, John 170
Biger, Robert 37
Birmingham 212
Black Dwarf, the 9
Black, Robert 38
Blackamoore, James 9, 29
Blackett, Honest Jack 72

Blackmore, William 180
*Blackwood's Magazine* 210
Blagrove, Frederick 142; Joseph 142; William 142
Blatchford, Mr 168
Blizard, Henry 98
Board of Trade 53-4
Bodley, Mr; Misses 168
Bole, Nicholas 180
Bonaparte, Napoleon 33, 184
Bond, Christopher 180
Boone, Jo: 36; Richard 38
Bowbier, Mrs 167
Bowden, John 38
Bowdidge, Mr 167
Bowring, John 169
Braddon, William 82
Bradninch 172, 200
Bradshaw, William 35
Branch, Charles 142
Brand, Nicholas 145
Braunton 12
Brayley, William 26
Briant, Andrew 36
Bridges, Amelia 144; Janette 144; Thomas 141
Bridestowe 200
Bristol 2, 5, 10, 35, 36, 37, 38, 42, 50-1, 85, 87, 91, 135, 149, 200; Channel 5
British human rights 11-12, 178
Brooks, George 142; Isabella 143
Brothels 129
Brougham, Mr 194
Brown, James 35; Mary 143; Thomas 33
Browne, Jo: 36, 38; Mr 167; Mrs 167; Thomas 38; W. 167
Bucland, Robert 36
Burford, Robert 37
Burgoin, John 180
Burke, Edmund 161-2
Burridge, John 42; Robert 42
Burritt, Elihu 201
Burrow, James 180; Mrs 167
Burwell, John 43-9

Butcher, Christopher 50; Thomas 36
Butler, Jo: 36
Buttell 145; Benjamin 53, 146; Nathaniel 146; Samuel 146
Byford, Jo: 37
Byrd, William 166

Cadbury, Joel 165
Cahill, Revd 205
Canada, Morocco 34-5; Newfoundland 33, 44, 52, 84, 147; Nova Scotia 159
Canary Islands 19
Candre, Teeke 36
Carbew, Lazia 29
Carew, Bampfylde 131
Caribbean, 6, 20, 23, 40, 51, 52, 69, 83, 90, 209-210; Antigua 95-105; Barbados 40, 50, 72-3, 84, 95, 147, 151; Bermuda 84; British Antilles 93; Cuba 24; Demerara 163; Grenada 93-4; Haiti 164; Jamaica 54, 84, 85, 95, 130, 139, 155, 162, 199-200, 221 n.89, 224 n.168; Nevis 135-8; St Christopher's 147; St Kitts 224 n.168; Tobago 84; Trinidad 163, 201-206
Carley, Jo: 37
Carrington, Revd James 183
Cartwright, Edward 38
Cary, George Stanley 199
Cary, Jo: 38
Cassada 64
Castillo, William 151-3
Caverly, Peter 12
Celly, Pascoe 35
Cerqueiro, Captain 80
Chagford 149, 189
Challenge, Jo: 37
Channel Islands 35, 37, 38
Chappin, Richard 35
Charles II 88
Chester 53
Chichester, family 83
Christopher, John 35

Church of England 171, 177
Churchill, Mrs 167; Revd 167; Samuel 167
Chute, Edward 168
Civet 28
Clapp, Mr 168
Clarke (Clark), Jon: 37; Joseph 168; Miss 167; Mrs 167; Peter 38; Richard Hall 169
Clarkson, Thomas 165-6, 169-71, 191
Cleather, Thomas 181
Clivedon, Mr 66
Cloth trade 5, 7, 22, 42-9, 87-92, 139-44
Clotworthy, Joseph 181
Clunn, John 35
Clyst St George 145
Clyst St Mary 200
Cocke, Abraham 37; William 35
Coffee 62, 71, 83
Cohen, Marian 143
Coleridge, George 180; Henry Nelson 135; James 180
Cole, George 200
Coles, Richard 180; William 180
Colleton, Sir John 88, 170
Colonial Office 202
Colsocke, Tippet 38
Colyton 26, 30, 135, 200
Combes, J. 180
Commonwealth 6
Cone, George 36
Congregationalism 195
Conworth, John 36
Cook, Mrs 167
Cookworthy, William 170
Coop, Richard 37, 38
Corker, Thomas 50
Cornwall 165; Falmouth 38; Fowey 36, 39; Helford 35, 36, 37, 39; Looe 35, 36, 37, 39; Millbrook 35, 36, 37; St Germans 37, 39; St Ives 38, 157; Saltash 35, 39
Cotter, Hannah 167
Couch, Philip 224 n.168

*Index*

Courtenay, family 83
Cousche, John 167
Cousins, William 224 n.168
Coventy, Thomas 38
Cowen, Jo: 36
Cowley, Hannah 130
Cox, Mr 157
Cranch, Mr 168
Cranst, Edward 37
Crape, William 36
Cratbert, William 37
Crawford, Doctor 72
Crediton 82, 149, 172
Creswell, John 167
Cromwell, Oliver 12
Cropper, Mr 188
Cross, Robert 169; Samuel 169
Cullompton 167, 172
Culmstock 166
Curfe, Paul, 190-1
Cursie, Thomas 37
Cutten, Stephen 38

D[?]gen, Thomas 36
Dagara Peace Commission 6-7
Dale, Mr 168
Daly, Cath 143; Robert 142
Damart, Miss 197-8
Daniel, Thomas 200
Dark people 8
Dartmoor 4
Dartmouth 35, 36, 38, 40-44, 51-2, 88-9, 172
Davie, Robert 37
Davy, family 221 n.89; William 14, 154-6
Dawe, Jane 38; Mr 167
Dawes, Thomas 93
Dawlish 200
Day, Mr 214; Richard 35; William 224 n.168
De Costa, Sabrina 79, 80
De Santo Serva, Francisco Feriera 80
Degeo, Mr 167
Delamore, Messrs 104

Delbridge, John 83
Delling, Richard 38
Demelly, Mr 126-7
Demerara 200
Denbury 37, 39
Denmark 178; factory of 64
Denning, John 180
Dennys, Mr 114
Densham, Miss 168
Derdoe, Thomas 38
Derry, Richard 181; Sampson 36
Devaynes, William 149
Devon County Council 4
Devorax, Thomas 36
Dickson, Henry 141; Richard 142
Diment, Henry 82
Disdale, Mr 68
Dodderidge, Richard 26-7
Domet, Mr 66, 72-3
Doone, Philip 36
Doricot, John 26
Dorrington, G. 79
Dorset, Dorchester 38; Lyme Regis 38-9, 42, 135; Poole 35, 38; Weymouth 37, 38
Downes, Michael 36
Downing, Francis 199-200
Drake, Sir Francis 2
Drestell, Teeke 36
Drew, John 167
Drury, Edward 36
Dugdale, Mr 167
Duncane, James 38
Dungwell, Edward 36
Dunning, Mr 156
Dunsford, Martin 175; Miss 167; Samuel 169
Duval, L. 167
Dyer, Mr 167
Dymond, John 169; Joseph Sparkes 169

Eagles, Thomas 37 (2)
Eastern Europe 12
Eastlake, George 181; William 181

Eaton, Rosanna 144
Ebford 167
Eddisford, Revd 167
Edwards, Bryan 162; Charles 37
Elford, Jonathan 170; Richard 38; William 170, 181, 182-3
Elizabeth I 26, 156, 210
Ellard, Charles 50; John 42, 50; Mr 67
Ellicombe, William 168
Elliot, Stephen 38; Thomas 37
Ellis, Ann 167; John 84, 180
English Channel 5
Equiano 159-60
Evans, Elizabeth 8; Jonathan 169; Samuel 180; W. Burd 167
Exeter 4, 8, 11-12, 26, 30, 35, 39, 40, 41, 43, 51, 52, 54, 89-92, 139, 145, 149, 154, 159, 165-70, 172, 175, 176, 177, 184, 186, 188, 201, 212: bishop 177; castle 77, 82, 170, 183, 199-200; Cathedral 3-4; Cathedral Yard 169; Chamber 169; City Bank 169; Dean 4; Duryard 200; General Bank 169; George's Meeting 169; Guildhall 172-3, 183; Heavitree Road 207; Hill's Court Road 208; Martin's Lane 169; Pennsylvania Road 208; Rose Cottage 208; Royal Clarence 169, 188; Royal Public Rooms 212; St John's 177; South Street 9, 169; town clerk 170; Quay 7; Workhouse 207-9
Exmoor 4
Exmouth 88

Farming 5
Feard, Ben 35
Feres, Peter 36
Fickett, Isaac 35
Firearms 44
Firth, William 35
Fish 20, 59
Fisher, Richard 38
Fishing 5, 44, 52, 59, 62, 68, 69; plantations 83-4

Fittham, Garrett 37
Fitz Thomas, Cormocke 36
Fitzmorris, Cornelius 36
Flattery, Andrew 36; Jo: 36
Flee, Elias 33
Floss, William 36
Flowhaven, Thomas 37
Floyd, Mr 167
Follett, Mr 175
Foot, Thomas 167
Fop, Elias 37
Ford, Joseph 167
Forester, James 142
Foster, Sylvia 143
Fownes, Mrs 167
Fox, Charles 170; Francis 165, 170; Frank 191; James 170
France 5, 39, 43, 69-70, 71, 91, 163, 191; Isle of Rhe 33; prisoners 145; privateers 52; Revolution 12, 171; war 52, 53, 54, 56, 178, 184 Francis, Elenor 142; Frank 142; Revd 167
Francisco, Juan 81
Frankland, Arthur 74-6
Freeman, William 38
French, Leonard 8-9
Friends of Devon's Archives 5
Frust, William 35
Fry, Robert 166; Sarah 166
Fuge, Robert 181
Funeral 61-2

Gale, Joan 8
Galloway, Christopher 36
Gandy, John 170
Gard, Alexander 167
Gardner, David 36; Thomas 35
Garland, Patrick 37
Garrett, William 38
George III 70, 157
Germany 91, 92
Gibbs, Philip 170
Gibraltar 191
Gilbert, Adrian 30; family 83
Ginger 20, 50

## Index

Glanville, Thomas 180
Glasgow 53
Glevely, Lord 201
Gloucester 39; bishop of 161
Gloyns, Francis 131
Glyde, Mr J. 167
Goard, Henry 37
Godfrey, William 180
Gold 22, 28, 90; ackeys 44-9
Goodwin, Valentine 38
Gore, Mrs 167
Gorges, Sir Ferdinando 30, 87-8
Gould, James 42
Graham, Dahlia 207; George 141
Granger, Mr 167
Grant, Bernie 6; Mr 167
Gray, Nicholas 36
Great Torrington 167
Green, Alicia 144; Ancilla 143; Camilla 143; Elizabeth 143; Felicia 143; George 141; Henrietta 143; Henry 141; J. 168; James 141; Judith 144; Louisa 143; Maria 143; McKenzie 141; Olive 144; Richard 38, 142; Richard 38
Greens, Timothy 142
Greig, James 141
Griffey, Messrs 167
Griffin, Daniel 35; Nicholas 37; William 38
Griffith, Arianna 143; Cecelia 144; Chloe 144; James 141; Johanna 144; Maria 143; Mo 141
Griffiths, Colin 142
Grimelstone, Thomas 37
Grimeth, Samuel 37
Grimfield, Grace 38
Grister, John 36
Guinea Company 26-30

Hagon, George 38
Hague, Sam 213
Halberton 130
Hall, George 36; Thomas 142
Hallaren, L. M. 168
Hamilton, Sir Alexander 145; Mrs 167; Rowell 98
Hampshire 38, 106; Portsmouth 68; Southampton 35, 38; Winchester 161
Handerson, George 224 n.168
Hardie, Wiliam 35
Hardin, Henry 33
Harding, Abraham 180
Harold, Messrs 167
Harris, Abraham 37, 35; Andrew Hector 88; Edward 168; Jo: 37 (2); John 42, 51; Mr 167; William 180
Harrison, John 139
Harrop, S. 180
Harry, John 36
Harvey, Thomas 180; Wilken 141
Hatherleigh 30
Hawker, H. 188
Hawkins, Sir John 2-3, 5, 17-25, 215, 218 n.7; William, senior, 13, 17-18; William, junior 29
Hawthorn, Linn 142
Heard, Thomas 168
Heath, Arthur 142; Rebecca 143; Rodney 142; Thomas 141
Heaven, William Hudson 200
Hele, Sir Warwick 88
Helvert, William 36
Hems, Harry 155
Henson, Hugh 37
Henton, D. 167
Herbert, George 167
Hey, Richard 166
Hides 20
Hill, Mrs 167; Thomas 169
Hobson, Miss 130
Hodge, Charles 180
Hodges, George 146; Nathaniel 145-6
Hogg, Mr 114; Robert 37
Hoggett, Roger 29
Hole, Peter 167; Revd 167
Hollwill, Henry 33
Hollyday, Charles 35
Holman, John 38

Holmes, John 169; William 167
Honiton 149, 172, 174
Honyhood, Mrs 168
Hoode, Adam 36
Hooper, Frederick 12, 195-6
Hope, Peter 224 n.168
Horsey, Joseph 180; Peter 180
Houdver, John 36
Houlditch, Richard 180
House of Commons 53, 88-91, 161, 174
Howe, John 37
Howell, Hinds 200
Huddy, Charles 180
Hugh, John 35
Hunt, Jo: 38; Joseph 168
Huntingford, George 161
Hussey, William 167
Hutton, Mrs 167

Iceland 44
Ilfracombe 6-7, 149, 188
Incledon-Webber, John 57-73
India 44, 211; cottons 44
Investment 83-147
Ireland 8, 31, 35-39, 44, 83, 84, 92
Iron 42, 44
Isaacke, Thomas 35
Islam 25, 31, 195
Isles of Scilly 35, 37, 39
Italy 52
Ivory 28, 40, 50, 54, 90
Ivy, Daniel 42, 51

Jacobson, William 197
Jamaica 200
James, Dido 143; John 82
Jeffery, Arthur 42, 51
Jenkins, Henry 37
Jennings, Abraham 30
Jervoise, Mr 167
Jerwood, John 167
Jews 6, 85, 193
Joaquim, Antonio 81
Jones, James 151-3; John 37; Philip 167; Rosan 144; Thomas 142, Thomas 180
Jope, John 35
Judgson, Mrs 167

Katherine, Richard 38
Keen, Ellis 33
Keene, Daniel 168
Kegwin, Thomas 29
Kelly, William 35
Kembe, Abraham 38
Kember, James 37
Kemble, Mr 167
Kemp, William 167
Kennaway, Abraham 167; J. 180; Richard 180; Robert 167; Thomas 167; W. 167
Kenrick, Timothy 169
Kerry, John 35
Killerton 112, 183
King (Kinge), John 29; Thomas 35; William 36
King's Nympton 84
Kingdon, Joseph 169
Kingsbridge 172
Kitson, Revd 167
Knollman, Richard 35
Kruythoff, Mr 126

Laine, John 37
Lambe, William 38
Lancaster 53, 70
Land, John 167; Mr 174; Walter 38
Lane, Derby 38
Langdon, Jo: 37
Lange, William 38
Langford, William 37
Langmead, William 181
Lanyon, Mr 27
Larkworthy, A. 167
Lathrope, Jos. 180
Law, James 35
Le Conte, Harry 95
Leach, George 170
Lead 44-9

*Index*

League Nations 11
Leatt, Benjamin 180; James 180; William 180
Lee, J. 167; Mathew 169; Thomas Huckle 169; W. H. 213
Leekes, John 38
Lerry, Jon: 37
Levercombe, William 51
Levy, Moize 193
Lewis, John 167; Mrs 167
Ley, Henry 170
Lighter, John 35; Richard 35
Lightfoot, Southy 33
Linch, James 35
Littlefear, Joseph 169
Littleton, Edward John 199-200
Livermore, William 180
Liverpool 2, 10, 54, 57, 68, 70, 150, 173, 188, 190, 212
Loane, Thomas 37
Lockie, Thomas 38
Lockyer, Nicholas 186; Revd 167
Lokens, Mr 119, 122
London, 2, 5, 6, 10, 19, 35, 36, 37, 38, 42, 43, 51, 91-2, 139, 149, 155, 172, 190, 199; Chatham 38; Freeman's Hall 194; Gravesend 38
Lopes, family 84; Sir Mannaseh 85
Lovell, Nicholas 35
Luccraft, Mr 167
Luke, John 168
Lundy 200
Lushington, Stephen 194
Lutie, Philip 35
Lyde, James 222 n.93
Lyle, William 33
Lyme, Dr 66
Lympstone 201-202

Macilland, Mo 142
Maddocke, Richard 36
Madge, Philip 170
Maglin, Michael 37
Majaval, Janus 81
Mamhead 84

Man, Rebecca 35; Thomas 35
Manchester 92, 212
Manley, James 180
Manning, George 166, 169; Mrs George 167; Revd James 165, 169;
Manning, Mr 79
Manumission 29
Marchant, Elizabeth 88
Maristow 84
Marks, Mr 72
Martin, Grace 37; John 35
Martinos, Jozi Maria 81
Marystow 157-8, 197-8
Match, Richard
Mathew, Roger 46
Mathews, General 72; Richard 194
Matten, Henry 38
McKanzie, Mo 141
McLean, Donald 141
McNally, Blagrove 141; Richard 141; Robert 141
Mearce, Jon: 37
Melhuish, Henry 167
M-ell, John 180
Mellowes, Jane 38
Mends, Herbert 170
Merchant, Wal: 37
Merivale, Elizabeth 167
Merrit, William
Mersie, John 38
Mervey, Robert 38
Meskell, William 37
Michell, Walter 38
Milford, John 168, 169; Misses 167; Mrs 167; S. F. 168, 169, 177; Samuel 165, 169, 177
Miller, Bessy 143; Henry 141; James 141; Robert 36
Milward, Richard 166; Thomas 167
Mingus, Peter 27, 28
Minstrels 212-214
Miskoll, Dot. 36
Mitchell, Jos. 180; William 157
Modbury 95
Mohun, Buxton 184

Mole, Robert 168
Moody, Martha 200
Moore (Moor), John 170; Mr 170; Philip 169
Morehead, John 54
Moretonhampstead 149, 172, 186
Morgan, George 141; Hugh 37; Jo: 37; Samuel 167; Thomas 169
Morn, John 167-8
Morris, James 37; Toby; Mrs 168; William 36
Morsey, William 36
Moune, Richard 38
Mountjoy, Mr 167
Mowbray, Robert 36
Mudge, Aubry 38; John 170
Muggin, Nicholas 37
Murray, Col. A 163-4
Mursen, Da: 37

Nation, Mr 167
Native Americans 30
Naylor, General 72
Netherlands 5, 42, 43, 51, 52, 85, 91, 112, 114, 129, 130, 131, 178; people of 29, 39, 126
Newcombe, Captain 72
Newspapers 183; *Courier* 183; *Devonport Telegraph* 186; *Exeter Flying Post* 168; *Exeter Gazettte* 175; *Morning Chronicle* 183; *Times* 210; *Trinidad Standard* 204; *Western Luminary* 207
Newton Bushel 38, 39
Nicholas, William 37
Nicholls, Thomas 82
Ninues, Ignacio Joze 191
Noble, Walter 38
Norfolk, King's Lynn 39
Norrington, Charles 180; James 180; William 180
Norris, Jo: 36; Mr 27
North America 12
Northcote, Samuel 170
Nouger, Jo: 38

Ogborn, Mr 167
Okes, Dr 167
Oliver, James 224 n.168; Richard 97, 100; Rowland 105
Orme, Robert 145, 146
Otterton 38, 39
Ottery St Mary 82, 167, 178-9
Oxnam, Revd 177

Pafrey, Walter 35
Page, Christopher 37; Richard 33
Palmer, Jane 143; William 180
Parish registers 26-30
Parker, Elizabeth 6
Parminter, Elizabeth 51; John 42, 51
Parnell, Richard 168
Parry, Governor 72
Pasmore, J. 167
Passmore, George 180
Paul, Robert 166
Payne, Edward 93
Pearce, Philip 37; Thomas 167
Pearcey, Henry 36
Pearl, William 141
Pearls 19
Pearse, George 200
Peckford, Mr 168
Pedro, Don 29
Peece, Robert 36
Penman, James 107
Penn, William 169
Pepper 50
Pering, Revd 168
Pewter 42
Philip, Arundel 167
Philips, Reuben 174; George 37
Philpotts, Charles 141; Henry 177, 199
Pill, Peter 35
Pine, Mrs 167
Pinkstan, Mrs 167, 168
Piracy 17, 30-9, 50
Pitcher, Jo: 37
Pitman, John 175
Pitt, Mrs 167; William 151, 170
Pitter, Thomas 141

*Index*

Plymouth 4, 12, 15, 19, 29-30, 36, 37, 38, 40, 41, 51, 53-6, 57, 58, 74, 77, 89, 145-6, 147, 149, 151-2, 159, 165, 170-3, 181-8, 190-4, 195, 224 n.168; Athenaeum 186; fort 87; Grammar School 171; Guildhall 170, 186, 193; Pope's Head 170
Pole, Sir Charles 149; Sir William 30
Pollard, Jo: 37; William 84
Pole, William Templer 199-200
Poodam, Thomas 35
Pope, Edward 37; Joseph 167
Popham, Sir John 30
Pophams, Home 142
Porter, Henry 200; Thomas 200
Portugal 13, 17, 19, 22, 28, 51, 58, 66, 71, 74-6, 77, 91, 191-2
Poucee, Henry 142
Poulter, Thomas 36
Powderham 83
Powell, Emma 143; Harriet 143; Richard 141; T. D. 168
Presbyterians 170
Prickman, Esther (see Swete)
Prideaux, John 157, 170, 193-4; Walter 165, 175; William 181
Pridham, Joseph 181
Primsom, John 36
Privateering 28, 50, 52, 53
Proude, Walter 38
Prowse, Roger 42
Pulman, Thomas 180; Walter 180

Quaite, Edward 36
Quane, Nicholas 37

Rabbe, William 35
Raleigh, family 83; Sir Walter 30, 44
Randell, Peter 37
Randton, Nicholas 38
Ranke, Borne 36
Redes, Adrian 38
Reed, Henry 167
Reid, John 180
Religion 12

Remmell, 181
Ribeiro, Florenco 80
Rice 20
Richards, Aaron 190-1; Bessy 143; Bill 143; Edward 141; John 35; Katherine 35; Molly 143; Susan 143
Rickett, George 35
Ricketts, Mo 141; Mr 72
Rider, Nicholas 36
Roberts, Bob 141; Eve 144
Robertson, Charlotte 144; Henry 141
Roche, Francis 142
Rochester, Charles 142; Fran 143; Joe 142; Johnny 141; Sally 143
Rockbeare 200
Rodin, James 141
Rolle, family 106; Dennys 106-111
Roman Catholicism 205
Ronaldson, John James 139
Rosaigre, Emanuel 81
Rose, Tristram 38
Rosendaal, Countess of 131
Rossiter, Thomas 200
Rowcliffe, Thomas 8
Rowe (Row), Bessy 143; John 167; Joseph 168; Lucy 143; William 180
Rowland, Nathaniel 180; Peter 38
Royal Adventurers into Africa 88
Royal Africa Company 40, 50, 52, 84, 88-92
Ruddock, Mary 143
Russell, Mary 35
Russia 12
Ryder, Mr 175

Salcombe 37, 39
Salter, Abraham 180; Charles 180; John 180; Richard 180; Roger 180; Thomas 180
Saltram 188
Sampson, Mr 174; J. 175
Sander, Hugh 37
Sanford, Nathaniel 180
Saunders (Sanders) Andrew 170; Benjamin 180; John 170; Joseph

169
Scarborough, Mary 135; William 135
Scotland 35, 39, 66
Scott, John 201-206
Scutt, Richard 36
Seaman, Edward 36
Seaton 135
Seaward, Richard 180; T. 180
Selby, Nicholas 33
Sexual relations 117, 119, 122, 124, 125
Seymour, Edmund Percy 210
Shaffe, George 8
Sharland, Mr 168
Sharp (Sharpe), Granville 169; Tristram 36
Sheere (Sheer), Cuthbert 29; Richard 29
Shenstone, William 168
Sheppard (Shepherd) James 180; Richard 180; Misses 167; William 135
Shilbe, Richard 38
Ships, *African* 54; *Amity* 54; *Angelique* 54; *Ann Elizabeth* 54; *Ann Mary* 155; *Anna* 51; *Beginning* 50; *Besney* 54; *Betsey* 54; *Betty* 40, 42, 43, 50, 51; *Bonetto* 72; *Brocenteur* 54; *Brooks* 171, 173; *Cygnet* 80; *Dartmouth Galley* 42, 52; *Daniel & Henry* 40-56, 216; *Dragon* 40, 42, 50; *Duchesse de Gramond* 54; *Echo* 77; 79-80; *Elizabeth Galley* 42, 51; *Eolus* 68; *Felicidade* 77, 79-80; *George* 68; *HMS Helms* 191; *Heureaux* 54; *Hunter* 151; *Intelligent* 191; *HMS Jaseur* 74-6; *John Robert* 42-3, 52; *Jonas* 19; *King George* 53; *L'Amitie* 54; *L Elorte* 191; *L'Etoile* 191; *L'Heureaux Union* 54; *La Sultan* 191; *Le Rosalie* 54; *HMS Maidstone* 73; *Mary Joseph* 54; *Messney* 54; *Minion* 20; *Neptune* 151; *New York* 147; *Northumberland* 151; *Norton* 33; *Phoenix* 66; *HMS Pomona* 57-73; *Pole* 19; *Prince of Brunswick* 54; *Prince George* 54; *Providence* 35; *Regard* 147; *Prudence* 28; *St Ann* 54; *St John* 54; *Salvador Mundi* 191; *Senegal Packet* 54; *Solomon* 19; *Speedwell* 40; *Star* 80; *Supplement* 54; *Surprise* 52; *Susan Abigail* 147; *Swallow* 19; *Sylvia* 42, 51, 52; *Traveller* 190; *HMS Wasp* 77
Shobrooke 200
Short, George 167; Thomas 33
Shute 200, John 167; Stephen 167
Sidmouth 8
Simms, Philip 35
Sinclair, Marian 143; Sophia 143
Slavery, definitions 10-11
Slaving, voyages 15-82
Smith, Anne 143; George 180; Gilbert 26; Henry 168; Robert 141; Thomas 37; William 141
Snell, James 36
Snelling, William 35
Society of Friends 58, 67, 146, 150, 169, 190
Somerset 30, 106; Ilminster 95; Minehead 37; Staunton Drew 222 n.93; Taunton 37, 39; Wells 39
Somerset, James 13, 154-6
Sorrell, James 180
South America 98; Brazil 19, 77-82; Surinam 112-31
Spain 5, 12, 17, 23, 28, 39, 51, 52, 56, 91, 163, 191
Sparke, John 20
Sparkes, Thomas 166, 169
Speke, Miss 167
Spicer, Josias 37; Nicholas 26; William 37
Squire, Humphrey 168; T. 168
St Croix 199
St Kitts 199
Stabback, George 168; John 168
Stannill, Adrian 36
Stedman, Adriana 129-32; Joanna 123-30, 132; John 2, 112-134, 175-6, 216; Johnny 114, 129, 130-4

## Index

Stephens, Jo: 38; Robert 35
Stevenstone 106
Stewart, Charles 155
Stocker, Thomas 180
Stoke Gabriel 30
Stone, Edward 36
Stonehouse 37, 149, 184
Stoodleigh 200
Stoodley, John 167
Stooke, Revd 167
Stoud, Ocdo: 37
Stouth, Richard 38
Strange, Philip 36
Stupart, Lieut. 79
Suffolk, Colchester 37, 39; Ipswich 37, 39
Sugar 7, 19, 50, 54, 83, 95-105, 119; embargo 175-6; factory 7, 145-7
Sutton, James 139; Robert 139
Swaby, James 139
Sweden 42, 92, 178
Sweetland, H. D. 167
Swete, Esther 95, 104; family 95; Grace 95; John 95, 146; Maine 95-105
Symons, Samuel 168

Tarrant, Henry 167; Revd M. 167
Tavistock 149, 186, 188
Tawstock 29
Taylor, Henry 50; Mr 168
Tea 62
Teignmouth 35, 39, 44
Templer, Thomas 168
Ten-percenters 40-56
Thomas, Hannibal 35; Jo: 37; John 6; Jonas 36; Samuel 6; Thomas
Thompson, George 224 n.168
Thorne, John 180
Tilly, George 33
Tindall, Edward 38
Tingcombe, John 170, 181; Jonathan 170
Tin-mining 5
Tiverton 2, 112, 114, 130, 131, 149, 171, 172, 174-5, 200
Tobacco 7, 50, 51, 59, 83, 83
Tobin, Richard 35
Toby, Edward 36, 37; T. 180
Tonkin, Digory 170
Topsham 33, 36, 37, 38, 39, 40, 50, 51, 145-7, 149, 167, 172, 183
Torbay 36, 39
Tortures 32-3, 115, 116, 120, 204
Totnes 8-9, 172, 199; Follaton House 199
Towgood, Micjah 167; Mrs 167
Tozer, Abraham 168; Revd 167
Trathorne, Nicholas 36
Treffry, Joseph 181
Trefife, Thomas 35
Trelawney, Robert 84
Tremayne, Arthur 157
Tremlett, Anna 168; Anthony 168; James 167; Misses 167
Trevor, William 36
Trewman, R. 167
Tricke, Augustine 38
Trickey, Henry 166; J. 167; W. 167
Trinidad 200
Tripe, John (see Swete)
Tucker, John 168; Jonathan 169; Mr 167; William 169
Tucker, Mr 175
Turkey, Istanbul 31
Turner, Francis 167; Richard 167

Uffculme 166, 167
Unitarians 150, 169
United States 178, 190; Civil War 210-211, 212; Florida 106-111; Georgia 106, 213; Maine 84; Maryland 224 n.168; Massachusetts 152; New York 95; North Carolina 146; northern 210-211; Revolution 12, 157, 159; South Carolina 88, 146, 157; southern 84, 210-211; Virginia 13, 222 n.93

Upottery 161

Vassal, Louis 141
Vaughan, Thomas 37
Venison 62
Vianna, Jose 193-4
Victoria 209, 210
Vidal, R. S. 169
Vinson, Peter 224 n.168
Vowells, Richard 8

Waight, Jon: 37; Walter 36
Wainwright, William 95
Waldkeeper, William 37
Wales 39; Swansea 213
Walker, Alexander 141, 142; Amelia 144; Bessy 142; Francis 143; George 141; James 141, 180; John 36; Josias 180; Judith 144; Kitty 144; Lavenia 143; Marian 143; Mary 143; Michael 142; Rose 143; Sarah 142
Wallis, Susan 144
Walrond, Miss 168; Humphrey 95
Walte, Thomas 37
Warde, Gregory 38
Wardrobe, Harriet 208
Ware, Henry 180
Warren, John 180
Waymouth, G. 167; Henry 169
Webb, Charles 180
Webber, Thomas 36; William 36
Wells
Welsford, W. A. 185-6
Wembury 88
Were, Elizabeth 167; M. 167
West, Lieut. Humphrey 168; William 37
Westchester 38
Weymouth, Richard 35
Wheaton, Joseph 180; Peter 180
Whicker, John 180
White, John 29; Margaret 142
Whiteford, Mr 66; Sir John 66; Joseph 181, 184
Whitlock, George 180
Whitterne, Edward 37
Wichehalse, Nicholas 27

Wightwick, George 197-8
Wilberforce, William 183
Wilcox, Mr 167
William III 89
William, John 224 n.168
Williams, John 169; Miss 167; Mr 167; Mrs 167
Wills, Christopher 36; Richard 36
Wilson, Lieut. 79; William 107
Windover, John 180; Richard 180
Winfield, Jo: 36
Winkleigh 6
Withers, John 169
Withycombe Raleigh 88
Wood, Beavis 174; John 175; Richard 37
Woollcombe, Henry 74, 181, 182, 188. 190
Woolmer, Shirley 168
Worcester 37, 39
Worthy, J. D. 167; Jonathan 167; Mr 167
Woster, Ralph 35
Wreford, John 180
Wright, Bully 144; Charlotte 144; Edward 142; Jo: 36; Kath 143; Mr 214; Nicholas 142; Robert 142
Wyatt, Adam 28

Yonge, John 26
York, James 157, 159

Also by the Mint Press

*Not One of Us;*
*Individuals set apart by choice, circumstances,*
*crowds or the mob in Exeter, 1451-1952*
By Todd Gray

Distribution through:
Stevensbooks: www.stevensbooks.co.uk

sales@themintpress.co.uk

Telephone: 01392 459760